James L.
Hymes, Jr.

The Child under

Prentice-Hall, Inc.,
Englewood Cliffs, N. J.

by the same author
Understanding Your Child
Behavior and Misbehavior
Effective Home-School Relations
A Child Development Point of View

Eighth printing........March, 1971

© 1963, 1961 by James L. Hymes, Jr.

Library of Congress Catalog Card Number: 63–17318
T 13220

Contents

CONTENTS

why study
young children?

Chapter 1

Youngsters under six are fascinating to watch, to read
about, and to think about. One good reason for studying them,
whether one is a parent or teacher, is the sheer interest, excitement and fun that come from understanding their growth
and development.

Children under six are tremendously active. During the first
four months or so of life, babies stay where you put them.
If you like peace and quiet, this is the honeymoon. From four
months on, these youngsters are everlastingly on the go. Their
first big achievement is building the power to turn over, all
by themselves, from tummy to back. With that start, they are
off! Crawling develops quickly threafter, then standing, then
walking; and then, except for sleep, these children are hardly
ever still. Some years ago, as an experiment, a trained athlete
attempted to duplicate the movements and activities of a two-
year-old which had been recorded on film. The athlete gave
up, exhausted!

1

Why Study Young Children?

Children under six have extremely active minds, fully as busy as their active bodies. Older youngsters in high school or college often lack interest in a new book or a new idea; they have to be prodded. This is not true of children under six. These young ones are interested in everything—all of life is appealing. They are full of curiosity. They are sure to find your missing lipstick, the one long lost under the chair or behind the sofa. Finding it, they are not content until they know how it works. They must try it out—possibly on lips, walls, chairs, windows, or paper. These are the children under six, whose bright, eager eyes spot the dustball under the bed, or the cigarette butt on the floor. And they always want to know: What does it taste like? What can you do with it? Does it come apart?

Most parents, even those who have never read a book about children, have learned one lesson—beware of silence! They are suspicious if everything is too quiet. Silence is a sure signal that something is up. The chances are that busy legs have carried a busy child to some fascinating place where busy arms and hands and fingers are exploring. Under-six is the time when cupboards are ransacked. It is the time when drawers are emptied, when waste baskets are overturned, and when nothing has quite the appeal of a pocketbook—preferably a woman's huge carryall and, best of all, one belonging to a guest!

Great Lovers of Noise

For about a year under-six children do not talk. This is another brief honeymoon! They have language from the time they are born, but in the first year the language is their own and it is a limited one. Soon, however, they pick up our words. From about the first birthday on, their tongues become as busy as their eyes and bodies and fingers have been. They talk constantly. They talk to adults, they talk to other children, and they even talk to themselves, if need be! Apart from words, young children are great lovers of noise—just noise for its own sake. They make motor noises—brrr, buzzz—when they ride their tricycles; they shout when they talk. And hammering is heaven!

Much of child-talk is questioning. Young children are old enough to want to know, but not old enough yet to realize that there is a time and place for everything. Or that "nice people" don't ask some questions—at least not in public or in a loud voice.

At an early point in development young children expect mother and father to be walking encyclopedias. We are supposed to have answers to one ever-ready question: *Whaddat?* At a later age these children have a genius for making adults realize sadly how little we actually know. Fours and Fives persist, like attorneys for an investigating committee, with their embarrassing *why?* and *how come?* These children want the truth. Mothers and fathers often build a real sympathy with those witnesses who hide behind the Fifth Amendment. They, however, don't have such an easy way out.

Just as the youngsters are forever wanting to know *why?* many an adult keeps asking himself the same question—*why?* For these are the children, under six, who specialize in "doing the darnedest things." Somewhere in this age range it is not the least uncommon for a child to run outdoors without a stitch of clothing on. Why? (And if your child is the one who runs out, you would write the word in capital letters—WHY?) Somewhere in this age range it is not the least uncommon for children to explore the charms of the Mohawk haircut or the flat top or the Italian bob—but each youngster is his own barber. Why do they do it? If you loved your child's hair just as it was, you may ask the question with tears in your eyes.

3

Somewhere in this age range it is not the least uncommon for children to have an imaginary playmate. Adults cannot see the playmate, yet we are accused of not giving her (or him) juice and milk. These imaginary playmates are very sensitive creatures. Their feelings get hurt, their knees get skinned. The children can see them. We cannot. Why do children dream up these creatures?

Adults even find themselves asking the child's earlier question: *Whaddat?* For early childhood is an age of intense imagination. Three-to-six children live in their own special world—the world of play and make-believe. Adults are the strangers, the foreigners. We are newcomers to the shore. At times we stand baffled by what we see, not understanding the secret language of childhood, confused by the goings-on.

We look at a young child's painting and can only ask weakly: *Whaddat?* The youngsters work in their sandbox, and they really work—intense, absorbed. No thought of a coffee break crosses their minds. We watch. To us, sand is sand. We see a block of wood, some little toy cars, a strainer, a bottle-cap, and a leaf, but we cannot see what the children see: the town they have made, the river, or the people. We have to ask: *Whaddat?*

The urge of these three-to-six children to rearrange and to re-create is not confined to easels, sandboxes, block corners, and other official play spaces. Make-believe crops up in living room, bedroom and bath. It is the rare family of a four-year-old that sometime or other has not had its living room "improved." All the chairs, end tables, stools, and lamps are carefully placed in a special arrangement. There is order and precision—but not adult order and precision. There is plan and purpose—but not adult plan and purpose. A blanket has been brought from the bedroom. Pots have been brought from the

4

kitchen. The wastebaskets play some role—steering wheels? hats? caves?—but certainly not their intended role. Adults look and ask: *Whaddat?* (Or, if you are irritable, perhaps you scream your question!)

Why study youngsters under six? They are fun. They are fascinating.

OFF TO A GOOD START

There are other reasons for studying young children. Under-six children can be infuriating if you don't understand them. Mothers and fathers of young children can save themselves wear and tear as well as headaches and heartaches, if they know what this age is all about. There are some answers to our adult *why?* and *whaddat?*

A little understanding can preserve the peace of mind of grandparents, of aunts and uncles, and of any other close kin who live with or near young children.

Many of these under-six children are in school. Almost 50% of our five-year-olds go to kindergarten. Some Fours and Threes and even Twos are in nursery schools. Throughout the whole age range children go to Sunday School. Teachers who work with young children—and nurses and baby-sitters—can make their own lives more peaceful if they know what to expect from young children, and why these youngsters do what they do.

More important: With study we can make children's lives under six more peaceful and productive. To some adults these are simply the "pre-school" years—play years, waste years, years of waiting until school begins. To the child living them, these are *real* years. They can be six years of health and contentment, or six years too full of distress. Six years is a long span of life, whether they come at the beginning of life, at the start of a marriage, on a job, or even in prison. As an act of simple kindness, we all need to know how to make these first six years healthy, happy, good years for a child to live.

In addition, these early years have a special significance. They are the child's first turn at bat. Youngsters meet for the first time, for better or worse, almost all the basic problems in human living that will come up, over and over again, through the rest of their years. The early days are full of simple acts: eating, dressing, toileting, sleeping, and playing. But each simple act carries its own underlying lesson about this world—a lesson the child confronts for the first time.

The very first feedings—the schedule, the amount of food —are experiences in discipline. Children are making their first discoveries about this society's expectations and how to meet them: Easily? Comfortably? Or fighting with fury?

Very early, children have their first confrontation with reality. Toys break, and they are broken. Toys get lost, and they are gone. Time—for the next feeding, for a birthday, for grandmother's visit—plods its fixed and steady pace. Children learn their first lessons about how they will fit into this world: Capably? Taking life in their stride? Or retreating, rebelling, resisting?

In the under-six years children have their initial dealings with people—with mother first; with father; with adult relatives and brothers and sisters; with baby-sitters, neighbors, doctors and storekeepers; with friends their own age; and with teachers. At the first meetings, how do these people look to the child: Formidable or friendly? People will be a part of their lives in all the years ahead—teachers; classmates; dates; supervisors, bosses and fellow-workers; neighbors; a husband or a wife. The under-six child has his first dealings with people and he makes his first responses: I have to keep my guard up; I have to watch them; I can trust people, they are good to me and nice to have around.

6

Most important of all, under-six children are beginning to know themselves. A picture of what they can do, how they feel, how people seem to respond to them gradually builds up in their minds. Children meet pain in these years. Can they take it? There is fear in these years. Will the children stay frightened? These early years hold jobs and challenges. Will these children learn confidence (I can do it!) or despair (I mess things up!)?

First impressions are not necessarily lasting ones. A lot of life, important life, follows in the years after six. But first impressions are first and they are real. If we know what young children are like, what they seek and what matters to them, we not only make these beginning years six good years to live; we give these children a good start toward the years that lie ahead. A start is only a start, but a good start heads youngsters in the right direction. It increases the odds that they will continue going in the right direction. We all have a stake in their doing that.

ILLUMINATING THE YEARS AHEAD

Studying young children can also be an excellent way to understand all human behavior. Teachers of elementary school children and high-schoolers, parents of older children, all who work with people (even those who work with adults) benefit by understanding the beginnings of development.

Young children are not monsters or fiends or little devils who have taken human form. Children under six are people. They have the same feelings the rest of us have. Their brains are working, just as our brains work. Their life is lifted up or depressed, just as we all have our ups and downs. The general principles that govern their growing are the same general principles that govern all growing.

Young children, however, offer us one very unique ad-

7

vantage as subjects for study: They hide nothing! They are not smart enough yet to put on disguises. Their behavior is all out in the open. If they have an idea, they say it. If they have an inclination to do something, they do it. When they feel an emotion, they express it. Children under six give us human behavior on a silver platter, sometimes an overwhelming dose of it.

Humans cover up as the years go by. We use our expanding language to mask our feelings. We become polite, discreet, and full of devices and detours and double-talk. But not young children! They think primarily of pleasing themselves; they have not yet learned all the arts of pleasing others. They do not put on a show. By studying how they grow and how they act, we can understand children at later ages better. We can understand ourselves better, and other adults too.

There is an especially close tie between early childhood and adolescence. The early childhood years are often called "the first adolescence." Adolescence is often called "the second early childhood." In the under-six years the child is first finding himself. This identical concern, broadly speaking, is what adolescence is all about. The youngster who scored a hit in his first turn at bat can come up again in adolescence more sure of himself, more confident. The adolescent who struck out the first time is more apt to swing harder, to swing more wildly when he comes up the second time. His teen years look to him like his last chance to score.

The bond between early childhood and adolescence is especially close but early childhood is a part of later childhood. Early childhood is a part of adulthood and a part of old age. This should be no surprise. Each of us was once a child, and we carry that childhood with us. When you know what a good childhood is—the satisfactions a young child must get out of life to get off to a sound start—you are in a better position to understand an individual's behavior in the later

8

years. When you know what hurts young children, you can better appreciate the scars carried by some of us on into adult life.

FOR INDEPENDENT STUDY

1. Check whatever library you use for other books about young children. Materials on child growth and development are usually listed in the card catalog under 136.7 or 649.1. Look particularly for *The Magic Years*, by Selma H. Fraiberg (New York: Scribners, 1959) and *Helping Your Child's Emotional Growth*, by Anna W. M. Wolf and Suzanne Szasz (Garden City, N.Y.: Doubleday, 1954). Both are beautifully written and full of insight; the latter tells its story through excellent photographs. If you have an interest in the more technical research background, look for *The Psychology of Early Childhood*, by Catherine Landreth (New York: Knopf, 1958). If you want to buy other books, the best bargains are *Your Child From One to Six*, Publication #30 of the U.S. Children's Bureau (20¢) and *Infant Care*, Publication #8 (20¢) both available from the Government Printing Office, Washington, D.C.

2. Access to magazine material will also help you. *Parents Magazine*, published monthly, $4.00 a year at Bergenfield, New Jersey, includes excellent material about the under-six child. *Today's Child* is a much smaller publication but it focuses exclusively on this age range (monthly except July and August), published at 1225 Broadway, New York for $3.00 a year. The best buy, although not confined to young children, is *The PTA Magazine*, 700 N. Rush Street, Chicago 11, Illinois, published monthly except July and August for $1.50 a year.

how children
are studied

Chapter 2

For most of the centuries of man's existence children were taken simply for granted. A child was a child. No one stopped to wonder: How does a youngster grow? What helps him? What hurts him? All children were Topsy—they just grew. Some grew strong and some grew weak; some were healthy and some were sickly. But whatever happened, happened. A child was a child.

Parents used one guide—tradition. They raised their children as they themselves had been raised. Child rearing was a fixed and repetitive process. If a youngster thrived, fine. If a youngster became an angry, fighting child, or a very silent, passive, overly accepting child, well, *Que sera, sera*—What will be, will be.

Today we know quite a bit about children. Increasingly since about 1900 youngsters have been the subject of conscious study, of careful observation and of experimentation. We are moving away from tradition as the sole base for action: "Do this, because this is what we have always done." We are moving away from ignorance: "This is good to do . . ." but no one knows why!

The study of child growth and development is part and parcel of our whole scientific attempt to understand the world around us. We have come to know a great deal about our physical world—the properties of metals, for example. We know about their strengths and weaknesses, the strains they can stand and their breaking points. We have come to know a tremendous amount about plants and animals—one's special need for sunshine; another's need for acid soil or for a lot of water or a little. We have come to know many of the conditions that make cows, pigs and sheep thrive or grow skinny. We are at the beginnings of our explorations into space but we have been studying children and their special qualities for quite a while.

The Many Differing Kinds of Research

Youngsters have been studied in many ways and by many different groups of people. Some approaches have been so informal that they may not seem to rate the term "study." Adults, for example, have looked back on their own childhoods. They have tried to recall the events and happenings that, in later years, still stand out as having great significance. This is not a very scientific method. Memory plays tricks. And one child, after all, is only one child. But probably no single tool gives more flashes of insight than our memories of what it was like to be a child growing up. Too many parents and teachers forget that they ever were children.

In a more professional way, psychiatrists have the special

11

chance to look backwards and they have made a major contribution to our understanding of childhood. Many psychiatrists work directly with young children; many more have the
opportunity to hear the stories of childhoods recalled. They
hear the bitter experiences, the injustices that people still feel
unhappy about although years have gone by. They spot the
happenings in growing up that have so great an impact that
they last in memory over long stretches of time. Psychiatrists
see only troubled adults who probably had troubled childhoods; they see only troubled children. But their insight has
greatly helped us understand all children.

Still another approach has played the record backwards.
This is the case study which is an essential instrument in
clinics and a tool for research. Through the case study a team
of workers—parents and teachers, psychiatrists, psychologists,
social workers, pediatricians, ministers—reconstruct a child's
past, fit the pieces together, and tie them in to the present.
Many case studies deal with children or adults who, one way
or another, have run into difficulties. But other case studies
bring together the life histories of so-called normal children,
growing up in a standard run-of-the-mill way.

Much of our knowledge about children comes from obser-
vations made at the very time the behavior was happening.
The most informal records are those kept by parents. Parents
are not the most unbiased reporters of their own children's
behavior; and they do see only one or two children. But a
number of parents have conscientiously tried to record: This
is what my child did. This is what he said. This is how he
acted.

Much more objectively, a few research workers have followed a child—not their own—recording behavior through
every single minute of the child's waking hours. One child is
still only one child. But this research gives a complete graphic
record of everything one child said and did, to whom he said

it, and with whom he did it throughout one day of a seemingly healthy, happy youngster's life.

More commonly, research workers have taken down with stenographic notes the full record of parts of a day—a fifteen minute stretch, a thirty minute stretch—using many children, day after day. These slices of behavior capture for the record exactly the language children use, the ideas they possess, the materials they use and the emotions they express. Analyzed and studied, such records have thrown much light on children's fears, on their conflicts, on their use of material, on leadership, on aggression, on sympathy, on language and problem solving and on what children do as children in the child's life they lead.

Still more objectively than the stenographer's note pad and more fully than the tape recorder, the motion picture camera has been used to capture on film the behavior of child after child, on and on for hundreds of children: This is what they do, this is how they act.

Less formally, but having the great advantage of numbers, professional people from many fields have taken notes on the children and families they have served through the years. Thoughtful teachers, for example, have kept their eyes and ears open as they have taught children. Pediatricians, seeing thousands of children, have written down the results of their daily work with youngsters and their families. Social workers have drawn on their vast experience. No one sees all children. No one sees children under all conditions. But these sensitive reports from many professions have thrown light on childhood, and on the experiences that seem to produce healthy behavior and sick behavior.

EXPERIMENTATION WITH CHILDREN

In a much more formal and organized way, the scientists who construct tests—mental tests, achievement tests, infor·

13

mation tests—have helped us know what children can and cannot do at various ages. They select a task—drawing a circle, tying a knot, remembering numbers, following directions—and ask large numbers of children of different ages to attempt each job. Below a certain age, none can. At a certain age, most can. The results have become a part of our knowledge of children: What they are like, what is within their power and what is beyond them at different stages of growth.

There are limits to the kind of experimentation to which children can be exposed. You can break an object and start all over again with another just like it. Despite the obvious limitations, there has been significant experimental research on childhood. One child or one group has been deliberately exposed to certain conditions, and another similar child or group kept free of these conditions for contrast and comparison. Identical twins lend themselves beautifully to this kind of experimentation. Other matched groups of children have been used as "guinea pigs" in a safe way so that we could know more about the powers and limitations of childhood.

Animals are not people. There is always danger in applying to humans what is learned from experiments with rats, chickens, monkeys and geese. But you can experiment more freely with animals. When the findings from animal research dovetail with what is known from studies of humans, the information can have tremendous corroborative value. We have gained some very significant understanding about growth and behavior in this way.

Anthropologists also do a safe kind of controlled experimentation. They do not deliberately expose children to strange sets of conditions, but they go out around the world to find societies where the natural way of life is different from our typical way of living. Their contrasting pictures of childhood

14

in different societies have helped us to understand what our society demands of its children, and the ways in which children the world over are both the same and different.

Within our own immediate world, sociologists have studied different groups of children—Negro youngsters, urban children, children in small towns, rural children. Their reports, meshed with other data, have constituted a kind of controlled experimentation with humans, allowing us to see how children live and react in different settings—to spot what all children have in common and to note some things which are specific and individual.

We know a lot about children today. We have made intensive studies of their physical growth. We have analyzed their products—their paintings, their block building, their stories. We have used what are called *projective tests*—ink blots, for example, or general pictures which call for no particular answer but leave the child free to respond as he sees fit. These very wide-open tests have gotten down below the surface to the more hidden and deep-flowing parts of the human.

The United States has taken the lead in the study of childhood but workers in many parts of the world have played a significant part in the total process—Binet in France; Piaget in Switzerland; Sigmund Freud and Buhler in Austria; Anna Freud in England; Blatz and Chisholm in Canada. These are some of the famous names, but countless less well-known people in Latin America, in Europe, in India and other parts of the world have contributed both original insight and corroboration.

Of course, not all children have been studied. Research relies heavily on samples which are believed to be typical of the whole. And we are a far cry from having studied every aspect of all the behavior of which children are capable. In

15

the behavior that has been studied our knowledge is far from complete and the evidence is not completely clear-cut. Many parts of childhood are still almost a complete mystery.

We have, however, reached a point of enough knowledge so that we can say with some degree of confidence: This is what most children do. This is how they act. This is what they seem to seek. We know where children are vulnerable. No longer do we have to do whatever has always been done, just because it has always been done. No longer do we need to take whatever happens to children as "fate" or "in the cards." No longer do we have to be completely subjective, pairing one person's guess against another's personal preference: "Well, I happen to believe. . . ." We have reached a point of enough knowledge so that we have some solid ideas about what makes children strong, what makes them well, and what makes them good—good as people, good for themselves, good for all of us to live with.

FOR INDEPENDENT STUDY

1. In the Appendix you will find a highly selected list of materials which illustrate each of the ways of studying children mentioned above. This is a reference list, not a list of quick supplementary readings you can "zip" through. But whenever you can dip into these materials, you will build your knowledge of how children are studied and be less apt to feel: "Oh, that is just what someone happens to want to believe about children."

2. Several books have done this "dipping" job for you. They bring together what their editors think are representative studies so that the reader can know the various methods of research that have been used, and some of the specific research that has had the greatest impact on our thinking

about children. Among the most recent of these collections of research are: *Human Development: Selected Readings,* by Morris L. and Natalie Haimowitz, eds. (New York: Crowell, 1960); *The Child: A Book of Readings,* by Jerome M. Seidman, ed. (New York: Rinehart, 1958); *Readings in Child Psychology,* by Wayne Dennis, ed. (Englewood Cliffs, N.J.: Prentice-Hall, 1951).

3. This is the time for you to do a piece of "research" on your own. One possibility: Look back on your own childhood and write down what you remember of the "injustices" you experienced in the course of your growing up; the joys and delights and pleasures that still stand out; the times you were "bad" and did things you knew your parents would not approve of; and the times you were proud.

a child is born

Chapter 3

The human starts with one cell, the fertilized ovum. During the nine months of prenatal life this one cell multiplies until at birth the newborn has 200 billion cells!

The fertilized ovum at conception is about the size of the dot over an *i*. At the end of nine months the average baby at birth is about twenty inches long. He has grown 3,500 times in length!

The phenomenal process of change is rightly called "the miracle of growth." It is truly awe-inspiring. The ovum, the single cell to begin with, is one and undifferentiated. Within the first two months of prenatal growing this one cell divides and differentiates until heart and lungs, brain and spinal cord, head and face, arms and legs, hands and feet with distinguishable fingers and toes are all recognizably formed.

In this process canny and wise precautions seem always to be operating. The heart, so crucial to life, begins beating in the fourth week as if to give ample practice-time for its big

18

job ahead. The genital organs, so essential to our on-going world, are established as early as the twelfth week. Sucking, a basic skill for survival, is practiced *in utero*. The kidneys secrete urine. Enzymes are secreted into the digestive tract. The fetus lives in a fluid environment yet it takes small breaths as if to test out its lungs. And, as every mother knows, the unborn child seems indeed to be giving himself hidden but hardly secret practice sessions in some of the leg movements and body movements that he soon will be making in post-natal life.

Starting from a dot, growing for about 265 days, the child matures until he is able to make one of the most significant journeys of his life, "a journey from profound seclusion." He makes the transition from a fluid environment to our gaseous world of air. He comes from a safe secure sanctuary where oxygen passes from his mother's blood to him through the placenta, to this world where he now must breathe for himself. He leaves a constant temperature and a steady pressure for a setting where temperature and pressure vary. He moves from a protected environment in which all stimuli are at a minimum into a world of light and noises and smells. He comes from a cushioned haven, where he gets his nourishment effortlessly, into a world where he must suck, and suck vigorously, for food. And yet the child can do it. His growth has made him ready.

In 1960 the infant mortality rate in this country was only 26.0 per 1,000 live births. The maternal mortality was only 3.6 per 10,000 live births.

A child is born. Mother and father stare in joy and wonder. And well they may. Doctors and nurses may grow blasé, but here is a miracle—a child can grow so safely and perfectly; it can withstand the birth process; it can be ready to continue its growth in this different and demanding world. From a dot!

A Child Is Born

And now at birth: Heart beating, lungs working, circulatory system going, digestive system functioning, all except the brain and the reproductive organs able to carry on in about the same way that they will throughout a long life ahead.

The Baby Is Deeply Dependent

Stand in awe! Baby deserves it. Mother deserves respect, and there is no reason why father should look modest! But the most significant fact about the newborn—and the child throughout the whole span of his under-six years—is *not* the picture of his strength or the list of the things he can do. More important by far is the longer list of all the things he *cannot* do! The interminable length of this list is the key to understanding young children. The human baby is a helpless child. The human baby is a dependent child. The human baby is a weak child. These qualities—weakness, helplessness, dependence—set the tone for how a baby must be treated at birth, in the months that follow, and for at least the six years ahead.

The baby has come far and there are things he can do, to be sure. But you can name his skills on the fingers of two hands. You could go on indefinitely naming all the things he cannot do. The human infant is a *cannot* kind of person. He stays that way for a long time.

The baby's bag of tricks includes some of the very basic abilities needed for survival. He can cough and he can sneeze. He can blink and he can yawn. These are essential protective devices. The baby can cry, and this is a tremendous tool for summoning help. He has a few reflexes, largely hangovers from an earlier time in human history when once they too were safety devices. He has a reflex grasp, for example, so that if anything touches his palm—mother's finger now, perhaps the

20

branch of a tree in the long ago—baby clutches it and can hang on for dear life.

The baby can suck, but not too well at birth. He can swallow, but not perfectly yet—at least he swallows up as easily as he swallows down! This is another protective device. One thing you can say: There is nothing lacking in his ability to urinate, to defecate, or to sleep!

But this short list is almost naught stacked against everything the child *cannot* do. He cannot lift his head, for one example, and mothers know this. For many months, even after the ability has begun to develop, mothers wisely check on their sleeping babies. Youngsters can suffocate, and unfortunately do die sometimes, because they lack the simple power to lift up their heads to free the nose and mouth for breathing.

The new baby, miraculously grown in some ways, needs us. He needs us to bring him food. He needs us to change his position. He cannot turn over for several months; we must be on hand to relieve boredom and soreness. He cannot move himself from place to place for many months; we must do all the carrying and lifting. He has hands and fingers, but for many months—and even years—these are clumsy tools. We have to do all the picking up, fetching, and removing. He needs us. He cannot. We must.

You realize the dramatic helplessness of infants when you examine the very special provisions that must be made for those born prematurely. Premature infants need a special tent or incubator where the temperature can be carefully regulated. They need scientific control of the amount of oxygen in the air. Infection must be rigorously guarded against. Yet the premature is not a different kind of child. Usually a baby weighing less than 2,500 grams (about 5 pounds) is called "premature" and gets this extra-special care. (Prematurity is judged differently for different races and nationalities. For instance, the standard for Filipino infants is 400 to 500 grams less than ours.) We *know* that the premature child is weak. We are glad to do for him what he cannot do for himself—and for as long as he needs it.

The helplessness of the baby, premature or full-term, creates what is his dominant need—at birth, in the months that follow, and through all of early childhood. *He needs mothering.* He needs nurturing. He needs someone who will care for him—someone big and strong, able and willing and ready. He needs—the old term is probably the best—*tender, loving care.*

THE BABY IS IMPULSIVE

This need for mothering, arising out of helplessness, is accentuated by another dominant characteristic of the human newborn: He is a creature of the moment! The baby has no perspective, no long history of yesterdays, no awareness of stretching tomorrows. He can only know this very immediate present. He is egocentric, responsive only to his own feelings. He is impulsive, responding to whatever stimulates him. The expression, "When you have to go, you have to go," fits the baby to a T. He is capable of no modulation, no shades and shadings off. What he sees, he wants. What he feels, he yells about. And he wants what he wants when he wants it.

Touch the baby on the arm or leg and his whole body jerks. The capacity to localize responses, to control response, to hold in or hold back or put off or postpone has not developed at birth. All of his inhibiting responses will be slow to develop.

Anyone who has ever tried to show off a baby to doting grandparents or willing friends knows this characteristic full well. You make all kinds of elaborate arrangements for baby to put on a good show, but if the baby wants sleep he sleeps.

22

Nursing mothers know this. The baby nurses when he wants to nurse. He sleeps when he wants to sleep. He urinates when he wants to urinate.

Infancy is the prize time in life for the "Great I Am." Such impulsiveness, such egocentricity would be troubling characteristics in older children or adults. They are healthy signs in the baby—exactly how a baby is supposed to respond.

But because he is such a creature of the moment, the baby has an even greater need for mothering. He has to have the kind of loving care that gladly does for him what he cannot do for himself. When hunger hits the baby, it hits him hard. It does not blend in with other needs or interests or awareness. The baby is hungry. *This* is the feeling he knows and he knows it keenly. When the baby hurts, he knows only the hurt. His pain and pleasure, his comfort and discomfort are the real world to him. The result is that the baby (and, to a lesser degree, all of early childhood) is prey to panic, to desolation, to deep distress, with a depth of feeling unique to this time of life.

It is very hard for adults to recreate these feelings of sharp anxiety within ourselves. We are so far removed from this stage in development. Our capacities have grown so that we cannot imagine the helplessness of the baby. Our impulsiveness and egocentricity have diminished—we cannot go back to a time when our own feelings mattered exclusively.

The complete non-swimmer—afraid of water, utterly inept and helpless in water—may be able to sense just a little of what it is like to be a baby. Over his head, out of his depth, the non-swimmer knows panic, emptiness, inadequacy, and he knows them sharply. He has eyes only for the swimmer, the person who *can* do what he cannot. This dependency is the baby's plight. He is the "non-swimmer." He is the *non-everything!* He needs us, ready and willing and able by his side.

23

A Child Is Born

Time to Fall in Love

Fortunately, babies have a secret weapon. They have one secret strength hard to list precisely in any academic statement of physical and psychological characteristics. *Babies are charmers!* They possess the mysterious and exciting capacity to warm our hearts.

A child is born. Mother and father stare in joy and wonder —and warmth. They look at their child and feel soft inside. This is just as it should be. They look at their child and make tender, "gushy" sounds—loving sounds. And this is just as it should be. They look at their child and want to squeeze him, to hold him. When the baby seems to smile or sleeps contentedly, the parents feel good all over. When baby cries, they want to *do* something. And this is just as it should be. Especially at the very start of life this secret weapon of charm works like a magnet to draw out warmth from most of us. And this is fine!

The warm glow must keep on burning. During the first few months the baby needs food, to be sure, but his perceptions are still dim. The hands that bring the bottle or the hands that hold and nurse him should be gentle, of course. They should carry a message of security. But the crucial time for the communication of this message begins in the second, third or fourth month—at about that age the baby begins to build awareness. This is when the love affair must blossom! Now the hands that hold the child, the hands that bathe him, the voice that comes with the food, the smell of the human who holds him, all begin to sink in. From this point on, good physical care—doing the job and getting it done—is not at all enough. The child is beginning to look beyond the deed itself for the person doing it, and beyond and down into the person doing it for feeling tone.

From this point on the helpless, impulsive, egocentric child

24

wants to know and needs to know: Can I count on her? Can I trust her? Does this mothering person feel good about me and glad that I am here? The answering message—love means *yes*—comes through the child's experiences in all the humdrum routine activities that make up the baby's day—feeding, changing, dressing and bathing. Honeyed words—"Darling," "Sweetie Pie," "Cutie"—are not the communication that counts. Babies are non-verbal. They pick up non-verbal messages the best.

The baby is searching for a *sense of trust*. He gets it—or fails to get it—from the feel of hands and the feel of muscles. He has a special radar system that penetrates atmosphere and attitude to get through to the feel of hearts. Lucky is the child to whom hands and body speak an overriding message of pride and joy. Lucky is the child whose experiences with mothering speak to him of "unconditional love." His parents are delighted with him, just as he is. There is nothing he could do to earn more love; there is nothing he could do which would take love away. He is loved with no strings attached.

Lucky is the child who starts life lovingly mothered, and lucky is the child who gets the same supporting message of love from more and more people as his awareness widens. Luckier still is the child who keeps on feeling loved for a long time to come.

Helplessness and impulsiveness and egocentricity will be the child's brand and mark for quite a while. A puppy becomes a dog in about a year. A pony becomes a horse in about two years. A chick becomes a chicken in a shorter time. But a child stays a child. He feels like a child. He feels small for his whole first six years and even longer. It is natural for him to look up to his parents. Easily, comfortably, he holds his hand out to them. Not until eight or nine or ten will he feel and say, "I'm not a child any more!"

As early as the second half of the first year needs other than

25

this primary need for love will arise as the child grows. But this first need—a sense of trust in the people around him, a sureness that they are pleased with him—stays just under the surface, ready at any moment to bubble up to the top again.

FOR INDEPENDENT STUDY

1. Prenatal development is so briefly covered in this chapter that, unless your knowledge of this important time in growth is strong, you should read some additional material. One good source is *The First Nine Months of Life*, by Geraldine Lux Flanagan (New York: Simon and Schuster, 1962), a beautiful book.

2. This chapter makes no mention at all of heredity. To fill in this gap, you are urged to check with a book *Basic Facts of Human Heredity*, by Amran Scheinfeld (New York: Washington Square Press, 1961), available in a paperback edition.

3. A very inexpensive government publication succinctly states the framework of children's successive needs, beginning with the search for a sense of trust. You will be glad to own *A Healthy Personality for Your Child* (Washington: Government Printing Office, 1952. 20¢). This report is an outgrowth of the Mid-Century White House Conference on Children and Youth.

4. This is a good time to read one of the classics in the field of child development. Originally published in 1938, *Babies Are Human Beings*, by C. Anderson Aldrich and Mary M. Aldrich (New York: Macmillan, 1954, rev. ed.) is now available in paperback (New York: Dell, 1962. 95¢). It expresses a philosophy toward children, beginning with babies, which you will find highly stimulating and provocative.

26

What would you do?

At the end of each chapter hereafter you will find one "test" question. These are multiple-choice questions. Make a note of the answer that, in your judgment, comes closest to representing what you would do. These questions have four distinctive qualities.

1. They usually relate to material that lies ahead in the book, rather than to information that has already been covered. They are designed to alert you and to provoke you, rather than to "test" your reading and memory.

2. You can discuss your answers with anyone. In fact, you are urged to talk over what you have decided with as many people as possible. For once, this isn't "Cheating"!

3. You can go back and change your answer whenever you want to, and as many times as you want to.

4. If no one of the alternatives really seems right to you, you need not choose any. Instead, write out briefly what you would do. (Some of the questions are intentionally rigged; none of the alternatives is "right.") By all means keep a record of your answers so that you can compare your solution with the "right" answer which is given at the end of Chapter 33.

Question 1 You are a mother of a two-year-old. He is playing and running and he falls. You can tell that he hasn't really and truly hurt himself very much but he comes running to you. What is your inclination: *a*) Tell him that he didn't hurt himself, and to go back to his playing; *b*) Sympathize a little bit—maybe rub the "sore spot" and pat his shoulder; *c*) Be a little stern so you teach him that he shouldn't come running to Mother for every little thing; *d*) Accept the fact that children love to make-believe; put a bandage on the "hurt" and kiss the "sore spot" and give him lots and lots of comfort.

27

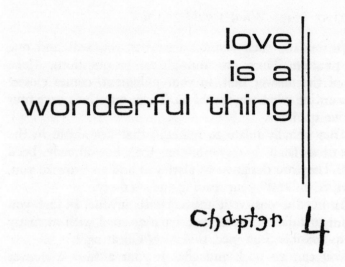

love
is a
wonderful thing

Chapter 4

We say: "Love makes the world go 'round." But is love
—mothering, nurturing, giving tender loving care—really that
important to little children?

One way of getting the answer is to look at children who
were unlucky in love. There is a lot of evidence about the fate
of youngsters who, because of special circumstances, were deprived of mothering. Often these children had good physical
care. They were fed good food. They were kept clean. They
had a good crib. Their diapers were changed. Their sheets
were clean. Nothing was wrong with their hygiene, but everything was wrong with their human relationships. They had
all that a baby could ask for *except* the one thing a baby
wants and needs most of all—someone who cares, someone
he knows he can trust and count on, someone he loves.

THE SILENT ONES

The picture is a scary one.

Most frequently these unloved children become silent. Very silent, strangely silent. When you visit them in an institution —the ward of a hospital, the ward of an orphanage—you hear no noise. You might expect no laughter but you hear no crying either! No talking. No face lights up as you come near. You get no smile. The children may stare at you but they do not reach out to you. These are quiet children—uncomfortably quiet, frighteningly quiet.

The air may be pure. The food may be good. The children sleep. Nurses are in attendance and doctors make their rounds. But frequently these children do not grow. Away from a mother who cares, twelve-month-olds often look like six-month-olds—they do not crawl or stand or walk. Eight-month-olds look like three-month-olds—listlessly, they simply lie in their cribs. Almost always these children are smaller in weight and height than they should be for their age. When they gain, their gains are small. They are as apt to lose and to grow backwards in size and abilities, just as they lose their emotional drive. Occasionally, if the shortage of love is especially severe, these children die. Complete deprivation of love can be as debilitating as complete deprivation of food.

If the children survive and continue to live in an impersonal, clean but non-caring atmosphere, their intellectual performance suffers just as their physical growth suffers. Somehow the common bits of everyday information—the names of ordinary objects, for example—do not sink in. The explanation could be that these children are in unusual settings; they are not surrounded by the daily bustle of a home. But there is reason to think: The children don't care and they don't ask and they don't notice. Their curiosity—the *whaddat?*—has been stilled.

29

Just as physical growth was stunted, intellectual power seems stunted. You can never be sure what any child's top ceiling is, but these unusually deprived children tend, almost all of them, to have low horsepower.

Vocabularies are limited. In particular, when they reach the age when other children are letting their minds range, these children have trouble with abstract thinking and with general concepts. They cannot get their feet off the ground.

It is hardest of all for them to grow socially. The laws of our world somehow never quite become a part of them. This is not because no one has tried to teach the lessons. Quite the contrary! Often the laws have been shouted at the children and pounded in: You must not take things that do not belong to you. Honesty is the best policy. Don't hit, don't grab. Don't fib. Wait your turn. But these very deprived children have learned, for the most part, not to care, just as no one has cared about them. They have never joined the human race. They do not think "in human" the way we think "in English." Our laws are not their laws. They have little conscience about breaking them and feel almost no guilt. Often these children grow up to be the major troublemakers in our communities.

Never having known love, they find it hard to love. It is difficult for them to be a true friend, a good husband or wife, and especially to be a good parent. To play these roles you have to think of the other fellow. You must be willing and able to give up something to make the other person—friend, mate, child—happy. The youngsters who were utterly deprived of mothering can only act like babies. They never grew well physically; they did not grow well intellectually; their emotional growth has been blighted. They are apt to stay impulsive and egocentric. Their one concern is the baby's concern: *What's in it for me?*

These youngsters want love. Sometimes they demand it excessively. They may marry and have children. Intellectually

30

they *know* that "to have a friend you must be a friend." But neither brain power nor willpower can supply what they lack. A healthy child grows emotional power and these children do not. They do not have the capacity to feel with the other fellow. This power does not stem from any one organ or muscle, but it can be missing just as if an actual organ or muscle had atrophied. These children simply do not have what it takes to build and maintain a human relationship.

Quantitatively, these severely deprived children are a drop in the bucket. Their significance is not that they are all around us. They are not. Their significance is that they became nature's "experimental" group. They had everything but love. Their retarded growth shows us what love does to humans.

Love is sunshine. Love is warming and relaxing. Love makes you glad you are who you are. These children were not happy.

Love is lubrication. Love oils and greases the wheels of growth and lets them mesh and turn smoothly. These children had ground to a halt. They were stuck in their growing.

Love is like glue. It helps life's lessons to stick. Love is like a meat tenderizer. It softens the fibres and lets life's lessons sink in. These children had hard shells. The lessons were all around them but they bounced off.

Two Important Notes

Love is a wonderful thing. When a child is unloved the results are very bad. But two things must be very clearly seen at this point.

One is that we have been talking about a very special group of children. To be sure, people were not mean to these children in the usual sense of the word. The adults in charge were not beasts or brutes. They were simply busy or impersonal. The trouble was only that these children were not their children to fondle and fuss over. And, very frequently, in the institutions where these children grew up, there simply were not enough adults to go around. But the result was that these children were severely and steadily deprived of mothering over long periods of time. They missed out on love almost completely, and not for just a moment.

If you are a parent, it is easy to misunderstand this point. We all have our moments when we are completely fed up with our youngsters. We have our moments when we would gladly wring their necks. We have our moments when bedtime is sheer delight. In all honesty, at the moment, we don't really love our child. We want him to go to bed or go to sleep or go anywhere so we can have some peace! It is all too easy to remember these moments and to think that they are the same as what you have just been reading.

The two pictures are miles apart. The children we have been discussing had no parents to care for them. Their experiences in lack of love or loss of love were not "once in a blue moon." Coldness, isolation, deprivation were their steady daily diet.

Two, the problem of gross deprivation has been recognized. There should be many fewer children hurt in this particular way and to this extreme extent in the future. Now we know what destroyed these youngsters. We are in a position to do something about it.

Inevitably some babies are orphaned. Some are abandoned. Some, because of their own illness or an illness in their families, or because of poverty or illegitimacy, cannot be brought up in their own homes. These sad happenings can never be completely eliminated. But we can manage the "next steps" for children born into misfortune so that they do not suffer additional, needless, and preventable emotional, physical and intellectual harm.

One effort today is to make sure that children do not spend a single minute more than necessary in an impersonal, "efficient" but not intimate setting. Social agencies are eager to make these babies available for adoption, just as soon as possible. Their aim is to get them into the kind of personal environment where they can know the love that comes from mothering, the love that only someone who cares can give.

Adoption procedures take time, to protect both the child and the adopting family. They cannot be handled overnight. In the time interval until adoption is possible, social agencies try to place young children in foster homes. These homes will not be the child's final home but they can, in the meantime, give the warm, intimate, constant attentions that the young child needs and that add up to security and safety for him.

Not all available children are adopted. This is another of the realities of life. But today we no longer take pride in huge orphanages, the massive structures which by their very size say "institution" rather than *home*. Some children who are not adopted remain in the more intimate setting of foster homes. Other children who live in institutional care today are more apt to be in cottages—home-like settings with, ideally, a house mother and a house father who have the time and the personality to give warmth to the children.

HUMANIZING HOSPITALS

We have made great strides in preventing illness but, in this imperfect world, there always are babies who need hospital care, sometimes for extended periods of time. Hospitals have been among the leaders in recognizing that the child's emotional needs must be met at the same time that his physical needs are cared for. Many have gone back to what is still the custom in so-called underdeveloped countries. The child comes to the hospital, and his family comes too—at least his mother. Doctors and nurses do their specialized jobs; but mother is present, living and sleeping right in the room with

33

her child, to do what is her equally specialized job: to mother, to nurture, to love. The pat, the gentle stroke, or the song can be as potent as our better known miracle drugs.

Not all hospitals let mothers stay. Not all mothers are free to stay. But hospitals are finding still other ingenious ways of meeting the basic need of young children for a sense of trust. One of the most promising new procedures is the use of the "case nurse." When this procedure is followed the child becomes one nurse's child. The youngster is hers to care for and to do all that needs doing. The idea of a "case nurse" sounds simple, almost obvious. But it is a major change from past procedures where one nurse took temperatures, another washed faces, and another changed sheets—a passing parade of busy people whose focus was on the job to be done and not on the child.

Rooming-in is worth mentioning at this point. In our society a high percentage of our children are born in hospitals. The hospital nursery—sterile, clean, shut off—has been one of our proud symbols of progress. The mother, an amateur, stays in her room. The nurse, professionally skilled, is in charge of baby. Babies are brought on schedule to their mothers for feeding; they are allowed to stay with their mothers as long as it takes to get the feeding over and done with. The days immediately following delivery have been a time of separation from their mothers for all of our babies born in hospitals.

Hospital deliveries and the antiseptic techniques of the nursery have drastically reduced infant and maternal mortality. Today, however, some medical people wonder whether, unwittingly, these advances have brought in their train a new hazard—separation, impersonality, the absence of the hands that alone say *love*. To maintain the new benefits in physical care, and to re-create the old virtues of emotional nourish-

34

ment, some hospitals make it possible for the newborn to "room in" with his mother.

At first glance rooming-in seems like a very minor development. Today mothers stay in the hospital following delivery for a very short time. Rooming-in goes on for only three or four days at most, and during those days mother sleeps some, baby sleeps a lot. Quantitatively the actual increased contact between mother and child can probably be measured in minutes.

But rooming-in does make possible those few minutes. It means a few minutes less crying and distress for the child because mother is right there to feed him, a few minutes more holding and cuddling because no nurse hurries in to carry the baby away, a few minutes when mother can, if she wants to, gaze admiringly—the baby is right there, a few minutes when she can count toes and pat a cheek and stroke the baby's back, and a few minutes at the very start when a mother can feel like a mother instead of like someone who has just "delivered."

The fact that only a few minutes are involved makes rooming-in so important. It is a symbol of our new concern to find ways so that no child—not the abandoned, the neglected, the orphaned, the sick *nor* even the child just born—suffers from lack of love. Love is sunshine. Love is lubrication. Love softens and readies the child so he can learn. Love is a wonderful thing, and every youngster must get his full share.

FOR INDEPENDENT STUDY

1. A summary of research the world over on the effects of lack of love, and a truly significant book, is *Child Care and the Growth of Love*, by John Bowlby (330 Clipper Mill Road, Baltimore: Penguin Books, 1953). This is a paper-

back, based on a study by the World Health Organization. There is also a recent WHO follow-up: *Deprivation of Maternal Care—A Reassessment of its Effects*, by Mary D. Ainsworth *et. al.* (Geneva: World Health Organization, 1962).

2. The book, *Young Children in Hospitals*, by James Robertson (New York: Basic Books, 1959) is also provocative and full of implications that go beyond hospital care.

What would you do?

Question 2 You can tell that your five-year-old is jealous of her new baby brother. She does all sorts of things just to get some extra attention from you. What is your inclination: *a*) Give in to her and give her the extra attention. *b*) Gently explain that she is a big girl now and that she has to do more things for herself and on her own because you are very busy with the new baby. *c*) Try to divide your time equally so you treat both of your children exactly alike, and so that neither has any cause for thinking that the other gets more attention and is the favorite. *d*) Very firmly, point out to your older child that she is acting just like a little baby and that she has to learn to grow up and act her age.

loving a baby

Chapter 5

We all say we love little children—except for the small handful who abandon or grossly neglect their youngsters. But children do not always feel fully loved—not only the few who are grossly hurt. Almost all children grow up less sure of themselves than they could be, less trusting of others, less at ease with others than they could be. We *say* we love little children but our message does not always get across.

The question is: How does a baby know he is loved? How do we get our good feelings over to him?

The caveman allegedly dragged his woman by the hair on her head. That was how she knew he loved her. In jokes at least, some modern men strike their wives regularly, "like a gong." Then the wives know that they are loved! (Others, of course, prefer that you "say it with flowers", and still others claim that "diamonds are a girl's best friend.") But how does a baby know that he is loved?

We parents proudly carry pictures of our babies. We proba-

37

bly all talk too much about our children. And we make long-range plans for their future. We buy a bigger, better house; we save for a college education "because we love them." But the baby can't get these messages. He simply does not hear very well over a long-distance wire.

We lavish money on children, even when they are young. We buy very fancy baby carriages, frilly clothing and expensive toys. But money doesn't spell *love* to a baby. Gifts and presents are not the answer, and they never will be, throughout life. One family may be "poor as a churchmouse" and its child may feel deeply loved. A rich child may have "everything" and still have nothing.

How does a baby know that he is loved? When you look at the children who were "unlucky in love" you might think that the answer would lie in some dramatic event or an outstanding happening. Quite the contrary! It's the little things that count. *A baby learns that he is loved through the very simple, humdrum, over-and-over happenings of his life.* The ordinary experiences of living tell a youngster when his parents are glad they have a child, and when they are glad *he* is that child. Honeyed words don't do it. Spectacular gestures don't do it. But slowly and steadily and gradually over time, the way a child is treated builds a sureness inside of him—a solid sense of trust—or leaves him feeling weak and shaky.

The Climate in the Family

The whole atmosphere that surrounds the child, the spirit in the air he breathes, is a key part of this process. From the very beginning a baby has to be enjoyed and appreciated for what he is—*a baby!* And a baby is something special. Not an adult. Not a teenager. A baby is a baby, and does very peculiar thing that are right for babies. He has weaknesses that are a baby's weaknesses, and strengths that are a baby's strengths.

The atmosphere is healthy when it conveys how glad two parents are that they have a *baby*—they wouldn't trade him in for any other age.

A baby's skin is soft skin. The atmosphere is right when someone thrills to touch its softness—to stroke a cheek, to tap a button nose.

A baby is a little tyke. The spirit in the air is right when someone yearns to cradle a whole head in the palm of one hand, or to touch and fondle and marvel at the tinyness of toes, the delicate quality of fingers and the fine features of an ear.

A baby is squeezable. All's well when someone feels a powerful urge to pick up the baby and hold him tight—and gives in to that urge!

A baby has a special smell. The tone and atmosphere and climate are good when someone cannot resist nuzzling into the baby's tummy while the baby laughs and pulls hair.

A baby is tender. He needs a gentle someone who lightly washes his face with a deft, quick touch—and a smile! A baby frightens and worries when his face is covered and when arms and legs are held down. He needs someone who is quick but not rough pulling shirts and sweaters over his head.

A baby loves motion. In a world good for him, someone likes to rock him, likes to sway with him, or bounce and walk and hold him.

A baby is timid. He takes to the new slowly, just a little at a time—a little taste, a little feel. A brisk efficiency in the air —let's-do-it-and-get-it-done—is unsettling. A baby needs a summertime pace, a slow and drawly tempo.

A baby loves sounds. The spirit is right when someone around sings (no matter what the voice is like!) and talks about anything in the whole wide world, through bath and feeding and dressing, as if the baby understood.

A baby loves strength so he can test his own growing

39

strength. The climate is good when someone takes the time to push against his feet, so he can push back.

A baby loves games, silly games. The world is in good shape when someone else also gets fun out of Bye-Bye and Peek-a-Boo. And then later, when someone has the strength and the energy and the time to make Ride-a-Cock-Horse a laughing time, and Piggyback a time of happy excitement.

Everything the baby loves, he loves again and again and again. Splash in the bath and the baby wants "more." Lift him up high and it's "Do it again!" Kiss his neck, and you have to kiss it again. Laugh and make a funny face—once is never enough!

Babies are strange creatures, with strange ways and strange pleasures. If you take them as you find them and are pleased, your baby senses your pleasure and feels loved.

WE DON'T HAVE TO BE PERFECT

But some baby ways and child ways are not always pleasing. A baby drools and spits up. This is how a baby is supposed to act. A baby wets. When he is older he squashes his cereal in his fists and squeezes it through his fingers. And all through his early years a healthy child will always have a special affinity for the gushy and the messy—for mud, for dirt, for paints, for water. He will rub his fingers on the butter, smear and pat milk on the tabletop.

Hold a baby and he pulls your nose or the hair on your head. He pulls your glasses off and he pokes at your eyes. As he grows older a child does other things, neither better nor worse, but they may be more irritating. The young child grinds the cigarettes and ashes in the ash tray. He squashes a tomato so the juice squirts and flows down his front.

A baby drops things. He breaks things. He is sure to spill his milk!

40

All this and more is a baby—and a child. No one can be pleased with all of it.

Fortunately, enjoying a child does not mean that you grin all the time, or that you have nerves of steel, or that you never feel exasperated or deflated or defeated. Babies do not need a climate of total sweetness and light. They do not need angels to raise them, nor paragons who never get a sore back from all the lifting and hauling, or tired feet from all the carrying, or aching hearts from the never-ending mess.

People will do. Ordinary people are all a baby asks for. We can be ourselves. We each have our own sense of humor, our own special tolerances where we are easygoing, and our own sore spots where we are touchy. There is no one golden pattern we each must follow, nor does everything have to fill us with joy. What counts is the overall weight of our responses, the way we feel most of the time. Our general spirit and tone can "say" to the baby: We're glad we have you! And we can each "say" this in our own way.

THREE WARNINGS

There are only a few warnings that we all would do well to remember:

First, it doesn't help if we are so stiff and standoffish, or so scared of spoiling the baby, that we hold back and hide the pleasure that we feel. Babies are not spoiled by our love. They are not spoiled because we fondle them and cuddle them and enjoy them. Love is the sunshine that nourishes babies, it doesn't rot them.

Second, it doesn't help if we are harsh. Harshness really worries a baby. A steady flow of anger or a fiery blowup really upsets him. Even when the baby seems to invite it, remember: Babies are the wrong people to slap or spank or hit. They are the wrong people to scream and yell at. They are the wrong

41

people to punish severely. You can hit a schoolage child, if you really feel you must, and you can hit an adolescent (if you really feel you can!). But it simply is not safe to hit or slap a baby.

We think that the incident is just a little storm. But very young children are so utterly dependent on our love and goodwill that our "little storm" always looks like a wild tornado to them. We run the risk of hurting much more than we mean to. Specific and explicit discipline becomes important later, as the child grows. But right now—with an infant, a baby, in the first year or so—there is no harm at all in being a "softy." Our gentleness will not make the children "soft." It gives them strength and helps them grow.

Third, it doesn't help if we rush in to take away from babies their own brand of comforters. Almost all youngsters in our society have something they turn to, their special "do-it-yourself" pacifiers and peace bringers. Many babies and very young children cling to a soft, fuzzy blanket. A great many suck their thumbs when they are very little. And many go whole hog—they suck, they clutch their blankets, and for good measure they twirl a wisp of hair or rub their soft ear lobes, all at the same time.

These "do-it-yourself" comforters serve a very basic purpose in early life. They are the baby's equalizers. He turns to them to make up for our stormy moments, for life's inevitable letdowns in this imperfect world, and for any shortages in the sucking which is so important to young children. We have a stake too (as well as the baby) in not abruptly ending these comforters. As long as the baby has his equalizers, we don't have to be perfect! Blanket and thumb let him make up, on his own time, for our being just humans.

Even if we didn't know the reasons why these handy comforters are so important, we ought to be willing to string along with them. Obviously, young children enjoy their thumbs, their blankets. Sucking, twirling, clutching may not be our kind of fun but it is theirs. They have, for a relatively brief time in life, a special sensitivity to soft feels, to rhythmic motion, to warming sensations. Babies are disconsolate when the blanket is temporarily lost. They relax and are contented when their comforters are at hand. Anything so deeply pleasing to the child ought to be pleasing to us! We have to develop real restraint about blocking any activity that a child does so eagerly and intensely, over and over.

"Peanuts," the comic strip, has probably helped many of us to hesitate before robbing children of their blankets. Page after page, however, could be written describing all the ingenious techniques that have been devised to stop thumbsucking in babies—alum, or anything nasty and bitter on the thumb, mitts that keep the thumb always under cover, splints to prevent a child from bending his arm and to keep his hand from reaching his mouth, bandages on the thumb, bribes and weird threats that the thumb will get swallowed or fall off or disappear.

We have to slow down. We must not rush in to take away from children what they so clearly seek unless we are completely certain that we can offer something in return that will make the child feel even better. The wise parent feels good when his child feels good. This happy acceptance helps a child know that we are glad he came, and that we love him in spite of his funny baby ways.

FOR INDEPENDENT STUDY

1. You will love one book which tells its story of good human relationships during the first year through beautiful photographs, accompanied by a minimum of text but very

sensitive text: *A Baby's First Year,* by Benjamin Spock and John Reinhart, with photos by Wayne Miller (New York: Duell, Sloane and Pearce, 1956; also available in a Pocket Book edition, 50¢).

2. One source of good pamphlet materials about children of all ages is the Child Study Association of America, 9 East 89th Street, New York 28, N.Y. Their booklet, *As Your Child Grows: The First Eighteen Months* (1955; 40¢), by Catherine M. Wolf and Aline B. Auerbach is appropriate at this point. If you send for it, be sure to ask for their whole list of publications.

3. You will also like *The Parents' Manual: A Guide to the Emotional Development of Young Children,* by Anna W. M. Wolf (New York: Ungar, 1962. Rev. ed.), now available in a paperback.

What would you do?

Question 3 Your five-year-old has a bad habit of whining and begging and pleading for things. He seems to complain almost all of the time that you buy things for the baby and for everyone else in the family but never for him (and this is *not* true!). What is your inclination: *a*) Buy him what he wants to shut him up. *b*) Let him complain if he wants to, but don't pay any attention and don't give in. *c*) Put your foot down and tell him, once and for all, that this kind of whining behavior has to stop and you mean it! *d*) When he is good and doesn't whine, buy him something so he learns how to behave; but whenever he fusses, don't budge an inch.

food and love

Chapter 6

Food, and all the activities associated with it, is another one of the main lines of communication through which a baby learns how much he is loved. Eating is a steady, over-and-over-again part of the baby's day. There are seven or eight feedings a day—day after day—at the beginning. The baby sleeps much of the time. These feedings, at the start, become almost the sole time during his waking hours when the lines are open and messages can come through to him.

Food serves a dual purpose. It is a source of energy. That is its physical meaning. Fully as important, maybe even more so, is that food brings a full feeling and pleasure. Food ends emptiness and pain and distress. An emotional meaning—a feeling of being loved—slowly emerges as good feeling flows after good feeling, as pleasure piles upon pleasure. Pain and distress, unrelieved, time after time, say the opposite to the child.

Physically, for energy, any way the food gets into the baby

is all right. The calories, proteins, minerals and vitamins simply have to get in, stay down, and go to work. Any way this can happen will do. Getting the right emotional food into the child is not so simple. A great many subtle and sometimes inconsequential-seeming elements—how the child is fed, when he is fed, how long he is fed, how the person feeding feels—determine the amount of emotional nourishment the baby gets.

BREAST-FEEDING

One of the first questions a mother has to decide is whether to breast-feed or bottle-feed her child. From the physical standpoint, doctors are well agreed: Breast-feeding is tops. Mother's milk is the perfect food at the start of life. It is hard to beat breast-feeding for its emotional content, too.

Breast-feeding is a very ingenious arrangement for bringing two humans close together. You cannot breast-feed at arm's length. You simply have to hold your child close to you—there is no getting away from it. Body touches body. Warmth melds with warmth. Mother's arms have to hold her child. Her strength is the child's support. In breast-feeding, a mother is one with her child. She gives herself. She feels like a mother, and baby feels that he has a mother. Inevitably mother and child get to know each other more intimately. It simply cannot be otherwise!

During the prenatal period nature's canny timing insures against a last-minute rush. All the basic developments are established early so that nothing is left to be done in the nick of time. But nature in her wisdom slows down some developments, too. She seems to know what we often forget with children: Haste makes waste! One of the underdeveloped parts of the newborn is his chin. The face is formed but every baby is chinless, a little Andy Gump. Seemingly there is a good

46

reason: So baby can hold a firm grip on the breast nipple and so that he can snuggle close to mother. This closeness, oneness, the holding and supporting, the fondling and caressing that are almost inevitable in breast-feeding are fundamental ways through which the baby builds his sense of trust.

Formulas can duplicate the nutritional content of mother's milk. Doctors are so experienced at prescribing formulas that they seem to do it almost offhand—so many ounces of concentrated milk, so many ounces of water, add this much sweetening if necessary. When called for, the formula is written out in such a jiffy that we sometimes forget that a great deal of specialized knowledge and effort, in chemistry and nutrition, lies in back of the words.

So, too, it is possible to create a "reasonable facsimile" of the emotional values of breast-feeding. A child does not have to be breast-fed to know he is loved. In every part of child rearing, at every age, there never is some one procedure which *must* be followed exactly. There is no technique which must *never* be used. Raising a child is not so mechanical and automatic a business. Children are too different; we are too different. If there is one trick that you should *always* do, it is to find the way that fits you and that fits your child—the natural way for the two of you.

Just as the doctor can make up the formula, the mother can duplicate in other ways the emotional vitamins and calories and minerals and proteins of breast-feeding. The one difference is that *Mother* must make the effort. The research chemist and the research nutritionist cannot do it for her.

Bottle-feeding has no automatic "built in" guarantees to insure holding and support and closeness. The bottle can be put in a bottle stand. The bottle can be propped up. There are countless devices to keep the nipple in the baby's mouth. As long as the milk flows the baby gets his physical nourishment—the chemist has taken care of that. It is up to the

47

mother to build in the emotional nourishment that she is responsible for.

Many mothers do make the effort. Bottle-fed babies can be held closely. Mothers can take advantage of the bottle-feeding time to caress their children. They can take the fullest advantage of this opportunity for two bodies to "speak" to each other. For at this stage in the baby's life it is not only tongues that speak or ears that hear. Every pore of the baby's whole body is a receiving station. When mothers know that food is not simply energy—*food is love*—they can make bottle-feeding a time when they feel like a mother and when the baby can sense their mothering.

SUCKING IS IMPORTANT

Breast-feeding has another advantage in addition to the closeness it guarantees. In its very nature, breast-feeding almost automatically has to be a leisurely, relaxed and unhurried process. Baby sucks. You burp him. He sucks again. Baby may seem to doze and perhaps you touch his cheek or touch his lips. He sucks again. You burp him and put him on the other breast. The baby sucks. The process is geared for mothers, not for engineers or mathematicians. There are no gauges. No indicators that you watch. No mechanical way to tell just how much milk the baby has consumed. Leisurely, comfortably, naturally, you keep your eye on your child. And you play your hunch. When your baby seems content, when he seems relaxed, you assume that he has had enough. A mother could weigh her child before and after feeding, but nursing mothers take the whole process with an easy feeling of trust.

The trouble with bottle-feeding is that you can see the milk. This "advantage" tends to throw mother's eye in the wrong direction. She watches the bottle, not her baby. The bottle is empty, the milk is gone. It must be time to stop! Some milk

48

is left. Wake up, baby, and suck! In a way, mother knows too much. Bottle-feeding sometimes becomes a tense and worrisome time.

When he is breast-feeding the baby sucks but you can't be sure that he is getting milk. He may be sucking for the fun of it! And sucking is fun for the baby. The lips are the most sensitive parts of his body. They are his most alert feelers out into this world. Just using them—to get milk, yes, but simply using them—is one of the baby's most pleasurable activities. Sucking is a soothing, assuring experience in and of itself.

Lips always remain one of the body's more sensitive areas. As the child grows, he builds other sources of satisfaction. Right now, in infancy, his lips are a prime source of comfort and contentment. Breast-feeding tends to guarantee the baby all the sucking he needs. No legal-eagle can watch and say: "Ah, you are sucking to get milk and that is all right. But now you are sucking and there is no milk; that is not nice." No "engineer" can measure the size of the hole in the nipple: It is too big. It is too small. The chances are that the breast-fed baby will suck vigorously to get his food. He will have more opportunity just to suck, for the sheer pleasure and comfort that sucking can bring.

Bottle-feeding can also become an unpressured time of mutual enjoyment between mother and child. It can become a time for mother's pleasure in her child undistracted by mechanical measurements, and for a child's enjoyment of his mother, on and on until he has had his fill. But we must create our own sensitive arrangements when Nature's own natural, "built in," automatic ways are not followed.

LOOKING AT THE WAY WE LIVE

Breast-feeding is no cure-all. Nor is it a disguise so that a resistant mother can show love she does not feel. The procedure itself is not the crucial thing. A mother can breast-feed her child, unwillingly and unhappily, conveying all the wrong messages to him. But the resistance to breast-feeding and the very common incapacity of mothers to breast-feed are worth some consideration. Some tragic forces are at work in our way of living to make so many mothers who could enjoy breast-feeding turn instead to a "formula" out of psychological or physical necessity.

Sometimes the blocks are overt and specific. Some nurses and doctors still ask the new mother the loaded question: "You are not going to breast-feed your baby, are you?" More commonly and more forcefully and more steadily, many silent pressures affect the decision. We are very modest about our bodies; and we have distorted attitudes. The breasts are over-emphasized as adult sex symbols; their physical and emotional role in nurturing a baby is constantly underplayed. Our children do not grow up seeing babies breast-fed as a matter of course.

We haven't found good answers to the whole question of women's education. Most of our girls go through high school and many go through college educated via words and books, perhaps educated away from their bodies. Many a woman has been subconsciously taught to shudder at feeding her own baby with her own milk: "I'd feel like a peasant." "I'd feel like a cow." Probably, too, our worship of science affects our attitudes. A formula sounds so scientific; a bottle seems so up-to-date. Breast-feeding looks old-fashioned.

We are all products of the way we live, just as baby is shaped by the simple experiences of getting his first food. An individual has to accept himself, just as we have to accept babies as they are. Our world makes us, *but* we make our world, too. We must be sure that we do not become overly thing-conscious, overly gadget-conscious, machine-minded

50

rather than human-centered. We may have to strive more self-consciously to preserve the simple, natural, easy ways of good human relationships that most of us are basically ready to follow, and would find deep satisfactions for ourselves in following. Our babies offer us a place to begin. Whether we breast- or bottle-feed, we must find ways of meeting their need for closeness, for oneness and warmth, for sucking and for skin and body contact, for leisurely and unhurried enjoyment.

FOR INDEPENDENT STUDY

1. There is not space to say enough about all that is involved in feeding children. Good physical nutrition is exceedingly important, for babies and for older children. And much more can be said about making mealtimes pleasant and enjoyable experiences. Two possibilities for supplementary reading are: *Feeding Your Child*, by Samuel W. Wishik, M.D. (Garden City: Doubleday, 1955) and *Feeding Your Baby and Child*, by Benjamin Spock and Miriam Lowenberg (New York: Duell, Sloane and Pearce, 1955; also available in a Pocket Book edition for 25¢).

2. Almost everyone today owns a copy of the *Pocket Book of Baby and Child Care*, by Benjamin Spock (New York: Pocket Books, 1946). If you have escaped, don't stay a refugee any longer. The book is outstanding, not only for its specific information (about feeding and a million and one other things) but for its general philosophy (about babies and the ages that immediately follow). You will also enjoy an English book, very informally written, almost in a Spock-like style: *Mother and Child: A Primer of First Relationships*, by D. W. Winnicott (New York: Basic Books, 1957).

51

What would you do?

Question 4 You take your five-year-old to Sunday School for the first time. He cries the minute you start to leave, clings to you, and wants you to stay with him. What is your inclination: *a*) Stay this first time but tell your child, so he knows without a doubt, that this is the last time you will stay. *b*) Don't give in. If you stay once, you will be trapped forever. *c*) Just stay. Why not? Let him sit on your lap or stay by your side or whatever he wants to do, and don't worry about it. *d*) Stay for a while but, the first time your child gets interested in anything and seems to forget about you, leave. If he misses you and cries a little, it won't kill him and the teacher can cope with him, if need be.

self-demand
schedules

chapter 7

Feeding a baby ought to be a simple business. Babies get
hungry and they fuss. We have the food and they can suck.
The food and the sucking make them feel good. The full baby
is content and relaxed. He is easy to live with. The food makes
us look good to him—*we* are easy people to live with. Feeding
ought to be as simple as ABC, especially in America because
we are lucky. We are rich. We have the food that can make
babies feel good.

Parts of this world face a very different situation. Their land
is poor. Their mothers are tired and sick and overworked. One
more baby is one more burden, a drain on a mother's low
vitality. The milk supply is limited. In these countries babies
suck and get little or nothing. They cry because their stomachs
stay empty.

We are different. We don't have an "eating problem" so
we create one! We manage one way or another to make feeding a baby a very complicated business.

53

FEEDING THE BABY—ON WHOSE SCHEDULE?

One of the issues we have dug up to fuss over is whether to feed the baby when he is hungry or to feed him when we think he *ought* to be hungry. Shall the baby be on a self-demand schedule, or on a schedule that someone else prescribes for him?

One way—the self-demand approach—is the simple way for a baby to know peace and contentment, safety and love. Yet we have come through a period when the other approach was the one we chose. Many of our babies cried, as African and Asian babies cry when there is no food and when all life seems insecure. Today we follow self-demand more, but the two differing approaches are worth examining. They raise issues which go beyond infant feeding.

The basic differences between the two are very easy to describe. In one approach the doctor makes up the schedule. He takes into account the baby's weight and height and age. He knows from experience how much food such a baby generally can take in. He knows how long it usually takes for the food to digest and for the stomach to empty. He knows how much sleep most babies of the same general development usually need. Putting all the information together the doctor comes out with an average: Feed him every three hours. Feed him every four hours.

In the self-demand approach, you simply keep your eye on your baby. Not on babies in general. You look at *your* baby, the one right in front of you. You don't have to be a genius to tell when a sleeping baby is about to wake up hungry. The baby sleeps less soundly; he starts to squirm a bit; he often begins to suck a little in his sleep. If you miss these first signs and the baby wakes up, you can be even less of a genius and still tell when the baby is hungry. He cries! Then you know.

Some youngsters thrive on the doctor's schedule. The three-
or four-hour prescription is an average, but the average is
bound to fit some people exactly. This happens when a man
buys a suit. A few men can walk right out of the store, the
new suit on their backs, without a single alteration. Most of
us aren't so lucky. We need a sleeve let down or turned up,
the waistline pulled in a bit or let out. The average is close
but not a perfect fit. So it is with most youngsters. The three-
or four-hour schedule is close, but not perfect.

A generation ago most babies were fed on the doctor's
schedule. They woke up hungry and they cried. Their mothers
knew what was wrong but the doctor had said, "Feed him
every four hours." The poor mothers looked at the clock and
waited, anxiously, for the minutes to tick by until the "official" feeding time. Many mothers cheated, of course. They
couldn't bear to hear their children cry—a hungry baby really
yells! Other mothers, more law-abiding, left the room—they
simply couldn't take it. And some mothers stuffed cotton in
their ears to avoid hearing the cries.

At other times the babies were sound asleep when the feeding time, set by the clock, came around. Their mothers were
spared tears but they still had a rough time. It is not easy to
persuade a sleepy baby that he ought to be hungry. Instead of
an easy, natural feeding—we have the food, the baby can suck
—meal time became worry time and often a time for fighting.

Mothers did what they did because they loved their children
—they followed the doctor's orders. But the baby had no way
of knowing the reason, and it would have been small comfort
if he did. The baby who wakes up, empty and helpless, knows
only the hurting inside of him. If he gets no food he has
moments of feeling deserted, of being unsure. It is harder for
him—seven and eight times a day at first, then six and five and
four—to build the safe feeling that people care for him, that
this is a good world to have been born into.

ABRUPT VERSUS GRADUAL WEANING

The question of self-demand versus doctor's schedule arises with two other significant parts of the baby's early life—the early morning feedings, and weaning from the nipple to the cup. You have your choice. You can play the averages, *or* you can do what seems most comforting and right for your baby.

Early morning feedings at one a.m., two a.m., three a.m. are a nuisance—there are no two ways about it! Mothers and fathers both need their sleep. Life in the family takes on a whole new look once the baby sleeps through the night and lets everyone have a good rest. You can't blame anyone for hoping that this wonderful time will come soon. But when?

The doctor can say: "This is about the usual time." This is when most children, on the whole, for the most part, by and large, are usually ready to sleep through the night. If the baby wakes up, just let him cry, or give him a little water. Water isn't exactly what the baby wants but it will tide him over; and he will soon learn that there is no point in waking up.

The self-demand way is more gentle. The baby doesn't have to "cry it out." If he wakes up hungry, you feed him and help him feel warm and safe. As the baby grows and can take in more food, he will wake up less and less often. The house is quiet, the night is dark. It becomes easy for him to sleep through, and to sleep contentedly.

Self-demand is a very gradual process. It stretches out over a little more time, and it goes unevenly. A baby sleeps through one night, but not necessarily the next. This uneven quality is characteristic of all development and will show up time and time again in the coming months and years. Growth is up and growth is down, but the over-all trend is up. Gradualism is a little more demanding on the mother and father, but a lot

56

more comfortable for the baby. The baby misses some nights of crying until exhaustion—he gains some nights of peace.

So, too, weaning to the cup can be done abruptly or gradually. You can play the averages or watch your baby. Actually, either way there ought to be no great hurry about weaning. Nothing like precious sleep is at stake! It may even be a little cheaper and more convenient to let sucking go on until it tapers off of its own accord and disappears. But most people feel a great pressure to wean. They are in a hurry to stop sucking. The idea that babies like to suck, that sucking in itself feels good to them, is hard to accept. We are all a little like wives who cannot appreciate their husbands' golf, or like men who cannot see why a new hat is so important to women! We don't like the baby's idea of fun—it is not the way we would have a good time.

In some parts of the world babies suck until a new child is born. In a few places they suck until they are old enough to go off to school. We think we are very patient and generous when we allow our babies to suck for five months or six. Comparatively, we are hard on our babies. We start early to feel itchy and to worry: Isn't it time now for him to stop? Play the averages and the answer can be *yes*. Now. Today. Those who advocate this abrupt end often advise: Break all the bottles. Throw out all the nipples. Don't leave one in the house and then you won't be tempted to give in to the baby's sorrow and desolation.

The baby is sure to cry and scream. Abruptly taking away sucking can be a major shock, comparable to our losing our job and our house and our car and our wife. But the abrupt approach "works," people say. And it does "work" if you mean that the child eventually drinks from a cup. He has to. He has no choice. Some parents, however, have reported that their child became almost completely dehydrated before he faced up to this stark reality.

57

Self-demand also works. The baby is offered a little milk from a cup at each feeding. Little by little he takes more of his milk from the cup. Gradually he takes all of his milk that way—so gradually that often you cannot remember for sure just when the change took place. Self-demand works—a little slower but without the child feeling a sense of loss and deprivation. It works without a stormy crisis. The change comes when the child is ready for it, not when someone else thinks he should be ready.

DEMAND AND REGULATION

Today we rely more and more on self-demand for establishing schedules, for giving up feedings, for weaning. One of the interesting sidelights is that we give the process a name. Many people in the world do exactly what we do but have no fancy-sounding name for it. As far as feeding time goes, for example, mothers carry their babies on their backs or on their hips or in their arms. When the child is the least bit fussy or unhappy, mothers do what comes naturally. They swing the child around and let him suck. Their babies know many fewer moments of worry and unsureness. They suck when they are hungry or unhappy. There is no name for the process. The babies just suck, and feel better.

We actually have *two* names—"self-demand," and the name most people feel more comfortable with, "self-regulatory," schedules. "Demand" is evidently a nasty word. We don't like the idea of babies pushing us around. The notion that a little shrimp is free to demand something and we hop to it offends—even when all he is "demanding" is food because he is hungry, and we have the food and he doesn't.

"Self-regulatory" has a good scientific sound. As a matter of fact, there is no difference between self-demand and self-

58

regulation. Under either label babies follow a very clear-cut schedule. Careful records have made it apparent that, if you feed your baby when he is hungry, he does not go hog wild. The healthy, normal child seems to have a great deal of sense built into him. At least, he is so made that it is perfectly possible for us to live with him. He is human, after all, and a human is made to live with humans. The baby "demands" but his demands are not so unreasonable or so wild and overbearing as to make life uncomfortable.

Whether you call it self-demand or self-regulation, all babies have their own rhythm and schedule. Some babies' own schedules turn out to be exactly the same as the doctor would have ordered. More commonly, babies have a special rhythm but not necessarily a neat and regular three- or four-hour pattern. They may have one short sleep, followed by a longer sleep, and then a shorter one again—something like a two and one half-hour and four and one quarter-hour schedule. Very commonly, babies follow one clear schedule for a few weeks and then, as they grow, slip into another quite different but still very regular schedule.

Two things are very clear: The first is that *all babies have a rhythm*; the second is that *each baby has his personal and private rhythm*. It is his own, special, just for him. The choice is not between the doctor's schedule and no schedule, but between the doctor's schedule and the baby's schedule (call it what you will: self-demand or self-regulatory).

It is clear, too, that when a baby is recognized as an individual, his needs are more fully met. This is a profound discovery about babies. It gets them off to a good start; it keeps them growing well. A profound discovery *and* very sensible. Self-demand (in feeding and in a lot of the rest of child behavior) is the same as looking at your own gas gauge on your own dashboard to see if you need gas in your own car, instead of looking at other 1958 Chevrolets like yours!

59

BABIES ARE A LOT OF WORK

Many people object that self-demand schedules tie a mother down. Under the doctor's schedule, the three or four hours between feedings belong to mother whether the baby cries or not. You can go to a movie or shop or go to sleep or visit a friend. Even though self-demand does settle into a clear schedule, it is never a fixed-forever schedule. You can't be sure that you will get your three or four hours of time off.

This complaint is more serious than it may sound. The mother who feels cheated by her baby's demands can hardly be a loving mother at feeding time. If the baby has played a dirty trick on her by waking up "before he was supposed to," the baby can catch the mother's irritation; and attitude is a thousand times more important than technique.

To give mothers a break, many doctors today set a two-hour limit on self-demand. The baby is fed any time he seems to need food after a two-hour period. But, within the two hours, if the baby fusses the assumption is that he needs something other than food—a change, burping, something a mother-substitute can provide.

You can't quarrel with this two-hour leeway to give mothers some time for themselves. Being a mother is a tough and ever-demanding job. Mothers get tired, they get bored, and they feel very tied down. Baby needs a giving mother, not a griping one. He needs someone who is glad and not depressed. This fringe benefit of a two-hour limit—this is mine, not company time—is a fine arrangement if it helps mothers to feel less abused.

We should note, however, that the time in a baby's life when his needs hit him so hard is a relatively brief time. We must be sure that our culture supports the idea of *giving* to babies for this short span when they need our giving. We must be sure our culture supports a willing acceptance of the reality that babies are trouble. Not too much trouble. Not more than most of us can take. But they *are* trouble. You cannot have a baby and still lead your own sweet life. Babies are helpless. We have to be the ones who are willing to give.

Rooming-in has been discussed. Some mothers object to it because they feel "entitled" to the three or four days of rest in the hospital, all by themselves, after having a baby. There is no point in arguing over three or four days, but the attitude should concern all of us. We need to increase our awareness that babies are the ones with overpowering needs. Once we accept this fact, we feel stronger when we give in, rather than more tired and put-upon.

Childbirth-without-fear is also worth mentioning in this connection. The practice is by no means widespread, and almost surely it is not for everyone. But those mothers who have followed this approach have a head start in one important way. They know that babies are an effort. They have learned to feel good from the beginning about making the effort. Through physical and psychological preparation, and because they are not heavily sedated in childbirth, these mothers actively participate in the birth of their child. The baby is not taken from them by an expert, the obstetrician. The mothers work to give birth, and many find it a highly satisfying experience.

One way or another adults must help themselves to realize what is our adult job—to give to children. Not things, but ourselves. We give our time, our love, our care. Babies cannot do for themselves. We have to be on hand, gladly, to meet their needs.

FOR INDEPENDENT STUDY

1. One of the less well-known books by Dr. Arnold Gesell gives the fullest statement of the basis for a self-demand

approach to feeding, as well as to other experiences in the child's early life: *Feeding Behavior of Infants: A Pediatric Approach to the Mental Hygiene of Early Life*, by Arnold Gesell and Frances Ilg (Philadelphia: Lippincott, 1937).

2. *Childbirth Without Fear*, by Grantly Dick-Read (New York: Harper, 1953) is provocative reading, as is *The Battle for Mental Health*, by James Clark Moloney (New York: Philosophical Library, 1952).

What would you do?

Question 5 The mother of a seventeen-month-old is expecting a new baby in a few weeks. She has heard that there is a good nursery school in the neighborhood that takes one-year-olds. She is thinking of sending her child. With whom do you tend to agree: *a*) Grandmother says: "Send her. You will be tired and need all of your energy for the new baby." *b*) A neighbor says: "Kindergarten is early enough to send children to school. What do you want them to do—go to school all their lives?" *c*) Father is opposed to the whole idea. He thinks that the seventeen-month-old should stay at home. *d*) A maiden aunt thinks that nursery school is the perfect solution: "Sally will have things to play with and friends. If she stays at home, she will just feel out of things."

times
of separation
from mother

chapter 8

Almost every mother has moments, especially during the baby's first two years but even later, when being a mother demands more than she honestly can give. Mother wants her child. Most of the time she is glad she has a child and glad to do what a child needs. *But* moments of real depression come along. Baby seems like a monster who constantly drains the mother dry. Baby seems like a weight that presses down on her and squeezes the life out of her. At these times a mother cannot pretend that she loves. She doesn't. Momentarily she comes very close to hating—the baby is simply too much of a baby. It asks too much, too often, too steadily.

These blue moments of depression are very common and very human. Babies will be much better off if we recognize how universal such feelings are in mothers. It makes no sense to pretend that they do not exist or to pretend that every mother loves her baby every minute of the time or, at least, she "ought" to!

63

Wishful Thinking Is No Answer

We are trying with children to get away from wishful thinking, down to an honest and realistic approach. We are trying to respond to what the child actually feels. Is he hungry (whether he "ought" to be or not)? Let's feed him. Is he frightened (whether he "ought" to be or not)? Let's comfort him. Does he feel hurt (whether he "ought" to or not)? If he hurts, or thinks he hurts, let's sympathize.

We must apply the same realistic good sense to ourselves. The baby is not helped if we think we "ought" to breast-feed, but hate it; if we think we "ought" to follow a self-demand schedule, but don't feel comfortable with it. He gets no good at all from our company if we think we "ought" to play with our child when actually we are fed up with him.

One reason that mothers feel depressed is simple fatigue. Mothers have a tough job, like a ditch digger's job or a stevedore's. It adds up to a lot of hard work. Mothers lug and haul and carry and lift. Mothers bend and get down on their hands and knees. All the heavy physical work goes on around the clock, without the luxury of relaxed coffee breaks or recess times. Sheer weariness can make anyone feel emotionally low.

Mothers today are the victims of social change. Their old reliable helpers have disappeared from the scene. The chances are that the family—the new baby, mother and father—is living in their own home or apartment. The larger family—grandmothers, maiden aunts, sisters—is off, living somewhere else. Maids, if we have them at all, are apt to be the once-a-week variety. They no longer "live in," on tap constantly to take over. Today the mother is left to hold the fort alone, and the chances are that her back aches and her feet hurt while she does it!

A social change in another direction has created a balancing gain and a very constructive one. Fathers pitch in a great deal more than they used to. Fathers help directly with the baby when they are at home, sterilizing bottles, diapering and changing, taking the baby for a stroll in the carriage. Fathers do a bigger share of housework, too. They prepare some meals, cope with the dishes, shopping, vacuuming, dusting, etc. Their extra pair of hands and feet can be a real factor in preventing some of the exhaustion that makes it hard for a mother to show the love to her child that he needs.

Wise mothers and fathers lower their standards, too. A house without children can be spick and span, ready to be photographed for *House Beautiful.* Add one baby, especially a crawler or walker, and you get a very different picture. Mother doesn't have the time she once had to fluff every pillow. If she tries, baby is always two jumps ahead of her, making a new mess for every one she can patch up. Families who change their concept of what is "beautiful" save their mothers from some fatigue. A "beautiful" house is one that looks as if "a baby lives here," not a stuffed animal or a goldfish. A little healthy confusion can be a source of pride, rather than of embarrassment. Mothers who drive themselves to maintain the old pre-baby standards soon wear out their capacity to show love.

SHORE LEAVE FOR MOTHERS

Fatigue is not the only cause of depression, however. All the rest of us at least take off July 4th and Christmas Day. There are no vacations from baby. Fathers get a little variety on their way to work and coming home. If mother isn't worn down, she feels tied down! Her job is like that of a submarine crew, or of the radar watchers in the far frozen North. She faces the same isolated quarters day after day. Sailors get a shore leave to keep them from going crazy. Mothers need a "shore leave," too, or else there is danger that their love will be smothered and not get through to the baby.

No problem exists in the first few months of the baby's life. During this period others can feed the baby, change him, and do what has to be done while mother has some time off without real risk. By four or five months or so—once a child has grown enough to depend on the known face, the known smell and the known hands—"shore leave" for mother is not such a simple matter. It is not easy to meet baby's need for sameness and steadiness and for one person's constant love.

If a relative lives with the family and has shared steadily in the baby's care, the solution is simple. Mother can go out for an evening's fun or—how heavenly when finances permit! —go off for a weekend with her husband and be a bride again and not "just a mother." This solution is becoming rarer and rarer, however.

Many young couples spend evenings at friends' homes and take their babies with them. When baby wakes up, his mother is right on hand. This makes a lot of sense. Other families try very hard to find one steady baby sitter or maid. They look for a warm, loving person, not a model of cold household efficiency. They try to find her early so that she can build up a personal feeling for the baby. The families who find such a person are lucky. Mother can set off on "shore leave" with more confidence, her mind at ease; and there is less hazard that baby will wake up feeling lost or threatened.

Warm and loving baby tenders are hard to find in our society. Realistically we usually have to work out the best compromise possible so that mothers do not feel too worn out or too tied down—mothers are human—and so that babies do not feel too lost—they are human, too!

WORKING MOTHERS—THE MOST DIFFICULT PROBLEM OF ALL

The most common separation, and the most persistent, takes place when mothers go to work. According to the figures compiled for the 1960 White House Conference on Children and Youth, almost three million mothers of children under six are working—about 20% of all such mothers. This is a large number. It represents a significant increase over the figures of ten years ago—83% more mothers of children under six were working in 1958 than in 1948! This trend is full of hazard for young children.

The whole question of working mothers is exceedingly complex. You can say only one thing flatly and without qualification: *If a mother of a young child does not want to work and does not need to work, she should not work!* If a mother enjoys being with her baby and can be with her baby, that is exactly where she should be. Loving and caring for a young child and being thrilled by his growth can be one of the most satisfying experiences for a woman. Being loved by a willing mother is a fundamental experience for a child.

Some young mothers today are simply getting on the bandwagon. They see other mothers working, and in increasing numbers. The idea snowballs. Getting their cues from what seems to be the trend, these mothers take a job, not out of preference but because they think they "ought" to. This is a shame—for the mother and for the child.

Our society prizes people who achieve. We prize those who produce, and especially those who earn cash and a lot of it. Too often, mothers feel they are loafing even though they work like dogs at home. They feel they are not "doing anything" even though they are busy every minute of the day.

67

They run themselves down and guiltily say: "I'm *just* a mother." "I'm *just* a housewife." "I *just* look after my baby."

All of us—mothers especially—ought to recognize very clearly: Nurturing a baby *is* producing. Mothering is the way of producing a healthy, strong personality in a child. It is the way of meeting our greatest shortage, more severe than the shortage of scientists or mathematicians or engineers or doctors. Our greatest shortage is of completely sane people who feel secure inside of themselves and who are glad they are who they are. There is no more significant job than that of producing healthy humans. Mothers who enjoy being with their children and who find it easy to get their love over to their children are doing exactly that.

Another group of mothers, included in that huge total of three million who work, simply misunderstand. They say: "I'll work now, when my child is young and doesn't need me." These mothers are not eager to work. They face no pressing financial problem now. They plan to stop work when their child gets older and "needs" them. But they think they are doing the right thing to work now and put some money aside.

These mothers *underestimate* the young child's need for love, and its importance. They think: Anyone can feed a baby. Anyone can change his diapers. But a mother who is excited about her baby is by all odds the best one to help a child know that he is loved. Not everyone can do this!

These mothers *overestimate* the child's need for them when he is older. Later, when these mothers plan to stop work, their youngsters will be getting their fundamental satisfactions from achievement, from their age-mates, and from adults outside the home. These mothers have a mixed-up time schedule. Their clocks are all off. *The child under six needs his mother.* Older children do too, but not nearly so much—they have many other more pressing needs as well.

68

The problem of working mothers is much more complex when mothers *must* work. Many mothers do, for financial reasons. They are the sole support of their children because of the absence of their mate, due to divorce, separation, illness, death or desertion. Many other mothers from "whole families" feel real financial pressure because the one income of one wage earner simply is not enough to maintain a decent and satisfying life.

Another group of mothers work because they feel they must work. Money is not the pressure. Equally strong psychological reasons move them. These women feel unused at home, unchallenged, empty, unhappy. Or they want the companionship of people their own age, the fun and excitement of being with fellow workers. Many women in this group have specialized training and a strong urge to use their training for some productive end.

We tend to be indulgent if a mother of a young child works because she must for financial reasons. We can understand this one explanation—money! Generally we are not so sympathetic when the reason that a mother must work is simply her own need for satisfaction. Again we face the same old problem, the one we face in all our living with children: Do we approve only when the other fellow feels what we think he "ought" to feel? Do we disapprove when his honest responses conflict with our preconceived standards? The only sane and constructive solution whenever humans—adults or children—are involved is to respond to what people *do* feel, whether they "ought" to feel that way or not.

This acceptance of people moves in the right direction but, unfortunately, it still leaves unsolved the question of how to meet the young child's needs *and* the adult's needs (whether those be financial or psychological). The sad fact is that there is no simple solution.

69

Almost No Good Way Out

Under state and federal law, "Aid to Dependent Children" is available to help mothers in dire financial need so that they can stay at home with their children instead of going out to work. This is a step in a good direction, but in every state the sum is inadequate and only a very partial answer to a very sticky question.

Some mothers manage to find full-time housekeepers to take their place in the home. Such women are hard to find, and expensive. Hardest of all is finding, not a housekeeper, but a mother-substitute. It is difficult enough to find someone to vacuum, dust, cook; it often is impossible to hire someone who has warmth, patience, love and laughter. Housekeeping isn't the problem. Baby-keeping is. The baby and the young child's need for love must be the paramount consideration.

When children are several years older—mature three-, four- and five-year-olds—they can spend their days in day nurseries or child care centers with groups of other children the same age while mothers work. This is no solution at all for children under three. Children under three years of age are too young for group living. Children this young would be severely threatened in all-day groups by the separation from their mother.

Unfortunately, even for three-, four- and five-year-olds, day nurseries are only a theoretical solution, not a present-day realistic one. There are such groups, but there are very few good ones! *Good* day nurseries or child care centers are expensive. They need highly trained, sensitive teachers. They must have a very small class size so that children already separated for the full day from their mothers, can have intimate and personal attentions. The groups need expensive and special play equipment. When group day care is done well, the cost is sky-high. Day nurseries need generous community support, or generous charity support, or tax support because tuition alone can seldom pay the bill. In most day nurseries, unfortunately, the child's physical needs may be met but his psychological needs are ignored. Even three-, four- and five-year-olds feel damaging separation; they feel loss of love. The children return home each night seemingly safe. No scars show. But the children do not feel safe.

A few mothers find foster homes where their child can be cared for, while they work, by a woman who substitutes for them in love, personal attention, and face-to-face intimate care. This is the best solution for the child under three who cannot be cared for in his own home; it often is the best solution, too, for an older child. But foster homes are scarce. As physical dwellings they are hard to find. As true centers of interest and caring, they are rarer still.

The mother who must work, no matter why she must work, faces a very difficult problem today. And her child faces a difficult problem. Even in those lucky instances where a good plan can be made—a friendly maid or relative in the home, a supporting foster home, a truly sensitive group for older children—the working mother still faces the problem of her own time and energy. It is no easy task to do a full-time job and to have left the emotional resources to give a child the attention and boost he needs when the separation is over. Children who have been away from their mothers often demand more attention when they rejoin their mothers. Their demand is understandable, but it comes at the very moment when mother's energy is at a low ebb.

Three million mothers of children under six are working outside of the home. The fact is: We do not have a good answer to this problem. The solution is not the simple one of passing a law: Stay at home! Many mothers cannot, nor is the physical presence of a mother the answer. Children need a mother who is happy being where she is. The problem is too

71

large for individual mothers and families to solve by themselves. Unfortunately, right now, we are pretending the problem does not exist. We have created no new social devices in response to the new fact that so many mothers of young children are working and that the trend is up—an 83% increase in the last ten-year period.

Separation from their mothers is a real hazard to young children, one we must all think about. We each have a great stake in growing well-loved children whose daily experiences help them feel safe and secure. Only such children are easy to live with when they are young; only such children are easy to live with in the years to come.

FOR INDEPENDENT STUDY

1. The U.S. Children's Bureau Publication No. 382, *Children of Working Mothers*, (Washington: Government Printing Office, 1960. 20¢) is the most recent report on all aspects of this important and baffling social trend.

2. The general situation mothers today find themselves in is well explored in *The Many Lives of Modern Woman*, by Sidonie M. Gruenberg and Hilda Sidney Krech (Garden City: Doubleday, 1952) and in *Her Infinite Variety*, by Morton M. Hunt (New York: Harper and Row, 1962).

What would you do?

Question 6 J. Ellington Whitehurst says in his book: "Infancy is one of the most important times of all. As the twig is bent, so the tree grows. Unfortunately, too many parents do not realize that from little acorns big oak trees grow. They miss the opportunity in these early years to start children off on the right foot, establishing good ways of behaving early

72

and rooting out the bad ways early . . ." What is your inclination: *a*) To agree with Whitehurst—he knows what he is talking about. *b*) To disagree—he underestimates what parents try to do. *c*) To disagree—infancy isn't all that important. *d*) To disagree just in general—Whitehurst is talking through his hat.

the birth
of a new baby

chapter 9

A child learns his sense of trust from the way he is treated in the ordinary, everyday events of his life. But one event, which can hardly be described as humdrum or routine, has a lot to do with how thoroughly loved a child feels. *The birth of a new baby*—a brother or sister (a sibling, to use the technical term that covers either sex)—*is a crisis in the love life of the young child.* Of course the one exciting day of the birth is not the day that counts. All the little events before the birth and after are the ones that matter. From what happens during all of these days the child takes the meaning that matters to him: Am I fully loved or not?

Not all children experience the birth of a newcomer in their family while they are still very young. Older children—over six or eight, let us say—generally take this event quite easily in their stride. They are less apt to see a threat in it. By this

74

age they feel more sure of their standing in the family, and they are after satisfactions other than mother-love alone. Both the last-born and the only child never have the experience of a new birth. They remain, unchallenged, in the prize position to be loved.

These children might seem "lucky." But each particular birth order—the only child, the last-born, the middle child, the first boy, the first girl—has its special position of privilege. Each position also has its special disadvantages. No one child is all-lucky; no one child has all the cards stacked against him. It is closer to the truth to say that each particular birth order is different. Whether that difference proves to be lucky or unlucky depends on how things are handled as a child's life moves along.

The seemingly "lucky" ones—the last-born, and the only child—miss out on what can be a time to feel more sure of their position and more pleased that they are who they are (to say nothing of missing out on all the other joys and sorrows that come from having someone younger than they in the family). The birth of a newcomer need not be a great upset; it can fortify a child and help him feel bigger. But a hazard exists that we do well to recognize. Whether the danger materializes will depend on what happens. Either a good result or a harmful one can come along.

PREPARATION AHEAD REDUCES THE HAZARD

The hazard to the child increases if we try to keep the forthcoming birth a deep dark secret. Many parents assume that a two-, three-, four- or five-year-old is "too young"—he wouldn't understand and he doesn't care. Inevitably a pregnancy is bound to be one of the world's worst kept secrets! Pregnancies are even harder to hide from young children than from the neighbors; and, like all bad attempts at secrecy, rumors result which can be more disturbing than the truth could ever be.

A young child shielded from the news is bound to know that something is up. He becomes aware of his mother's growing figure but his questions are answered with all kinds of lies and evasions: "Mother is eating too much." "Mother ought to go on a diet." In many areas of family life we preserve the fiction that children will not know what is going on if we don't tell them. For example: "My husband and I have terrible fights, but never in front of the children." "My husband and I are going to separate, but we never talk about it in front of the children." We conveniently forget that walls have ears, and so do little children. They have ears and eyes and pores —even radar! The lies never satisfy. The silence never comforts. The child is disturbed by a dim, vague sense that "something" is going on.

Youngsters are unusually susceptible to atmosphere, to tone, to indefinable notes in the air. Kept in the dark, a child cannot know for sure what is happening. But he does know the one thing that matters most in the whole wide world to him—his position in our love. Not certain of what is happening, he reads into the goings-on the danger that would concern him the most: Maybe we don't love him anymore.

The child who is taken completely by surprise when suddenly his mother disappears and then returns with a little "bundle" that inevitably is the center of fussing and attention has his worst fears confirmed. The youngster is worried— someone has come to take his place; and he feels vaguely guilty—he must have done something wrong.

Safeguards against the vague, unsettling anxiety and this final devastating surprise blow are essential. A child should know that his mother is carrying a new baby. Any questions —young children's questions are usually very simple—should

76

be answered honestly. "A baby is growing inside of your mother" is a good start. Often this is as much as the three- or four-year-old cares to know. "Mother will go to the hospital to have the baby" is another important bit of information and preparation as the time draws near. This is a time when children often like to hear stories about new babies, and there are some excellent ones. At bedtime and story time they frequently like to see their own baby pictures, and to hear the story of how and where and when they were born.

But what we do and don't do is much more important than our words. The time near the birth of a new baby is not the time, for example, to enroll the "old baby" in nursery school or kindergarten. We may be glad to have him out from under foot, but this is exactly what troubles him and exactly why we shouldn't do it! This *is* the time for as much good companionship and doing things together as his mother's energy or his father's greater energy will allow. It is the time, too, to be sure that the child is really well acquainted and securely comfortable with the person who will stay with him while his mother is gone.

Before the birth, and more commonly afterwards, is the time when continued mothering is called for, the kind of mothering that gently overlooks and understands. Children unconsciously test us out at this period. Without their knowing why, they do little things they know they shouldn't do, or ask for the extra attentions that they know are unreasonable. They want to see if we will pass the test. If we are harsh (as they tempt us to be), if we slap them down (as they almost ask us to), we fail their test. We seem not to love them, despite all our words.

ACCEPTING A CHILD'S FEELINGS

The hardest problem is for us to accept how the child feels. We are apt to become salesmen, persuading him how he

77

ought to feel. Our cheery point of view may not jibe in the least with the child's actual state of mind. We keep telling him: "Aren't you lucky! You're going to have a baby brother or sister. Aren't you glad!" The youngster senses that *we* are lucky and glad, but he fails to see any good luck in store for *him*; and this is what counts.

After the birth occasionally a child puts his lack of enthusiasm directly into words: "Why did we have to have him? Why don't we give him back?" Sometimes children are even more outspoken: "I'd like to burn him in the stove or flush him down the toilet!" Most often, a youngster just doesn't know what to say. He *is* glad, a little bit, in a way. And yet he has many moments when he sees no cause for joy. He is a little mixed-up.

Whenever a child does express his opposition to the newcomer directly and openly, we are almost always shocked. The child's words go counter to that nice stereotype: *"Everybody loves little children."* We think "everybody" includes even little children. Little children do love little children—themselves! But we are asking young ones to stretch things quite a bit to include the new baby in their inner circle. It is easy for adults to stretch their love; it can be mighty hard for a young child to do it.

Our sales talk often tries to reassure: "You are going to be our *big* child now." This isn't always the good news we think it is. It can be the very thing that worries the youngster. He doesn't want to be big at the moment. He may be feeling very much like a baby, and wishing he were the only one.

Again certain safeguards are important. This is *not* the time to take away the child's things: "You want the little baby to have your bed, don't you." "You want the little baby to have your toy." When a new baby is born, the older child needs to get—not to give! The words, "You're big" sound hollow unless they are accompanied by an increased flow of the nice

78

things this big-little child can understand—more time, not promises; more love, not words; more companionship, not pep talks. So often we seem to be saying: "You're big, lucky you. Now you can pay income tax!"

It helps if children are allowed to participate in getting ready for the baby—fixing up the baby's room, taking some part in the shopping. After the baby arrives it helps if the older child can participate in the baby's care, to do what he is old enough to do—and wants to do. The jobs can range from shaking talcum powder on the baby's bottom to holding the newborn on his lap. But we must be careful not to push children too fast into bigness.

If we can accept that, at this time, being tiny a while may be all-important to the child, we make it easier for him to glide into bigness later on. If we push him, he may dig his feet into the ground to resist. If we help him feel sure he is fully loved, he stays free to grow. Our biggest efforts must be in this latter direction. The child will then, in his own good time, make his own efforts to go forward.

Fathers play a very special role when a new baby arrives. Not as fatigued as mother, not as tied down with the baby's care, fathers can find many ways to assure the older child that he is still *in*, and very much so. Trips together, stories together, more good-natured roughhouse and time for much good fun in the bath—these are some of the ways that say to a child: We do love *you*.

Twins, triplets, quadruplets and quintuplets are very rare. But in fact every birth is a multiple birth. The new child is born; the old child is born again. Almost inevitably, the two-, three-, four-, or five-year-old has moments, before the birth and after, of going back a bit to babyish ways. He may want to be held more. He may say that he needs more help with dressing or eating. He may want more stories, more drinks at night, more time in the bath. He may increase his thumbsucking or start again. He may be much less well toilet trained than he has been. In a way, nature plays a dirty trick. Just when the new baby gives everyone less time, the old baby demands more time. And there are still only twenty-four hours in the day!

It is tempting to be angry with the old baby because he doesn't understand. But we must be gentle because *we* understand. The young child cannot truly know the jam we are in —that we have only two hands, that we have only two feet, that there are only sixty minutes in the hour. But we must understand the jam *he* is in. He feels unsure of our love, and our love is the most precious thing in the world. If he thinks he has lost that, he has lost everything.

The solution isn't anger, although we may well be tempted to get angry. It isn't impatience, although that is very understandable. The solution isn't pep talks, although it is mighty hard sometimes to keep still. The solution lies in more of those gentle supporting actions that make a child feel good.

The youngster who experiences this support becomes "luckier" than the only child or the last-born. He is treated well. He gets a second strong shot of love. And he is free to see, without anxiety or threat to himself, how well the new baby is treated. This lesson can be very reassuring. Right before his eyes, if he can look without worry, he sees a demonstration of mothering—the kind the baby gets now, the kind he got once, the kind he will get again if ever he is the one who needs it.

JEALOUSY

Despite the wisest handling, however, you seldom can cope with the birth of a new baby perfectly. If we are sensitive, we can save the older child from being snowed under by great moments of deep depression and worry. But few of us have the time, energy, and skill to ward off every single second of bad feeling. Some jealousy, some antagonism, some hostility —backfires from the child's fleeting sense of being unloved— are almost inevitable.

Youngsters with a sturdy sense of trust can handle these momentary feelings. They even thrive on them, getting from them the vinegar that spurs drive, ambition and determination. We don't need to worry if the feelings come out only once in a while as a child goes ahead living his life well for his age. We don't need to worry if a child only *says* his feelings once in a while: "I don't like him." "He's no good." "He stinks." The sound may not be pleasant but feelings that can be spoken out are never too strong. They become weaker once they are out in the open and not bottled up.

A little jealousy is so common in children and so understandable that you have to beware when it is totally missing. If a child seems only full of love, watch out. If he is "devoted" to his baby brother or sister, if he talks the same glad game that you do, he may be raising a danger signal. Constant sweet talk can mean that a child is so swamped with distress that he doesn't dare open up for fear that his honest feelings will get out of hand. You have to beware too when a youngster does not cover up, but shows his jealousy constantly and in everything he does, when jealousy has become the one theme of his life.

Either way—disguised or out in the open—jealousy is the child's way of saying: "I'm unlucky in love." There is no point in going back to the past—why he feels left out, whether he honestly has cause for feeling left out, whether he "should" feel so jealous. The job to be done lies ahead. Not through words but through deeds, you have to make the youngster feel the way every young child must feel: I am glad I am who I am. I'm lucky in love!

81

FOR INDEPENDENT STUDY

1. Two quite different books make rewarding reading at this point. *Jealousy in Children*, by Edmund Ziman (New York: A. A. Wyn, 1949) is a serious professional discussion of the question; *Baby Makes Four*, by Stanley and Janice Berenstain (New York: Macmillan, 1959) is a light-hearted and gay approach.

2. Good books for children are worth knowing in themselves, as a part of our literature; they also deepen our understanding of what children are like because sensitive authors know youngsters well. Get to know some of the books that have been written either to give children information about how a baby is born or to help them express their feelings about the new baby. Among the best are: *The Wonderful Story of How You Were Born*, by Sidonie Gruenberg (New York: Doubleday, 1952); *A Baby Is Born*, Milton I. Levine and J. H. Seligmann (New York: Simon and Schuster, 1949); *All Kinds of Babies* (1953) and *All About Eggs and How They Change Into Animals* (1952), by M. Selsam (New York: William R. Scott); *We Are Six*, by Clara and Morey Appell, with photos by Suzanne Szasz (New York: Golden Press, 1959); *We Are A Family*, by Inez Hogan (New York: Dutton, 1954); *When You Were a Baby*, by R. Eng (New York: Simon and Schuster, 1949); *The Very Little Girl*, by Phyllis Krasilovsky (New York: Doubleday, 1953); *When You Were a Little Baby*, R. Berman (New York: Lothrop, Lee and Shephard, 1950).

What would you do?

Question 7   A two-year-old acts very badly whenever his mother takes him to the park to play. He hugs his own truck, for example. He stubbornly says "mine" and won't share it at all with the other children. With whom do you tend to agree: *a*) His mother, college educated and very liberal in all of her thinking, gently but firmly insists that he share, if only for a short time. She says: "If we are ever going to have a peaceful world we cannot bring up a generation of little possessors who want to hug everything they own to themselves." *b*) Father thinks they should send the child to nursery school so he can begin to learn to share. *c*) Another mother on the playground is very casual: "Why make such a fuss? Let him keep his toy if he wants it." *d*) Whenever grandfather sees how selfish his grandchild is, he blames the adults for being too soft. He would make the child share, and no two ways about it.

the awe
of habits

Chapter 10

Helplessness does not last forever. The child grows and changes and develops. As he does, he seeks new and different kinds of satisfactions. Impulsiveness and sheer egocentricity do not last forever. The child grows and changes and develops and, as he does, he acts in different ways. Humans change—constantly, inevitably. Change is a basic human characteristic, but one that many people have grave difficulty in accepting. Seeing is not believing, somehow. The evidence of change is constantly before our eyes, yet we put little stock in it.

One reason why we lack faith in change is our very strong fear of habits. It is more accurate to say: We stand in awe of habits. We fear bad habits, we worship the good ones. We all *know* that "big oak trees from little acorns grow." We are completely *sure* that "as the twig is bent, so the branch grows." We haven't a doubt that "well begun is more than half done."

Our awe of habits sets the stage for how we act time after

84

time. When we see a child doing something unattractive at six months of age we immediately start to worry: Suppose he does the same thing at six years of age, or sixteen, or sixty-six? The minute we see a "bad habit" rear its ugly head, we feel we must trample on it, or, if the six-month-old behavior happens to be attractive and easy to live with, we think we have it made! This is the start of a good "habit" and there is one thing we are positive about: Children are creatures of habit!

Unfortunately, the one idea that has really taken hold of our thinking is only a partial truth about children. The awe of habits catches one little piece of childhood. When you think that habits are everything, you get a completely distorted picture.

HABITS HOLD NO DEATH-LIKE GRIP

Children have habits. Adults have habits. We all have good habits and bad ones. Habits save us time. They save us energy. They save us thought. They let us do certain acts unconsciously, automatically, simply and easily. We set the blinker on the car to signal a turn—you can call that a habit. We button the button on our wallet pocket—that's a habit. We always put our house key in our right-hand pants pocket—a habit again. Thank heavens we don't have to think out each of these acts every single time the need arises.

Habits are a very valuable part of everything we do all day long, but there is no need to stand in awe of them. We control habits; they do not control us. Every day we are constantly sloughing off old habits and taking on new ones. Habits do not have the death-like grip on the human that we give them credit for. It is relatively simple to put habits in their proper place.

Before blinkers were invented we habitually put our arm out of the car window to signal a turn; now, just as automatically, we flip the blinker. Once we habitually shifted from first to second to high gear; now, just as automatically, we cope with the four-speed shift or push the button marked "D" or set the lever in drive. Once, day after day like an old milk wagon horse, we turned left to head homeward; now that we have moved, we turn right just as automatically. With only an occasional lapse at the beginning, or maybe with none at all, you can shed the old habit and take on the new.

There is a very simple explanation of why it is so easy to change a habit. Once the satisfaction is gone and the thrill is gone, momentum keeps the habit going. A little counter-push is all you need to stop it. True habits start through a very simple application of pain or pleasure (and they end as simply, in the same way). We did something once; it brought us some pleasure. We did it again, and the sweetness came again. We did it again and again; soon it became an unthinking part of our bag of tricks. The act is a true habit if it keeps rolling along and we no longer need the reward each time.

Perhaps we did something and met some form of pain—a physical hurt, disapproval, some deprivation. We tried it again and bumped into the pain again. Soon we stopped doing it. The avoidance of the act is a true habit if the pain no longer has to be present or threatened.

A little pain or pleasure start our habits; a little pain or pleasure end them. Do you have a habit of waking up at the crack of dawn? Change your job so that you don't have to get to work so early. Suffer the pain of nothing-to-do when you wake up and you can break the habit. Do you have a habit of always turning to Channel 9 at seven o'clock? If your favorite program changes its time—you suffer the pain of not seeing what you want—you will have no trouble breaking the "seven o'clock habit!" Once the satisfaction (or pain) is gone, then the habit is easy to break.

NEEDS VERSUS "HABITS"

When the satisfaction persists, however, you have a very different job. We do many things over and over, habitually, not because once in the dim dark distant past we got some satisfaction from doing them—the satisfaction continues right now, in the present. We do them over and over, not because once long ago they made sense—they make sense right now, in the present. These acts once brought us satisfaction, *and they still do*. If you have a "bad habit of eating," it would be a hard "habit" to break!

It is misleading to call such acts "habits." They may look like habits. They may sound like habits. But they are totally different. In a true habit, the satisfaction was long ago. In these continuing acts the satisfaction is *now*. Simple momentum is not carrying them along. *Need*—a fundamental reason —is.

You can tell in almost a jiffy whether an act is a true habit or a need. *If it is easy to break, it was a habit!* If you run into any major difficulty at all, *beware*. You probably are not dealing with an old outworn habit. The chances are that you are tampering with a human need.

Habits fade away with a little counter-push. If you ignore basic needs, or try to block them, they shoot sky-high. Stop eating, and you get hungrier and hungrier and hungrier. Don't sleep, and you get more and more tired. Don't drink water, and your thirst becomes more and more fierce. If you treat needs as if they were habits, all you do is to make them go on longer and stronger and more powerfully than ever.

The young child's need for affection is a very basic need. Meet this need and it stays in its proper place and proportion. But treat it like a "habit" and try to break it and the chances

87

are that it will become more keen, more sharp, and will persist as the child's paramount concern a lot longer than it otherwise would. We should stand in "awe of needs," not in awe of habits!

Unfortunately, our awe of habits begins to govern what we do from the start of our children's lives. We love little children but we hate "Mama's babies." We are all for mothering, but we hate children who are tied to their mothers' apron strings. We can go along for a little while doing what a baby needs but we dread "sissies" and "mollycoddles" and "cry babies." Soon we hesitate to give in and do the simple, obvious, kindly deed that a child needs. We hold back. We are stingy. We are half-hearted or hard-hearted, lest children go on forever behaving like infants, "caught in the force of habit."

A baby wakes up in the middle of the night and cries because he is hungry. The temptation is to ignore this and let him cry. We don't want him to build a "habit" of thinking he can always get his own way.

A two-year-old comes running, crying, because he has fallen down and skinned his knee. He hurts right now and wants some sympathy. The temptation is to push him off and tell him that it really doesn't hurt. We don't want him to build a "habit" of always running to his mother.

A four-year-old is frightened at night. She has had a bad dream and, at the moment, wants a little reassurance. The temptation is to tell her to go straight back to her bed and not be such a baby. We don't want her to build a "habit" of crying over every little thing.

A three-year-old starts to nursery school. Everything looks strange to the child—the teacher, the room, the children, everything. At the beginning the child needs familiar company so he clings to mother's side. The temptation is to sneak out when he isn't looking. We don't want him to build a "habit" of clinging to his mother.

A two-year-old sucks his thumb when he falls asleep at nap time, and this drives us to distraction. At two the thumb makes him feel safe and secure, but suppose he still sucks his thumb when he goes off to college! Suppose he sucks it when he is drafted into the army or when it is time to get married! We worry needlessly because of our foolish fear that acts will go on forever and ever. We can't believe that true habits can be easily broken. We can't believe that as needs are met, new needs arise to take their place. We stand in awe of habits.

Change Is the Human Characteristic

Our trouble may be that we are such an industrial society. We have wide experience with *things*—the inanimate, the inorganic. And things do stay put. They never change. They remain the same forever (as far as the naked eye can see).

Put a chair by the table. It will stay there until you or someone else makes a deliberate effort to move it. The chair has no motor power of its own. It is stuck wherever you place it. If you are dealing with *things*, you must be sure to put them in a good place (establish a good habit), because the chair will stay wherever you leave it. You have to be leery of putting it in a bad place (or letting a bad habit get by) because the chair is not going to move of its own accord.

Children are different. Change is their trademark. All living things—plants, animals, people—change. Babies suck for months, time after time and with the greatest satisfaction. And then they start to drink and chew. They crawl for months, time and time again with the greatest satisfaction. And then they start to walk. For years children wallow in dirt; taking a bath is the greatest nuisance. Then they change—you can't get them out of the bathroom! They play with a gang, and nothing is more fun—until they change. Suddenly, "two is company, three is a crowd."

Change operates continuously in adult life. We sleep for hours—nothing could be more heavenly. Then we have had enough; we want to be up and doing things. Once the satisfaction is gone, it is easy to "break habits." All it takes is just a little new reward in some new direction, or a little counterpain.

The most significant fact of all is that, once the satisfaction is gone, children break hundreds of "habits" themselves. No one has to do it for them. They constantly go through a *developmental revision of habits.* The old ways no longer bring the satisfaction children want. They take on new ways all the time—ways that are appropriate to their new stage of development. Babies do what babies must, and five-year-olds act quite differently! A two-year-old is a Two and acts like a Two, but a four-year-old's pattern of behavior is not the same thing.

NEW SEASONS, NEW REASONS

There is no reason on the face of the earth to stand in awe of habits. No reason to fear the "force of habit." There is no reason not to give a child what is right for him *now.* We simply have to remember that tomorrow is another day!

Farmers probably have the least trouble of any of us in seeing this point. They are close to the changing seasons. Snow and cold wind and ice and hail come, but the farmer knows that winter can't last forever. The farmer's experience in growing crops teaches him the same lesson. He checks his tomatoes. They are green now, and what can you do with green tomatoes? He checks his peaches; they are small and hard. What can you do with hard peaches? The farmer knows the answer: *Let them grow!* Let them change and develop. The tomatoes will ripen, the peaches will soften. The crops go

90

through a "developmental revision of habits!" They don't stay green or hard forever.

The farmer doesn't chew his nails or get frantic about the future. He accepts the great lesson of Nature: Everything in its own good time! He can't plow in the winter, but he can repair fences and order supplies and fix up his machinery. He can't sow in the early spring, but he can plow and harrow. He can't harvest in the early summer, but he can fertilize or weed or spray for pests. Everything in its own good time. Nothing lasts forever.

Can all the rest of us, growing our crop of *children*, learn the same lesson? The infant and the very young child have the deepest need for security, for affection, for kindly deeds that buck a child up and make him sure he is loved. In the "season of the baby," all acts must be judged by one standard alone: Do they help a child feel a sense of trust? But the seasons change. New needs arise and they will take precedence. At the start of life, being loved is the child's one big concern, but the single-minded search for proof of love does not last forever (unless the child fails in his search). Normally, time moves along. New developmental tasks must be faced.

FOR INDEPENDENT STUDY

1. One good source of pamphlet material, for both parents and teachers, about young children is the Bank Street College of Education, 69 Bank Street, New York. Among its publications is a *Packet for Parents* ($1.50), a collection of 15 brief articles about young children, all helpful, and some of them applying specifically to this business of habits.

2. Several books, while not exclusively dealing with "habits," have an underlying point of view which expands the idea

suggested in this chapter. Among them: *Developmental Tasks and Education*, by Robert J. Havighurst (Chicago: University of Chicago Press, 1948); *A Child Development Point of View*, by James L. Hymes, Jr. (Englewood Cliffs, N.J.: Prentice-Hall, 1955); and *Personality in the Making*, a publication based on the fact-finding of the Midcentury White House Conference on Children and Youth, by Helen Witmer and Ruth Kotinsky, editors (New York: Harper, 1953).

What would you do?

Question 8 Whenever Mrs. B. has to discipline her twenty-month-old she tries very conscientiously to do it in the nicest possible way. She says things like: "Mommy loves her little Dianne very much. Don't touch the stove," or "Mommy loves her sweet little Dianne. Please don't splash the water." With whom do you tend to agree: *a*) A neighbor admires Mrs. B. greatly for her patience and calmness; she feels Mrs. B. is on the right track. *b*) Grandmother is very impatient with all the soft soap: "This modern psychology stuff! Why doesn't she just slap her hand and then she would stop." *c*) Father feels that he doesn't have the patience that his wife does, but he is all for what she is doing: "That's real tender loving care for you." *d*) Grandfather almost blows his top: "Hogwash and baloney and syrupy soup. All those words don't mean a thing!"

a great surge
of power

Chapter 11

A child is born. He grows and develops through his first year of life. Then comes the first birthday time. That first birthday is an exciting event in every home. The one-year-old gets more gifts from parents and relatives than he can use in a month of Sundays. No matter how lavish these external presents are, they pale in comparison with the "internal" gifts that come to a child from all the growing of his infancy.

TRULY DRAMATIC CHANGES

The prenatal time is a time of exceedingly rapid growth. In the first few months following birth there is a settling down. These first few months are a time for consolidation, for salting down the gains that have been made and getting set for what lies ahead. The child changes some, to be sure. By about the end of a month he can hold up his head and look straight ahead, when lying on his tummy. Baby has a bright-eyed look at this point which creates real excitement in the home. In the first two months or so some pleasing social advances also take place. Baby smiles, and that is very good to see. He smiles on his own, and he smiles when we smile or talk or laugh at him.

Baby starts vocalizing, too, in the first months. He begins to make those little vowel sounds—*eh, ah, eeh*—that are the very beginning of the flow of words that will come later. His cheerful little chirps go on when we talk to him, and he chirps seemingly just for his own amazement too. These sounds are pleasing to hear.

During the early months the baby grows in weight. He is likely to double his birth weight in the first five months or so —a satisfying sight to see. He also grows in length, probably about four inches or so in these early months. Despite all these changes in the first few months, however, you are not apt to say: "My! He is getting big!" Baby still looks like a baby, he still acts like a baby.

The dramatic changes begin to be visible near the end of the first half year. Around five months of age the usual baby starts to turn himself over from a prone position to his back. Now this *is* something. It is the obvious beginning of mobility, that same process that later sends the adolescent scooting all over town in his automobile! At the moment it takes place this turning over can be almost as nerve-wracking. Mother can no longer leave the baby on the top of the table or the bassinette while she answers the phone. Now he can go places! He can't go far, but he *can* go, and he may go right off the table down to the floor!

As early as the third month or so, the muscles in the child's neck have grown strong enough so that he can manage to hold his head up when mother holds him on her shoulder. This is a major step forward, but not a very showy gain. In just a

94

few months more, however, around mid-year a spectacular change takes place that the whole world can see. You can sit the baby up and he stays up! Neck muscles and back muscles have really grown strong. Now this baby is beginning to be someone. The whole world sees the change and baby begins to see the whole world (or, at least, a part of it!).

Just past the midyear mark baby is apt to start to crawl. He is not a good crawler at first by any standard. He may move backwards as much as forwards. At the beginning he may even go in circles. But he is really moving, and going somewhere. Those earlier gains—holding the head up, turning himself over, being able to sit up—are beginning to pay off. By this time we gasp: Will you look at what that child is doing!

Crawling of one kind or another generally begins somewhere around the seventh or eighth month. From that time on there is a steady procession of changes, all visible, all exciting, and one right after the other. A child crawls. He pulls himself up. He walks, hanging on to the side of his crib or his playpen or to the arm of a chair. He stands alone. Then —that climactic event—baby takes his first step! This is often the one specific birthday present the child gives himself. That step frequently happens right around birthday time. It is the climax, but the whole latter half of the first year has been one long spectacular: "Onward and upward, Excelsior!" combined with the "Charge of the Light Brigade."

All this dramatic progress toward upright posture and forward locomotion has still other fabulous developments sandwiched in with it. Another big achievement is the capacity to oppose thumb and forefinger. This is a distinctively human power. The acquisition of it is a major landmark in our development as humans, and it too develops in this great blooming period when changes flow in such overwhelming profusion.

Precise pincer prehension—the technical name for this capacity to bring together the thumb and forefinger—begins far back in that unspectacular, seemingly quiet time of the first few months. When the one-month-old is lying on his back, and you hold a rattle up above him, he cannot see it yet. In just a little time his eyes mature so that he can see the rattle, and he stares. By two or three months he not only sees the rattle but his whole body goes into motion. He "reaches" for it with his torso, with jerks of his legs, and with a thrashing of both arms. By four months or so there is more progress. The legs do not move as much, the body does not move as much. Two arms alone now come up, like a giant pincer. They can close in on the rattle, but the arms and hands are like rakes—relatively clumsy tools. And both arms work together at this point.

You have to give the child more time for growing. Usually around eight months of age or so, the truly impressive achievement takes place. Now the child uses one arm, one hand, and his fingers have become more precise instruments. He can pick up objects, even very small ones, between his thumb and forefinger. He has the beginning of one of the most basic tools for all his later living.

THE FIRST WORDS—STILL MORE POWER!

Nor is this achievement the end! Somewhere around the first birthday, a little before or a little after, the child says his first words! That little chirping that began far back in the first month of life now comes off the assembly line, a finished product that someone else can understand (although Mother will be best at understanding for some time to come!). You have heard of "Bo-Bo, The Monkey Man! He walks and talks like any man!" This is the child around his first birthday time. In the short space of about a year, with mounting crescendo as that one year nears its end *he walks and talks like any man,* or at least he has begun.

At the start of life the baby lived on a fixed plane. Without control of his head, with underdeveloped vision, his world was a small, small world indeed. Now his world miraculously expands, as it does for us when we climb a tree or reach the mountain top. Suddenly we see stretches of a world that previously had been hidden. The child does too. He can turn his head. Now there is a north, east, south, west. At the start of life the baby is tied down. Now he has motor power. He can go places and do things. The child has his hands. He has words. Such a heady experience, to come so suddenly into so rich an inheritance!

We find it hard as adults to recapture the helplessness of infancy. It is just as hard to recreate the tremendous surge of power within the child that begins at about six months of age, grows more potent at twelve months, and increases from then on in intensity. To sense what this surge of power is like, we would have to imagine ourselves as poverty-stricken, with not a penny to our name. Then, suppose that suddenly we become millionaires. Even this transformation would not begin to equal the change within the child. We become millionaires and then suddenly we open our mouths and discover that we can speak all the known languages of the world! And, as suddenly, we flap our arms and lo! We can fly! All these new strengths together, piling in on us, might come close to the child's great surge of power.

A Whole New Way of Looking at Life

We all know what new wealth does to people. It often corrupts. The result is so common that we are surprised at the exceptional person who remains "the same old Joe" despite a big new inheritance. Great new possessions and impressive new powers change us. And they change the child. The toddler is the *nouveau riche*. All his new-found wealth does something to him.

From as early as six, seven, or eight months on, the child does not want to sit on your lap—he wants to crawl. Around the end of the first year, he does not want you to feed him. He grabs the spoon and aims it toward his mouth. (If only his aim were better, and if only he knew that spoons should stay right side up!) He is beginning to develop a vocabulary but a very selective one. Almost universally in this country at around age two the word "no" is more popular than "yes." "Won't" is much more popular than "o.k." It is not that "no" and "won't" are easier words to say. They are not. But they are more expressive of "self." "Yes" and "o.k." are compliant and agreeable; their opposites, the child's favorites, give him a chance to throw his new weight around.

Most youngsters from their second year of life on have another favorite slogan: "Me do it." Try to help them dress and this is your thanks: "Me do it." Try to help them with eating —"Me do it." Try to button a button, open a door, carry a bundle—"Me do it!" The refrain comes when the job is one the children can manage and, as often, when the task is beyond even their new powers. These children have "eyes that are bigger than their stomachs." Small wonder! Recently it was as if they had almost no eyes at all.

Now the whole world is their oyster. Kind souls and gentle people are still exceedingly important (and always will be). Increasingly now, however, *things* have even more appeal. Everywhere the child looks he sees something fascinating and inviting. He has to touch it, handle it, poke it. He has to squeeze it and, almost always, put it in his mouth. Most parents know all about this urge. The toddler is the child who is "into everything" and "always on the go." After all, he has just inherited his body and he is bound and determined to use it.

The Search for Autonomy

A basic principle of development shows clearly in the toddler's behavior. It is the "principle of wholeheartedness." This principle operates at all ages. One-year-olds, two-year-olds exhibit it best but all ages go overboard in using whatever is new. Even adults. We buy an air conditioner and leave it on all the time. We buy a new car and ride everywhere. When we first saw TV we even liked the commercials! Wholeheartedness is a human tendency.

The child, from about six months of age and continuing until around year three, has something super-special and brand new—himself! A short time ago he didn't know he existed. He could look in a mirror and not realize that he was seeing himself. Now he knows himself and it is quite a self he has. Wholeheartedly he wants to explore and exploit this new-found possession.

The toddler searches for a *sense of autonomy*. This is his new need. Autonomy now—not a sense of trust—is "top banana." The one-year-old, the two-year-old goes all out in search of independence. He judges all experiences now by one standard: Do they make him feel big? Do they build strength and selfhood and power? Children this age take on a new vulnerability and become prey to a new hazard—experiences that will cut them down to size.

We are living in a period of history when, all over the world, former colonies and so-called backward countries are becoming *autonomous*. Proudly they declare their independence. Fiercely they proclaim it. And, because they are so newly free, these countries are often touchy. They are super-sensitive to

99

anything which seems to threaten their new sovereignty. From six months of age on until about three, the child is very much like them. He has one grand passion—his independence. Anything which makes him feel strong and big is fine. Anything which knocks him down and takes the wind out of his sails and keeps him small hurts him most keenly.

FOR INDEPENDENT STUDY

1. Dr. Arnold Gesell produced a fine picture book, with more than eight hundred photographs, showing *How A Baby Grows* (New York: Harper, 1945). It portrays very vividly all the developments during the first year that lead up to this great surge of power. And there is an excellent book, just about two-year-olds. It is very rare to find such readable and delightful material—or material of any kind!—about one particular age level. By all means get to know the *Life and Ways of the Two-Year-Old*, by Louise P. Woodcock (New York: Basic Books, 1941).

2. The Public Affairs Committee, 22 E. 38th Street, New York 16, N.Y. is another excellent source of simple, inexpensive pamphlet material for parents and teachers. The booklet, *Enjoy Your Child: Ages 1,2,3*, by James L. Hymes, Jr. (25¢), is appropriate supplementary reading at this point.

What would you do?

Question 9 A twenty-one-month-old crawls a little bit but he doesn't walk and doesn't talk yet. With whom do you tend to agree: *a*) Father thinks he and his wife should be more active in encouraging the child to walk and talk, and try harder to teach him. *b*) Mother is very relaxed: "Just give him time. Everybody is different. He will walk and talk when he is good and ready. What's the rush?" c) Mother-in-law lives with the family. She is a woman with very definite ideas. She thinks the parents certainly should check with their doctor. d) A neighbor says: "I know another child who was the same way and he turned out all right. I wouldn't do a thing."

helping a child
to feel big

Chapter 12

Little babies with their charm draw warmth out of most of us. So, too, youngsters who are first seeking a sense of autonomy usually strike a very responsive chord. We are glad to see a youngster "stand on his own two feet." Independence is in the American tradition.

The child's strong urge to do things for himself ties in with our whole feeling for progress. When the child takes his first step, falls, and gets right up again to walk some more, we smile very contentedly. A good American expression describes him perfectly: "You can't keep a good man down!"

As we see our children venturing out into the wide world —whether they venture crawling or toddling or even at times running away from us—their ambition reminds us of the very spirit that conquered the frontier in the past and that today is conquering space. We nod approvingly: "Go West, young man!" And the children do. They go west and north and east and south, and they try to conquer all the space they can find. This is usually fine with us.

Without realizing it, we are harder than much of the rest of the world on little babies. We give our infants less time to suck, much less close holding and fondling, much less physical contact than many babies the world over receive. In contrast, we find it easier than the rest of the world to be pleased and to encourage a one-year-old's and two-year-old's concern with power—at least, at the beginning.

Our attitude is tremendously significant. Children are sensitive to the general climate of approval or disapproval. They grow best when we are glad they are growing. They worry when we worry. Attitudes always get over to children. You cannot code them or stamp them "top secret." Initially, at least, our attitude toward their concern with independence is a very favorable and supporting one.

Fortunately, too, a child gets much of his sense of power through using the *things* that surround him. Things cannot convey love, but they *can* contribute to bigness and independence. America is very good at things. We are an inventive, mechanical, industrial people. We find it easy to cook up all kinds of objects that let a child try his wings. We don't create super-dramatic arrangements. The little things count. A child builds his sense of autonomy, just as he built his sense of trust—through the ordinary, everyday experiences of his life.

THE DO-IT-YOURSELF APPROACH

Clothing is a good example. We have always had a head start in this area. We have never swaddled our children or bound their feet. Our way of clothing has always given them a great deal of leeway at this stage of development when a free-swinging style is so important. Our warm comfortable

103

houses and clean floors have expanded children's freedom. Our toddlers go barefoot, which is all to the good. We have even developed blue-jean training pants. Often at home these are all a child wears and they really let him scoot around.

Not too long ago we dressed our children in real "baby clothes." The neckhole was tiny; the buttons were tiny, like the baby. The clothes were designed to test the mother's sense of power (and her patience!). But in even so small a matter as buttons, we have been moving more and more toward a do-it-yourself approach. This approach is what children want when they are searching for autonomy.

The first step was to move the buttons from the back to the front, so the child stood some chance of getting at them. The next step was to eliminate most of the buttons. There used to be six or eight—enough to drive anyone crazy. Then we made the buttons, the two or three that were left, much, much bigger. We moved away from the silly idea that "baby things" should be "baby size."

But even the best buttons can be defeating. Zippers came along and were a boon to this "Me-do-it" age. Yet zippers were not the perfect answer. We kept experimenting to find more simple fasteners that children could manage—snaps they simply push together, elastic bands that do the holding so a child only has to pull the clothes up, loose-hanging, big-necked shirts and sweaters with no fasteners so he pulls on the clothes and they hang on his shoulders, zippers that zip with no zippers!

SELF-SERVICE IN EATING

We have shown the same inventiveness in creating eating tools that help a child to feel big and more able to manage his own feeding instead of being dependent on his mother. Long ago we discarded the traditional baby spoon—so cute-looking but designed to be held only by clever, highly educated fingers. A good children's spoon today is more like a snow shovel. It has a broad edge to scrape up the food; a wide face so the food doesn't fall off; and a straight handle that a child can grab with his whole hand.

Plates for children usually have straight and high edges. The beginning self-feeder can corner his food against the edges and get it on his spoon without forever chasing it around his plate. Suction cups on the bottom of plates are very useful skid chains! They keep the plate from running away, just as the edges keep the food from escaping. Our genius for inventing unbreakable materials has been another boost for independence. When the plate or cup fall off the table—and they are sure to!—it is no longer a major calamity. The unbreakables let us take a chance with children, which is what they want at this stage.

We have been moving away from the high chair, too. The high chair is useful for a brief span of time, probably in the second half of the first year. It does its best job when the child can sit up but isn't yet too active. As the child gets older, lifting him up and lifting him down at each meal becomes more and more difficult for mothers—and more and more difficult for the children, too. They don't want to be lifted; they want to do-it-themselves. Nor do they want to be tied down and cramped in, once the strong urge to be "up and at 'em" comes along. The low chair and low table have taken the place of the high chair and play their part in feeding the child's sense of his own power.

At this stage in development the challenge to adults is to cut the world down to manageable size, rather than to cut the child down to size. Many homes have boxes or steps in the bathroom so children can get up to the washbasin and the toilet bowl on their own. Homes have low hooks and big hooks so children can get at their own towels and face cloths.

105

They have low rods in closets so children can reach their own clothing. And homes—like good nursery schools and kindergartens—often have low shelves for children's toys so they can be out in the open and within reach. These devices all help youngsters to feel less and less dependent, more and more independent.

We are becoming more tolerant about letting young children play with things in the kitchen—the pots and pans and measuring cups. Our technology has helped us here. Utensils are no longer iron, heavy and unmanageable, or too expensive. A child can play safely, contentedly, and for long periods ot time with the fascinating odds and ends of kitchenware. As he bangs and piles and pushes them around, he feels very important.

Store-bought toys bring this same good feeling to the child. Often we buy toys to show love—this doesn't work. But toys that are right for one- and two-year-olds stand a chance of giving the child a sense of power. The youngster just learning to walk, for instance, is the world's most eager "pusher." A baby carriage, a toy lawn mower, anything on wheels that he can hold onto for support mean both good walking and good feeling. A little later the slightly more skilled walker is the world's most eager "puller." He toddles along pulling his wagon or cart or truck behind him. The wagon is sometimes empty, sometimes loaded, but the child is always full of feeling "big as all get-out."

At around two years of age children love to hammer. Watching them you might say that they are not making anything. One of their favorite toys, for example, is a hammer bed. With a big wooden mallet the child pounds a peg through a hole; then he turns the hammer bed over and pounds the same peg back in the opposite direction. He is not making anything? He is making noise! And making noise is a major means the child has for feeling strong. (This is not a recommendation, but a warning—at this age the child's favorite musical instrument is apt to be a drum!)

BODY MASTERY BUILDS POWER

Of course, the hammering and pounding are important, too. The child's control over his body is a basic means of his feeling good about himself and about life, from the time of crawling right on through and long after year six. The changes in his body—the ability to crawl, stand, walk, and the control over his hands and fingers—stirred up his new self-awareness and triggered his need for power. The more skilled the child becomes in mastering his body, the more he feels a full and pleasing sense of autonomy.

The result is that young children—two-year-olds, and three-, four- and five-year-olds—love to live dangerously. They cannot know the thrill of body mastery if they stay swathed in cotton batting. Watch them on their tricycles, one of the favorite toys from about year three on. At first, the challenge is to make the tricycle go, and that is more complicated than it seems. The beginner pushes down with both feet and goes exactly nowhere. But children work at it and soon get the hang of pedaling. Then their great thrill is in seeing how fast they can go, how abruptly they can stop, how sharply they can turn. If youngsters get their fill of derring-do when they are young, they may be under somewhat less pressure to prove their bigness later, as adolescents, with speeding automobiles or one-hand driving!

Watch the young child on a slide. At two and three the big thrill is simply climbing all the way up to the top, to sit, and then slide down. We probably feel more comfortable when children "play it safe" but there is no bigness unless youngsters

107

expand their skills. By four and five, they want to climb up the slide instead of up the steps, or to slide down backwards, or to slide head first.

The same drive to expand body mastery shows itself on swings. Adults have to push the two-year-old. As soon as the child feels safe he wants to go "higher, higher." By three or four the child gets the knack of pumping. Then the higher he can go, the better he likes it. Before this under-six age span is over, sitting and pumping, no matter how high, are too tame. Youngsters want to stand on a swing and make it *go, go, go!*

When they climb, children show the same push toward more and more power. At two they may walk across a low board, from one packing case or saw horse to another, holding on to your hand. Once they have mastered this, they want the board higher. Soon, by three or four, they are on their own. Now the board must be narrower, as well as higher, so that more skill in balancing is called for, or at an angle, so the task is harder still. The three-year-old climbs slowly and carefully to the top of the jungle gym and that is an achievement. Four- and five-year-olds scoot up, hold on with one hand, and always jump down part of the way. These same children love to hang head down from the climbing ladder, clinging with their knees. And one of their greatest thrills is to stand on top of a play house in the middle of a play yard, boss of all they survey.

During all the years under six children devise more and more ways to use their bodies freely and with increasing skill. Our children are fortunate because we give them a reasonably free rein, at least in the beginning and especially in play. We are glad when they feel strong. If toys, equipment and facilities could do the whole job of building their sense of autonomy, our youngsters would have the raw meat they need to make them feel like lions.

108

FOR INDEPENDENT STUDY

1. Another government pamphlet, the Children's Bureau Publication No. 238, *Home Play and Play Equipment for Young Children*, by Adele Franklin is full of good ideas on inexpensive materials for young children to use (Washington: Government Printing Office, 1960. Rev. Ed., 15¢).

What would you do?

Question 10 In a kindergarten three five-year-olds are sliding different objects down the slide. First, one of their hats. Then a little toy car. Then a small stone. Then a paper cup. If you were the teacher, what would be your inclination: *a*) Let them alone, as long as they are not bothering anyone. *b*) Find some additional toys and things the children could slide down the slide—a small wooden block, a toy fire engine. *c*) Talk to the children in a friendly way, but firmly, explaining that the slide is just for people to slide down. *d*) Enough of the fancy explanations! Just tell them to stop. By this time children should know the right and the wrong way to use the slide. It has been on the playground all year, and they have been in the group all year.

the
training period

Chapter 13

In face-to-face situations, where human relationships rather than things count, we do not do as good a job as we might in nurturing strength and bigness in our one- and two-year-olds.

One of the obstacles is an unfortunate conflict of interest. The same span of years when the child is seeking autonomy is also the time for the *training period*. This is when we expect a youngster to learn some of the hardest lessons of his life.

Most people assume that school begins at six, or at five, if your community has kindergartens, or at four or three, if your child goes to nursery school. This education is almost *graduate* education! A child's toughest "school days" come when he is six months old, and twelve months old, and eighteen months old, and twenty-four months old.

Most adults have some moments of wishing they were children again. We dream of how wonderful it would be if

110

only we were young, carefree, happy, without a worry in the world. This is the adult's eye view of childhood. It can be quite a wrong view!

During the first few months of life, if we are wise, we cater to our babies, doing all we can to make them feel at home. We enjoy giving in to them, and demand little or nothing in return. But this honeymoon ends in a jiffy, usually long before even the first year is over. We act like the "Armed Forces." We are as sweet as can be at the "Recruitment Office." Nothing is too good for our new little soldier! But before the child knows what has happened to him, we send him off to "boot camp." We throw him into "basic training." We pile on lesson after lesson in how he must act.

A RIGOROUS PROGRAM OF TRAINING

Some of the hardest lessons center around toilet training. Not that the child has to learn to urinate or defecate. He is wonderful at both of these skills from the time he is born! His assignment is to learn *not* to urinate and *not* to defecate. This is why the lessons are so hard. Our teaching cuts directly across his skills.

The child has to learn to hold in and hold back until the time is right, by our particular local standards. He has to learn to wait until the place is right, by our particular standards. He must also learn the many verbal rituals that accompany his toileting—the right words to say, when to say them, how loudly to say them and to whom they may be said.

A child also must learn what we think are the right ways of regarding this whole business of urination and defecation. To a youngster his own eliminating performances are quite amazing. A child concerned with power would naturally be fascinated by his phenomenal capacity to produce such products all by himself. Many young children stare with wonder into

111

the toilet bowl and sometimes touch their feces. They didn't
know they had it in them! But our local customs all say *no*.
A child must learn not to talk about his bowel movements.
He must learn not to look too long at what he himself has
done. He certainly must learn to keep his hands off his defecation. In a sense he must learn to pretend that he didn't do
it! And if he did, it wasn't anything wonderful anyhow.

A child also has to master certain other very difficult
lessons about his body. He may touch certain parts of his
body if he wants to. It is legal for him to pat his hands or rub
his arm or touch his toe, but some of the most fascinating
parts of the body are taboo—taboo in our particular society,
that is. The parts he must learn to stay away from are the most
pleasing parts of all. The mouth, so sensitive for the child,
begins to be a forbidden area. The penis and the vagina, both
much more sensitive than other parts of the body, are strictly
out of bounds. We send our children to "schools" that have
a very demanding curriculum. Woe to the child who can resist anything but temptation!

In the training period the child runs headlong into many
other areas that are "out of bounds." We are a very prop-
erty-conscious society. Things all belong to someone. Robbery
is a major offense. "No trespassing" signs are all around. In
simpler societies where people do not own as many things as
we do, or where things belong to everyone, the lessons relating
to property are not too hard. But we own a lot of things;
we are wedded to private property; and we have a lot of special rules that apply to property. Very early, and insistently,
the child begins to hear: "Don't touch." "That's not yours."
"Mustn't." He has to struggle to pass our course on property
rights.

Again, the difficulty is that our rules cut across the child's
natural ways. Nobody has to teach a child to touch—that
would be easy. In the training period we teach the child *not*

to touch, *not* to take, *not* to handle, *not* to use. Nor does anyone have to teach a child to own. At around two years of age children are very strong believers in private property themselves. An intense possessiveness is one of the child's natural means of feeling strong. *He* owns something, and it is *his!* But ownership is not the lesson we want to get over. We try to teach children to share—some things, some times, with some people—and to share only his own and *not* the other fellow's belongings. These are hard lessons.

We begin to train the emotions in this period, too. Our young "student" carries quite a heavy schedule. Once more the same old difficulty exists. Obviously children do not have to be "trained" to express their emotions. They do this quite well, starting as early as the birth cry. In the training period the child has to learn *not* to express his emotions, or, at least, he must learn which emotions are legal to show and which ones are not highly thought of. He must learn our special ways of showing the emotions we approve of, and our special ways of keeping other feelings bottled up.

LEARNING THE PASSWORDS

It is in this period, too, that we start teaching all the little mannerisms that we happen to think are polite. We sit for our meals, at a table—not all people everywhere do. We use a knife, fork and spoon—not all people do; some prefer fingers, some use chopsticks. We leave our plates on the table; some people lift their bowls almost up to their mouths. We hold the fork in our left hand, the knife in our right, and then we switch the fork to our right hand to bring the food up to our mouth. And we have very specific notions about how much food that fork should carry. No child has to learn to eat. He comes born with that ability. There is nothing wrong with his capacity to get food inside of him. But mastering all our local

113

customs, the refinements and embellishments of eating, can be quite a problem. "Boot camp" has no snap courses!

Certain verbal rituals that accompany eating must also be learned. In some families a blessing is said before the meal —the child must learn to wait. In almost all families it is not considered right to reach across the table for food. We send our words across instead: "Please pass the. . . ." "May I have the. . . ." And then we say: "Thank you." We have our special rules about when it is legal to begin to eat: Wait until your hostess takes her first bite. And one very strict rule that is difficult for children, in particular, to learn: *Don't talk with your mouth full!*

There are many other little rites a child must begin to master. When he receives a gift, for example, his gratitude usually beams all over him. His eyes sparkle, he eagerly reaches out, he instantaneously puts the gift to use. But none of this "body talk" is enough once the training period begins. Now he has to say the magic words: "Thank you." When a child hurts someone or does some damage, his sorrow usually streams from all of him. His eyes widen; sometimes he pales; often he looks worried and moistens his lips. But few children get through the training period with only this sorrow. They must learn to say the passwords: "I'm sorry." "Pardon me."

Theoretically there need be no conflict between the child's search for autonomy and the training period. The two could go along together quite happily. After all, one of the main reasons for any school—elementary, high school, college, the "school" of the home in these early years—is to help children know their way around. Youngsters go to school inept and uninformed. They should graduate feeling more self-confident and a thousand times more able. "Knowledge is power," we say, and power is what the young child seeks.

The hazard is that we may teach badly in the training period. Then, instead of building strength, our lessons can

114

show the child how small he is. He wants to stand on his own two feet and hold his head high. But if we do not do a sensitive job of teaching, his head is bowed and he drags his feet. This is the great challenge of the training period: to teach so as to strengthen the child's sense of autonomy, and not undermine it in the least.

FOR INDEPENDENT STUDY

1. Reports on how and when different families go about training their children make fascinating reading. *Father of the Man*, by W. Allison Davis and Robert J. Havighurst (Boston: Houghton Mifflin, 1947), is based in part on a study of what 202 mothers in the Chicago Area did; *Patterns Of Child Rearing*, by Robert R. Sears, Eleanor E. Maccoby, and Harry Levin (Evanston: Row, Peterson, 1957) is a report on how 379 mothers in the Boston area brought up their children from birth to the kindergarten age; and *Child Training And Personality: A Cross Cultural Study*, by John W. M. Whiting and Irvin L. Child (New Haven: Yale University Press, 1953) compares one group of American procedures with reports from many other peoples in different parts of the world.

What would you do?

Question 11 Suppose you were teaching a five-year-old group of twenty children. Almost every child in the whole group wants to hear the story you have chosen to read at story time—all except two! One wants to sit at a table by himself and look through a different book, and the other doesn't want to come to the story circle—he wants to work on a puzzle. What is your inclination: *a*) Let them do what they want to

115

do. *b*) Explain that they can do these other things at different times in the morning but now it is story time. *c*) Make them come, but read the book the child has chosen, as well as the one you picked, if you possibly can find the time. *d*) Insist that they hear at least the beginning of the story. Then, if they don't like it, assure them that they can go back to their own activities, if they are quiet.

readiness
to learn

Chapter 14

The single most significant secret to all good education —whether in the training period or any other "school"—is *timing*. The trick is to teach when someone is able to learn, and when he wants to be taught. Good education is the art of striking while the iron is hot.

Sometimes we lose this art in the training period. We find it hard to hold our horses. We hate to put off until tomorrow what we think can be done today. This is a wonderfully aggressive spirit *but* we jump the gun! We plunge into a sensitive area where a sure feeling for timing is extremely important. Instead of a deft touch, we have a very heavy hand. Our haste in the training period hurts children, instead of building their strength.

First—The Sheer Physical Power

Many conditions must be right before a child is ready to learn. The most basic requirement is for sheer physical power.

117

Solid internal development must go on so that a youngster "has what it takes" to do whatever is demanded of him. He must first mature physiologically. His muscles must grow. His central nervous system must grow and develop. His bones and skeletal structure must grow. His organs must grow.

Teaching children calls for great realism. You cannot teach whatever you want to teach, just because you want to teach it. You have to accept that "first things must come first." A child cannot learn to walk at six months—no matter how much we may want him to—because his bones and muscles are not strong enough to support him, and his head is too large in relation to his body size. He simply has not yet grown the physical power to do the job. A child cannot sit up at three months—no matter how much we may want him to. His back and neck muscles are not strong enough. His head is still too large. He is not ready physically.

We accept certain physical limitations on behavior and do not fight them. We are even glad for some of them. We know that a seven-year-old probably cannot conceive a child and that a six-year-old is not apt to show the secondary sex characteristics of breast development or pubic hair. We are realistic here and probably say: Thank heavens! And, of course, no one seriously expects his six-month-old to walk or his three-month-old to sit. But these are physical performances, we say. Physical performances obviously depend on gland functioning, on organs, on bones, on muscles.

Physiological readiness underlies every single aspect of human functioning, not simply physical deeds alone. This is a key fact we must learn to accept. Physical maturation holds the key to *social* behavior. Internal growth sets limits on the child's play and his playmates—how many children he can play and work with, how he will play, what activities and materials he can play and work with. Physical development

118

—the development of glands and organs and muscles and bones and nerve endings—basically controls *emotional* development. It sets the pace for the emotions the child can feel, for how he must express them, for whether or not he can control them. Physical development underlies and regulates *intellectual* performance. It controls what the child can think about, how he can think about it, what he can remember. No matter what the lesson, the child must first have the sheer physical power inside of him to be able to learn it.

SECOND—THE DESIRE TO LEARN

The power to do the job is basic to readiness. The *desire* to do it is only slightly less important. Desire is the second essential ingredient which must be present before our timing can be right.

We tend to minimize the importance of interest and to think we are being "soft" with children when we take it into account. But adults should know the importance of desire better than we know about other factors. In our advanced state of physical maturation, we have the internal power to learn many different kinds of lessons. Our organs and muscles and bones and our nervous system are just like Kansas City: "They've gone about as far as they can go." From the standpoint of power alone, we have all the physiological readiness we need to give ourselves to a wide variety of possible activities.

We could study Greek or archaeology. We could take courses in Victorian poetry or Renaissance art. We could learn to ski or skin dive or to play chess. But a selective process is always at work. We shun many activities because they are not "our dish." If we worked on them, we would be "out of our element." We give ourselves to other activities where we

119

have the desire. We can learn them and remember. Because we have the interest, we are willing to go to whatever trouble is necessary.

Children respond in the same way. A child must have a keen, sharp persistent fire that makes him want to achieve a certain end. When this strong urge exists, then the time for teaching is right. A child (or any of us) may have some momentary, weak and passing interest in almost anything under the sun. But this is not desire. A flabby, flagging, wane response is not enough.

BUILDING POWER AND DESIRE

The physical power that is basic to readiness to learn is purely a matter of internal growing. There is nothing any of us can do to speed up the process of growing or to hurry it along. An individual's rate of growing is one of his inherited characteristics. His rate of growing is established at the time of conception when two cells join, each bringing special characteristics from the whole line of paternal and maternal ancestors. There is only one way you can speed up the process of growth so that your child will be an early bloomer, always ready at the first possible moment; and that one way is far from foolproof and not very practical: You must choose a mate who comes from a long line of early bloomers, and be one yourself!

Growth—in its own good time—builds power, and only growth can do it. Power comes first. Desire never exists without it. But often the desire comes almost hand-in-hand with power. A kind of spontaneous combustion takes place. Very frequently the child gets a strong urge to put to work the power that is developing inside of him. But desire also stems from the child's experience. It is the cumulative result of all the living the child has done—the things he has seen, the

120

feelings he has had, the lacks he has become aware of, the mistakes he realizes he has made.

When power is missing, there is nothing we can do but wait—we have to let the child grow. When a child has the power but desire is missing, there are things we can do. We can set out deliberately to provide the kinds of experiences that will stimulate interest and whet desire.

Two things must be kept in mind, however. The first is that *he process of building desire is usually a long, slow job. You cannot get impatient. Sometimes we act as if all a child needs to do is to turn on the tap. The urge to do something, a strong sense of caring, is by no means that easily developed. Desire is not some little force at the child's disposal, to turn off and on as he wills. It takes a heap of living before a child can "catch on fire." Desire is deeply rooted in experiences—a lot of them—just as power is deeply rooted in maturation—a long time to grow. Both of these basic controls are strong forces. They boss the child; he does not control them.

Secondly, we must remember that children, and all of us, are capable of only a certain number of passions at any one time. Some one interest is always uppermost in our minds and it steals the show. The one overruling concern may be the result of our physical growing at the time. It may have its roots in the highly satisfying experiences of our yesterdays or in the deeply disturbing experiences. Whatever the cause, the fact is that humans are not "even-Stephen" creatures. We cannot keep any number of balls balancing nicely in the air. Nor are we able to shift gears with the greatest of ease. We simply cannot shrug off what matters most to us and easily give ourselves to a lesson someone else thinks we "ought" to be excited about. Adults say about their great enthusiasms: "I had to get it out of my system." Children do not use these words but they, too, become consumed with interests and activities which, to them, are all-absorbing.

121

WHEN YOUR TIMING IS OFF

We find it hard to wait until children have both the power and the desire. The slogan of the army service forces has great appeal: "The difficult we do immediately; the impossible takes a little longer." We are really eager beavers. We are apt to take the attitude: What's so wrong with trying to teach? What's the harm?

A lot of harm occurs when your timing is off. For one thing, you waste your own time and energy. Every parent and teacher has experienced this (but not everyone knows why). If a child is not ready to learn, your lessons simply cannot sink in. You teach, but your teaching is like "talking to a stone wall" or "talking to the wind." When your timing is off, you work like a dog to get a point over that could be learned later, when the time is right, in a jiffy.

Still the question comes: What's the harm? After all, we have a lot of time. But something bad happens to our attitude when we teach unsuccessfully. We make our demands, but the child does not respond because he cannot respond. At first we blame ourselves—*we* must be doing something wrong. But very soon we blame the children. *They* are not trying. They are not paying attention. We feel we have a lazy child on our hands or a stubborn and willful one. Soon needless anger and conflict fill the air. What's the harm? When we ignore readiness to learn, we run the risk of ruining relationships.

We run the risk, too, of retarding the very learning that we want. After all, we teach the lessons we teach because they are good things to know or to do. We teach them because through the ages they have proven their worth. They make life richer and fuller and more pleasant for all of us. It is better to be dry than to have wet pants. It is better to eat many foods than to be limited to one or two. Food is good, and so is sleep!

122

Sleep is one of life's precious joys. It should never be the cause for fights and arguments. It is better to have rules about property and some formulas for politeness; life runs more smoothly and safely when there are some regulations. Later, it is better to be able to read than to remain illiterate. Reading is fun, a source of pleasure and of power. None of these learnings is a dirty trick we play on children. They are all good lessons—ones any child would want to master, if we only give him time.

The trouble is that we spoil the learnings when we push for them too soon. We run the risk of turning very attractive goals into nasty ends. When our timing is off, we increase the chances that children will resist and resent and reject what they could otherwise so easily accept graciously and grate-fully, later on. Simply because they do not yet have the power and the desire, the learning becomes so difficult that the children often turn their backs on it.

Eventually the lessons are learned. Many a parent who has started too soon finally can say: "See. It works." But we have to look not only at the lessons but at the children who have learned them. We often weaken the children when we try to make them do what they cannot yet do. This is the greatest risk of all. During the training period overemphasis and too-early emphasis hits children at their most vulnerable spot. They want to feel big; our premature lessons make them feel small. Our zeal takes a toll that different children pay in different ways. Some lose self-confidence and become more quiet than they need be, more tense and guilty and more worried. Some fight back to protect themselves. They become more rebellious, more hostile and more aggressive than they need be.

All of the dangers are on the side of jumping the gun. This shows up clearly in the statistics on infant mortality. When a child is born at full term—that is to say, when the timing

123

is right and the child is ready to be born—birth is a simple, easy, and safe experience. Figures in a special U.S. Public Health Service study in 1955 (Publication No. 449) show that out of 1,000 live births of white children weighing 2,500 grams or more—the rough standard for "full term"—995.2 children come safely through the hazardous first twenty-eight days. Only 4.8 children die—an amazing record!

The difficulties arise when a child is born too early. He has not yet had a chance to build the power to let him meet the challenges of the birth process and of independent life. Here the figures are not good. Out of 1,000 live births of premature children—those weighing less than 2,500 grams—156.9 do not survive the first month. These figures are a dramatic lesson for all of us about readiness. We tend to think: "The sooner, the better." *The better way is for everything in its own good time.*

WE SHOULD BE SKILLED IN TIMING

We adults ought to be good at timing. We work with timing and accept the need for it constantly in our everyday lives. Mothers know about the need for good timing from the cooking they do. "Take the roast out of the oven *now*." Earlier would have been too soon, the meat would have been raw, but now!—the time is right. "Ice the cake *now*." Earlier the cake would have been too hot and too soft, but now!— the time is right. The jello is ready; it has hardened enough. The ice cream is ready; it has frozen solid. The water hasn't yet boiled, the vegetables haven't yet cooked through, the omelet has not risen. But *now!* The time is right. Mothers are constantly reaching for the right moment, and waiting patiently until it comes.

Fathers are equally aware that they cannot do whatever they want to do, just because they have their hearts set on it. Men have to watch the clock, or whatever else gives them the sign that now the time has come. Businessmen can tell when the moment is right to clinch a deal, or nail down a sale, or push home an argument. Around the house fathers are constantly saying: "Wait. The glue must harden." "The cement must set." "The paint must dry." Fathers, too, ought to be experts at waiting until the right moment has come.

Anyone who has done any farming—on a little patch of ground or in a flower pot or on a thousand acres—should have the best sense of timing of all. The farmer is always watching for readiness. He cannot plunge ahead in his own sweet way. He must keep his eye on the weather, the condition of the soil, the growth of the crops, on the many different signs that tell him whether or not the time is ripe. When you teach children, you need the same kind of weather eye.

Most of us have a good sense of timing. The trick is not to forget to use it! We can make the training period what all good education should become: a source of power, of competence and of confidence. This is exactly what the young child wants. The big secret is simply not jumping the gun.

FOR INDEPENDENT STUDY

1. There have been many studies on readiness in many areas of behavior. You will enjoy reading one of the best known research studies, *Growth: A Study of Johnny and Jimmy*, by Myrtle McGraw (New York: Appleton-Century, 1935).

2. Parents generally hurry their children along when the children are young—despite all the signs youngsters give that they are not ready—and then try feverishly to put the brakes on when their children are adolescents—despite all the signs youngsters give then that they are ready. You can sharpen your understanding of readiness by recalling some

125

of the times in your own adolescence when your parents said: "You're not old enough—you haven't grown enough yet," and you felt that the time was ripe.

3. Much of the literature on dog obedience training is full of references to readiness. You will find such advice as, "The pup must be at least three to four months old or he simply will not have enough muscular control to be house-broken. The only thing you can do is to wait for the right time to come along . . ." and "The pup should be at least six months old before you begin serious work on obedience training. . . . Dogs have been started in training earlier (but) . . . we have seen too many dogs who've had their puppyhood shattered by too-early attempts at the imposition of the concentration and discipline necessary and who, though trained after a fashion, never worked happily or well. . . ." (from *Dog Obedience Training*, by Milo Pearsall and Charles G. Leedham. New York: Scribners, 1958). Check on animal literature in a pet shop. You may come to believe that the best thing we can do is to treat our children like dogs!

What would you do?

Question 12 You are the teacher in a four-year-old group. One child is playing with a beautiful doll, a new toy in the group. She spanks the doll and shakes it and scolds it and slaps it and finally puts it in the toy stove and says: "I'm going to burn you up." What is your inclination: *a*) Ignore the whole thing; just let her alone. *b*) Don't make an issue of it now or embarrass this one child but later talk to the whole group about how to play nicely with dolls. *c*) Explain to the girl that this is not the right way to play with the doll. *d*) Don't say a word but play with the girl and re-direct her use of the doll into more social and constructive paths.

126

teaching children to talk
-a prize example of good teaching

Chapter 15

During the training period all of us teach one lesson very beautifully. We teach it with no harm at all to the child. We show a fine sense of timing, a respect for readiness. We wait for power to develop. We use good sense about providing many experiences so that desire, too, comes along in fine shape. In this one area we are very good teachers, all of us.

It is worthwhile to study the "movies" of this "winning game" where we perform in almost perfect style. If we can spot what we do sensitively and intelligently and with such good impact on the child in this one instance, maybe we can apply the same sensible techniques to all the other lessons in the training period.

We are very good at teaching children to talk their native language. We teach English with all of its complexities. Russian parents also succeed brilliantly in teaching their children to speak Russian—and Russian is a very hard language to

127

learn! Chinese parents are good teachers—their children learn to speak Chinese. And so it goes all over the world. The easy languages, the hard languages—it makes no difference. Parents everywhere teach the native tongue to their children and in such a wise way that the children gain power. The training period gives youngsters a boost; it doesn't bowl them over and knock them down.

THE AMAZING GROWTH OF VOCABULARY

The child at birth obviously has no spoken words. The teaching gets off to a slow, gentle start, and this is the wise way. Usually it takes us about a year to train a child to say three words of English; but from then on we are brilliant. By the second birthday the average child has a spoken vocabulary of about 270 words, a ninety-fold increase in only twelve months. You couldn't ask for better teaching than that! From age two on most children make a steady gain of about 500 to 600 words a year. By age six a child's vocabulary is apt to include about 2,500 words, a truly amazing result of good teaching when you consider that he started with only the ability to cry.

During the training period and in the years that follow, on up to six, we not only manage to build this very extensive English vocabulary—we teach all the parts of speech! When the child first starts to talk, around his first birthday, his words are apt to be nouns. In the first year or so we teach him only the names of objects or of people, the really important things in his immediate environment. Most children say "Ma-ma" among their first words. "Baby" is apt to be another one of their early achievements. "Da-da," "woof-woof," "bow-wow" —the nouns that stand for the most familiar—come first.

Youngsters quickly go on from this bare beginning. Verbs

are usually the next part of speech that we manage to get into the child's vocabulary. And before the child is six we will have taught him all the different kinds of words that exist—pronouns, adverbs, adjectives, articles, conjunctions. We do quite a job!

We are excellent teachers of clear enunciation, too. Most studies show that children have about three words around the time of their first birthday. Often the trouble is that only their mothers can understand them! Even fathers, who certainly are "true believers" and all too willing to hear what they want to hear, sometimes have difficulty understanding their children. Fathers have to take mother's word for it that the child is really saying something. There is steady progress, however. At eighteen months, about 25% of what a child says is usually articulated clearly. By age three, more words are clear but it still can be very difficult for someone outside the family to understand the child. Before the end of the under-six age span, however, we have made our impact. Usually by this age almost all of a child's language is articulated clearly. A good job of training!

We are very successful in still another way. When children first begin to talk they speak in one-word sentences. They are specialists in brevity. Maybe we should copy them, but they copy us! "Baby" can mean: I am your baby. Do you love your baby? Come to baby. This baby is hungry (or wet or tired or hurt or a million and one other things). By as early as the fourth year of life, we manage to train our children to use complete sentences most of the time. The usual sentence length then is about five words and, by age six, children generally are talking in still longer sentences. They begin with simple declarative sentences. Within the six-year span, as a result of our teaching, children say all the kinds of sentences that exist—simple, compound, complex, interrogative, commands, etc.

129

A Slow, Gentle, Gradual Start

What makes us such brilliant teachers of English? What are our secrets in this one area that let us train but not weaken? We use three good teaching techniques—techniques that apply to all teaching. We can use the same magic in everything that we want to get over to children.

First, we take our time. We relax. We are not in a panic or a tizzy or in a terrible hurry. Important as learning one's native language is, we don't try to cram the language down a child's throat. For once, we curb our impatience and wait until the child is ready.

There is a normal, natural, universal progression in the development of language during the first year and we are content to go along with it. We don't try to superimpose our own ideas. The natural way is good enough for us. As early as the first month or so, children begin to talk making vowel sounds —*ah, eh, eeh*. At this stage of development, when the lips and sucking are so important a part of life, the sounds that are articulated in the front of the mouth are easiest for the child to make. And that is all right with us. Even at the beginning a few consonants are audible. These are always the back consonants—*g, k, l*—probably because the baby has the capacity to swallow.

Other sounds depend on control of the tongue. The very young baby does not yet have this control. He has to grow some more, and we are willing to give him time. Still other sounds depend on teeth. We know the baby does not yet have teeth, so we are not impatient. Would that we could have the same confidence that "the time will come" in other areas of instruction where the missing ingredient does not stare us in the face!

By six months of age or thereabouts, the child usually can

130

produce as many back and middle vowels as front vowels. During the same first six months the number of consonant sounds increases. The next step is for the child to put vowels and consonants together to produce a syllable. Then he repeats the same syllable, and lo and behold! He has his first word: "Ma-ma"—"Da-da"—"bye-bye"! In his own good time, in his own way, with no pressure from us, when the child is ready, the word comes.

In language teaching we are good exponents of gradualism. And because we are not in a hurry, the learning process becomes a very simple, easy, effortless, and highly satisfying process for the child.

We are not even upset when a youngster stays on a plateau and, for a while, seems not to make great progress. The normal development of speech does not proceed evenly—"Day by day in every way we get better and better"—nor does any other learning! Children have their ups and downs. During the second year, for instance, children very commonly slow down at times in their language development. The reason is obvious: Mobility steals the show! Youngsters are completely wrapped up in perfecting their locomotion. The power for steady speech progress is there but, at the moment, not the desire. The average vocabulary consists of three words at twelve months; nineteen words at fifteen months; *only twenty-two* words at eighteen months; then a big jump to 118 words at twenty-one months, and 272 words by the second birthday. Such uneven growth ought to worry us. A six-fold gain from the twelfth to the fifteenth month, and then almost no gain in the next three months at all! We ought to panic and leap in with both feet and try to teach harder. We don't, with language. In this area we have the nice relaxed capacity to realize that children cannot give themselves evenly and equally to all possible interests. At the moment all their desire goes into walking, and it doesn't bother us!

131

Around three and four years of age, another event occurs which ought to panic us. Many children do some stuttering. They are full of things to say and so eager to say them. Seemingly, quite normally, they have more to say than they can get out. Stuttering at this age is a great challenge to our forbearance. A few of us do weaken and give in to impatience at this point. We "do something" to end the stuttering and when we do, we prolong it! Most of us, however, are not upset. When we hold our horses, this momentary difficulty disappears.

What is the secret that makes us such good language teachers? One part of the answer is that we go along with the child. We don't expect more of him than he can comfortably do. We take our time and respect his readiness.

AMPLE EXPERIMENTATION

Our second wise teaching technique is to *let children experiment*. We let them fool around with language. We are in no great hurry to imprint on them our own particular form. We let the right way emerge out of children's own experimentation with the right way, the wrong way, with all ways. This tolerance is the second secret of our success.

One of the nicest sounds that can be heard in a household is the baby doing his "speech homework." He drills himself. He babbles away, in his basket or crib, making all the sounds of all the languages in the world. We are not disturbed because he doesn't stick to the right language, English. We don't minimize his activity: He is *just* babbling. He is *just* exploring sound. He is *just* manipulating tongue and lips and palate and air. We don't disparage the child's way or try to cut it off. We let the baby babble, and we are glad for it. Somehow we seem to know that out of voluntary soundmaking, English will come.

132

Self-imposed drill goes on all through the under-six years. Word counts are by no means completely reliable but research studies show that children say words as many as 11,000 to 12,000 times a day when they are three, and as many as 15,000 times a day when they are four. One study reports that a three-year-old asked 376 questions in one day! Most mothers know that their youngsters never stop talking, but even mothers may be surprised at these figures showing how much children actually talk and practice and drill. All the asking, all the talking, all the noise wears us down at times, but fortunately we don't stop it. Children would never learn as well if we did. We are really letting the child teach himself, and this pays off in the long run.

IDENTIFICATION—OUR THIRD WEAPON

We set an example—this is the third secret of our good teaching. We speak English. We simply assume that, of course, our child will learn to speak English if we do; and, of course, he does.

Our language teaching is very unobtrusive. It is very non-coercive *but* very effective! Our words are in the air, all around the child. They are bound to stick and to sink in. Now and again, to be sure, we do correct our child when he mispronounces a word. Occasionally we show him specifically and explicitly how to say a word. These times of overt instruction are very rare, however. They do not begin to compare with the countless other times when we are simply talking and the child is listening; or when he is talking and we are listening. Yet we are teaching all the time! We are teaching even when we don't know that we are teaching.

There is a technical name for this silent process. It is called *identification*. The child likes us; he wants to be like us. He identifies with us. Identification is a quiet process but a very

133

persistent one. It goes on day after day, almost every minute of the day. It is a steady, slow process. Identification does not change children overnight but in the long run identification pays off a thousand times more surely than our "noisy" lessons—the explicit times when we know we are teaching. If we love them and they know they are loved, our children are bound to be like us—to talk like us and to act like us. They have no other place to turn, nor do they want any other.

The studies show very clearly that children learn to talk from having someone around them whom they love and who is talking. For instance, single children usually have larger vocabularies; they are apt to be with adults more than children who have brothers and sisters. Twins are apt to be with each other more than with adults; they tend to have smaller vocabularies. Children from upper income, better educated families, where there is apt to be a lot of talk in the air, have larger vocabularies. Children from lower income and less well educated families usually have fewer words at their command because they are surrounded by fewer words. Children in nursery schools—surrounded by other children more than by adults—make great gains in many areas but usually not in vocabulary development. Children raised in institutions fare the worst of all. They don't get love; they don't hear words all around them. Their vocabularies are very meagre.

When in Rome you do as the Romans do. Children at home obviously do as their parents do. We are the very best teachers when we seem to be making no effort at all! Our children are drinking us in. The learning is phenomenal but the bonus of this silent teaching is that the learning goes on without an exhausting, weakening struggle—either for the child or for us.

We have three secrets of success:

1. We take our time and respect readiness.

134

2. We let children experiment and we don't expect miracles overnight.

3. We do some explicit teaching but, most of all, we simply set an example. If we can use these same good techniques in all the other lessons we want to get over, the training period will not threaten children—it will make them strong.

FOR INDEPENDENT STUDY

1. We teach children to talk so easily and so naturally that you may spoil your success by reading about how to do it! If you think you can still keep your natural style and not become self-conscious despite some added knowledge, one excellent book is *How Children Learn To Speak*, by M. M. Lewis (New York: Basic Books, 1959).

What would you do?

Question 13 Two four-year-olds have a squabble out on the playground over a shovel. They tussle for it briefly and one child succeeds in getting full possession. The loser walks away and, as he leaves, calls back over his shoulder: "You stinker. You stinky, stinky, stinker." You are the teacher. What is your inclination: *a*) Pretend you didn't hear him. *b*) Stop the child and talk to him about being a good loser. *c*) Bring both the children together and talk to them both about sharing. *d*) Don't let the child get away with a display of temper like this. You don't have to be a beast or a brute but punish him in some way—perhaps make him sit for two minutes or so—to teach him that being a poor loser simply is not allowed.

135

good teaching
in the
training period

Chapter 16

There is no reason on the face of the earth why the same three "secrets of success" that work so beautifully for us in teaching children to speak cannot be applied to all the lessons of the training period. Usually we manage to turn out an oversupply of children who are finicky, fussy eaters; of children who regard sleep as an enemy; of children who are much more resistant and stubborn than they need to be. It takes a lot of skill to persuade youngsters that food and sleep are no good, and that it is better to argue than to live peaceably, but we have it! And we ought to get rid of it!

HOLDING BACK THE HEAVY HAND

You can hardly go wrong in the training period if your appreciation of gradualism leads you to temper and to gentle some lessons that you might otherwise try to pound home or, if it moves you, to postpone explicit and specific lessons

136

in some cases. It is wise with the crawler and the beginning walker, for example, to hold off any heavy-handed emphasis on property rights. At this early age children simply do not yet have the power to distinguish between their things and yours. They cannot yet tell the difference between breakable things and unbreakable ones. They cannot tell the difference between valuable objects and those not so precious. Such subtle distinctions are far over their heads.

Your best bet is to save the "noisy," overt teaching of these lessons until later. At the crawling-toddling time in development clear the decks; remove the things that a child might damage or destroy, put everything that is not for the child up high, out of reach. Arrange the rooms so he has clear sailing —anything he can reach he can have. This is the time in family life when a mantelpiece is a lifesaver.

It is the time when a sense of humor is a lifesaver, too. It is hard to keep up with the crawler-toddler, let alone to stay one jump ahead. Children are bound to knock over and destroy some things that were never meant for them. But you can smile a little and chalk up the breakage to "profit and loss." After all, you expect to spend a lot of money on your child later, in school and college. Children cost some money at this early age, too. Pick up the pieces and go rolling along.

When children are around two, it is wise to postpone or soften all the lectures about sharing. Sharing is an important goal—so important that you should save it for a more propitious time. Two-year-olds are firm believers in rugged capitalism. Just accept them the way they are and don't try to convert them now to some other "ism." If two youngsters are playing together, your best bet is to have two of everything. If one child wants something that the other fellow has, be ingenious and work out the best temporary solution you can. The "right" solution is any solution that lets each child end up with something precious he can have and hold and use.

137

You do well to go along with the selfishness of Twos, and save your sermons for later.

You do well to postpone a great deal of direct and specific toilet training, too. It is certainly understandable that mothers are often in a hurry to end the mess of diapers. But toilet training is one area where "haste makes waste." There is no point at all in working on bowel training until a child is seven or eight or nine months of age, able to sit up easily and steadily all by himself. This sitting power is the bare minimum the child needs. But even nine months is only the crack of dawn when the sun is just beginning to peek up over the horizon. If you start too energetically at this "minimum time," you will be teaching the hard way!

A youngster must also have the power to hold in his bowel movement and to push it out at the right time. This muscle control and the ability to give you some signal that he is about to have a bowel movement usually do not develop until a child is about two. If you can bring yourself to wait until about that age before you begin any direct teaching, bowel training is apt to be a very easy task. The child almost learns by himself!

The same slow-and-easy way pays off with bladder training, too. If you feel very ambitious you can start very early to train *yourself!* At some time after the first birthday most children's bladders and muscles have grown sufficiently so that they can hold in their urine for about two hours. Religiously, then, you can watch for your child's rhythm and carry him to the "potty" every two hours on the dot. But you will be the one who is being toilet-trained, not the child. And you run the risk of getting angry with your youngster, because he will disappoint you so often.

If you can wait, most children by two-and-a-half years of age are usually able to tell you when they have to urinate. By that time they can hold in their urine until you can get them to

138

the bathroom. Now the *child* is trained (except for occasional accidents that can happen for quite a while longer). But he has been trained so effortlessly and easily that you will hardly know how you taught him.

Nighttime bladder control takes longer to develop and calls for more patience. You can go to all kinds of lengths to speed up the process: Cut down on fluids. Awaken the child. Even buy an electronic device! But, if you relax and seemingly do nothing but wait, you "train" him as well or better. By three years of age or so, most children have grown enough to sleep through the night and to hold in their urine; or they can wake up in time to call you. The training period does not have to be a time of anger on our part, and failure on the child's part. If we are gentle and patient, success comes quite easily. After all, everything is on our side. The child is growing, and he wants the same things that we want!

TRAINING FOR GOOD EATING

The same gradualism pays off in our lessons about eating. Not too long ago, the dining room table was the greatest battlefield in the home. Pediatricians reported that "eating problems" were the greatest concern of parents. (Today doctors say that "sleeping problems" are the big concern; seemingly we make progress by jumping out of the frying pan into the fire!) Some of the headaches and heartaches associated with eating have lessened as more and more parents follow a self-demand schedule in relation to feeding times and weaning from a nipple to the cup. But these are only the first of many issues that arise in connection with food. We have to learn to cope with all the other teachings as gracefully and as wisely.

Very early in life, whether a child is breast-fed or bottle-fed, it is necessary to supplement his milk diet. Practices vary, but quite often within the very first weeks the baby is given cod liver oil or some source of Vitamin D, and orange juice or some other source of Vitamin C, because milk is low in both of these essential vitamins. Egg yolk, strained meats, cereals, vegetables and fruits are also introduced early to the baby's diet, in whatever order the child's pediatrician thinks best. Meeting these new foods is the start of a child's lifelong process of learning to like the foods that we in our culture eat. Every society has its special tastes. We serve pablum, not *poi*. We serve zweiback, toast and bread, not *tortillas*. We don't serve blubber or eel, frog's legs or rattlesnake, but we do have other equally strange-sounding dishes—liver, spinach, tomatoes, bananas. These happen to be *our* foods. They are all good. No child should have any trouble at all learning to like them (except in those rare instances where there is some physical incompatibility, an allergy, which makes the child unable to tolerate a particular food).

The way in which new foods are introduced determines whether a youngster easily and effortlessly will take on his society's tastes or whether he will be a little rebel. The road to success is the same old road: Go *slowly*. If you pile on too many new foods all at once, or press the new foods on the child too insistently, or demand that he eat more than he seems to want, you have hit on the technique for creating "allergies" where none need exist. You build resistance when you could just as easily foster receptivity.

When the doctor says the time is right to begin (remember that he is playing the average!), offer the child a tiny taste of the new food. Generally it is wise to offer this tiny taste along with other foods the baby knows and loves. In every new situation, all through life, we all feel more secure if we have an "old friend" along to keep us company. The most common thing in the world is for the baby to take the tiny taste, roll the new food around in his mouth, fool with it on his tongue and with his lips, and spit it out!

140

This is the child's way of getting used to the new taste of the food, its new consistency and texture. Such behavior is almost the direct equivalent of babbling in language development. The child is "fooling around"—but not wastefully. In good child style he is familiarizing himself with something new and getting the hang of it. Come back at him with another tiny taste, at the same meal or the next one. If a youngster continues to reject the food after several tries, there is no harm at all in beating a temporary retreat. Hold off, and try again in a few days or a week. The nice thing about living with children is that there always is a tomorrow. And the nicest thing about living with young children is that there are lots of tomorrows! What you don't teach today you can always teach him later on.

The one secret is to relax. Make an issue of the new food and the child must fight you. Insist, and eating becomes more than food—now a principle is involved. You have to beware of defeating your own ends. You want your child to like new foods. The more you worry and demand, the more likely he is to end up resisting them.

There are a few other little techniques. Children usually like lukewarm foods better than the extremes of hot and cold. They generally like bland flavors rather than those with a sharp and pronounced taste. At first they can cope better with foods that have a somewhat liquid consistency, rather than those that stick and require a lot of tongue-work. They also like finger-foods, anything they can pick up in their hands. As they get older, children seem to respond to the attractiveness of foods, just as we do, and to variety in textures and tastes.

APPETITE: STILL ANOTHER AREA OF INDIVIDUAL
DIFFERENCES

Too many of us have no confidence in food. We treat it as something very unpleasant that we must sneak into the child.

141

We bribe youngsters to eat by putting cute pictures on the bottoms of their plates. There is no need at all for payola with eating. Food is its own reward. We beg children or wheedle them or cajole them to eat—and even offer to dance a jig! Our rewards and entreaties are quite extraneous. Food doesn't need any superchargers. Food itself is good. When a child eats it, he feels much better inside. If we take our time and give the child time, there is no reason why any youngster should have to fight his way through every meal.

Battles often arise over the amount of food a child eats. Most doctors make the flat statement: "No child ever starved himself to death!" Most of us can't believe it. We want to play it safe and stuff the child. We have an image in our minds of how much a child "ought" to eat, and then we double it!

Appetites vary, of course. They vary from child to child, just as they did in babyhood when each youngster had his own feeding schedule. And appetite varies from time to time. Almost all children, for example, slacken off in their eating somewhere around the end of the first year. They are growing much less fast and need less food. Sometimes, too, at that time they get as much good out of playing with their food as they do out of eating it. Appetite also varies from day to day, depending on the child's activity, mood and health.

We are older and wiser but the fact is: Only the child knows his own appetite. With the newborn and during the first few months many of us have trouble believing that "Food is love." When children are older we belatedly and suddenly get this idea—but in a mixed-up way. We seem to think that stuffing food into children proves that we love them! We can show our love better if we respect the child's own appetite. The best approach is always to *underestimate*. Let the youngster come back for more. But if you overshoot the mark, remember: There is no point in making a fetish of clean plates.

142

PERSUADING CHILDREN THAT SLEEP IS HEAVENLY

Each child has his own "appetite" for sleep, too. Some need a lot, some need a little. You can't go wrong just so long as your child gets the amount he feels is right for him. You certainly meet resistance, however, if you try to stuff him with sleep.

Sleep is good, like food. When we sleep, we wake up refreshed, just as we feel better after we eat. You have to wonder why there should ever be any battles over sleep! The battles do flare up, however, especially over the daytime nap during the training period. It is understandable why mothers want their children to continue taking naps as long as possible. Mothers need a rest time even if their children don't. There are skirmishes, too, over evening bedtime hours. And it is understandable why we are all eager to shoo the children off to bed at night. "They need the sleep," we say. We need some peace and quiet!

At the start of life eating and sleeping are intimately intertwined. A child follows his self-demand schedule for food; at the same time he follows his self-demand schedule for sleep. If we can only continue this sensible approach on up into the second and third and fourth year of life, sleep time could easily become a time of peace, not one more conflict in the cold war.

It is just as simple to tell from a child's behavior when he has an "appetite" for sleep as it is to tell from the baby's behavior when he has an appetite for food. Parents learn their own child's sleep rhythm by watching their child, not the averages. They have a general idea of the time when their youngster is likely to feel tired. The actual time for bed is pinpointed by his behavior. A youngster may yawn—this is one of the obvious signs. His eyes may begin to look tired. He

143

may seem on the verge of becoming more irritable or excitable. These are his signals that he needs sleep.

There is no problem at all in persuading a tired child to go to bed. A youngster who isn't tired cannot help but feel that he is being pushed around. That is something that children seeking autonomy never take lying down. Resistant youngsters dawdle and drag out the process interminably. They call for water over and over. They pop out of bed again and again. Some parents, driven to distraction, tie a rope to the bedroom door or bolt it. And some—this is deplorable!—even give their children sleeping pills. The technique can be so easy: Just wait until your child is tired! Sleep will keep him in bed better than any other device.

Again a few minor techniques help. A darkened room, quiet and peaceful, makes it easier for the child to drop off. A quiet time as sleep-hour approaches, rather than a spell of wild hilarity, helps a youngster get in the mood. A relaxed pace on the adult's part as you go through the preliminary talking and toileting and story time is another real aid. Youngsters sense when you are in a hurry to get rid of them—then they want to hold on longer. But the best technique of all is to be sure your child is sleepy.

TEACH . . . AND TEACH . . . AND TEACH!

The best approach to all the lessons is a very easy-going one. But don't confuse this gradual, calm manner—or even your postponing the lessons—with "doing nothing." The two are miles apart. You may well be holding back on "noisy" specific lessons, but every single minute of the time you are teaching silently. The process of identification goes on and on. The fact that you do not push the child around but respect his readiness makes identification operate even more effectively.

You are teaching, whether you know it or not, through everything you do.

As long as you don't eat with your fingers, or grab your food, or talk with your mouth full, your children won't either. As long as you like to eat, your children will relish food. If you don't turn up your nose at one food after another, your children won't either as time goes along.

If you are toilet-trained (and fortunately most of us are!), your children are sure to follow your pattern as soon as they are able.

If you are polite, in the long run they will be about as polite as you are. Keep in mind that right now these children are still action children. They can talk but words are not yet their main style of operating—not through their own words nor through listening to your words. About the only way you can cram the passwords—"Thank you" and "Pardon me" and "I'm sorry" and "Please"—into them is by your being rude to them! You will get your lessons in consideration and thoughtfulness over much better if you bide your time, keep all the verbal fuss to a minimum, *and* demonstrate what you want them to learn.

If you show a decent respect for property rights—Don't steal from other people and don't steal from your children!—the chances are very strong that your children will end up as honest as you are and about as generous.

If you don't lose your temper—especially with the children themselves during the training period—they are much more apt to grow up as people who can keep their own tempers reasonably under control.

When we soften or postpone direct teaching, we think we are doing nothing. The reverse is true. We are teaching our hearts out, because we are teaching with our hearts. Our insistent, yet silent lessons do not threaten the child. He is learning all the while and he still feels big! When we teach too noisily, we run a double risk: We are more apt to lessen the child's sense of autonomy *and* there is danger that we will spoil our good relationships with our children. We make it harder for the unspoken, quiet lessons to sink in.

FOR INDEPENDENT STUDY

1. One interesting big volume is packed with good suggestions about the training period (and every other phase of development) with answers alphabetically listed, and with some excellent general discussions: *The Encyclopedia of Child Care and Guidance,* by Sidonie M. Gruenberg, editor (Garden City, N.Y.: Doubleday, 1954). You might want to balance your use of this professional book by looking at one written with tongue-in-cheek: *The Complete Book of Absolutely Perfect Baby and Child Care,* by Eleanor Goulding Smith (New York: Harcourt, Brace, 1957). Spock's paperback, *Baby and Child Care,* already mentioned, is also tops in its sensitive and yet so commonsense approach to training. You will enjoy all Spock's books, including his latest, *Dr. Spock Talks With Mothers* (1961) and *Problems of Parents* (1962) (New York: Houghton Mifflin). He writes so simply and with such great understanding for everyone involved—mother, father, baby, the whole family —that you seldom need an antidote after reading him. Just for fun, however, you should see *What Dr. Spock Didn't Tell Us,* by Butler Atkinson (New York: Simon and Schuster, 1960).

What would you do?

Question 14 Your four-year-old takes one look at the salad on the supper table and spouts: "Lettuce is junk. I hate it."

What is your inclination: *a*) Good-naturedly say something like, "I think it is junk too, but we are all going to eat it." *b*) Immediately, while the issue is right out on the table, send her to her room until she apologizes. *c*) Tell her that she doesn't have to eat the lettuce if she doesn't want to but she must eat the fruit salad on top of the lettuce. *d*) Explain, in words that a four-year-old can understand, that lettuce is an important food. Tell her about the many children the world over who never have lettuce to eat—or a decent meal at any time.

temper
tantrums

Chapter 17

Sometimes we are tempted to put a little extra pressure on children who are seeking a sense of autonomy just because we don't want them to "get too big for their britches." We say "no" to build character. We insist, not because a job really has to be done but to teach the child that he can't have his own way all of the time.

Actually, we don't need to go out of our way during this period to keep the child in his place. Every child, inevitably and inescapably, meets one major obstacle to his getting an overdose of power. The obstacle? *The child himself!* We don't have to create road blocks just to give him practice in overcoming difficulties. *The child is his own worst enemy!*

Frustration Is Inevitable

From six months on until about the age of three, the child has a "champagne appetite but a beer pocketbook." Desper-

148

ately seeking bigness and power, he works himself into situations time after time which are beyond him. He sets his heart on goals which are unobtainable. Inevitably in the training period we do our share to knock the wind out of his sails. Our actions can be improved, especially if we sharpen our sense of timing. But the child himself is responsible for many of the messes he gets into. He brings on his own deflation.

Typically, a youngster wants the toy on top of the table, or the ball high up on a shelf that he cannot possibly reach. He insists on buttoning the button that he cannot button. His wagon wheel gets caught in the table leg; he persists in trying to free it, even though he cannot figure out how to solve the problem. He wants to carry the package that is too heavy for him. He tries desperately to keep up with older children who run too fast for him. He struggles to put the square peg in the round hole; his eyes cannot yet tell him that the job simply cannot be done.

The power-seeking child constantly exposes himself. He climbs way out on a limb, lured by the job for which he does not have the strength, the necessary coordination, speed, height or balance. The result is inevitable, and it happens many times a day: Life cuts the children down to size. Life says, in effect: You're just a little shrimp. You're just a little shaver. You want to but you can't. This galling lesson is drummed into the child over and over: You are impotent (at the very time when he most wants to feel potent!).

The outcome, especially around the second birthday, is that young children have many temper tantrums. Three factors conspire to make tantrums almost inevitable: the child's strong desires; his limited powers; the fact that his controls over his feelings are still feeble and weak. Anger—sharp, keen, open—sweeps over children. It engulfs them. Youngsters feel a fury sharper than they are likely ever to feel again. Later their controls will be better; their skills will have grown; their

149

ambitions will be more tempered by reality; they will be less exposed. Right now, none of these mitigating forces operates. Full-bodied anger takes over.

Adults cause the temper tantrums sometimes. Often, however, we are the innocent bystanders. The child is angry with himself, with his own lack of power, and from that start he momentarily becomes angry with the world or us or anything that comes along. He is simply full of anger.

He throws himself on the floor. He pounds with his fists. He kicks with his feet. He even bangs his head on the floor at times. He screams. He cries and sobs uncontrollably.

Actually, of course, there is nothing wrong with anger at any age. Anger is a human emotion and a very good one. There is enough injustice around to make everyone angry. A few more adult blowups could mean that some of the real evil in this world would meet the opposition it deserves.

Especially at the tender age of two, there is nothing wrong with anger. It stems from a child's search for power—a worthy cause. It stems from his feeble controls—an understandable condition. And a child needs to practice all of his emotions—anger included—to keep them alive.

Too many tantrums are not good, however. They can frighten a child, for one thing. Youngsters know that they have lost control and this worries them. Too many tantrums, especially if a child has to fight his way out of his anger all by himself, can leave only a residue of anger. The child learns only anger, rather than a variety of ways of solving problems. Tantrums are exhausting, too—for the adult as well as for the child!

You cannot prevent all tantrums. This is especially true with active, vigorous youngsters who feel all things keenly and who always operate with high-speed drive. But it is worthwhile to try to keep the number of explosions to some reasonable limit. A good sense of timing cuts down on the number of tantrums.

150

You lessen the likelihood of blowups if you say "Eat" primarily when the child is hungry; if you say "Sleep" primarily when he is tired; if you say "Come" primarily when he is ready to come.

Another technique is to do all you can to brush away any obviously overcomplicated challenges. There is no point in luring children into frustration. Common sense says to keep the child's environment simple, and well within his powers. Unfortunately, you cannot always do this. You never know what will catch a child's eye or what a youngster will think of getting into. Whenever you do succeed, however, you score a point for peace.

Still another good idea is to guard against exhaustion and too much excitement. Weary and overstimulated children are more apt to lose control of themselves. This is one reason why you see so many tantrums in supermarkets and department stores. Long shopping tours, long visits, or long car rides were never meant for young children. Avoid them, if you can. At home, when you see overstimulation about to take command, you can sometimes provide the "stitch in time" that prevents a tantrum by initiating a story, or a bath, or by starting some other quiet and relaxing activity.

THE RIGHT AMOUNT OF ASSISTANCE

Perhaps the most useful way of keeping emotional eruptions in hand is knowing when and how to give the right amount of help to a youngster. Aid and assistance can range from the maximum—you do the job yourself—to a bare minimum. The trick is to adjust the help you give to the amount the child needs in order to feel big and successful himself.

If you give too much help, more than a child needs, you rob him of bigness. The job gets done but only you feel big. The youngster has had another experience in feeling small.

151

On the other hand if you give too little help—less than a child needs—a youngster meets only defeat. Unhappily, he again has the experience of feeling small. *The right amount*—we seldom hit it smack on the nose—*is the least help the child needs in order to be successful.*

Sometimes the right amount means that you simply stand by. The company of someone who is friendly and interested adds up to real support. You don't do a thing, you don't say a word, but you are there.

Sometimes you not only stand by but you give some general encouragement: "You're getting it." "Don't give up." "You can do it." Or you might give some general sympathy: "That's a hard job." "That really is a tough one." Your general cheeriness and understanding may be enough to spur the child on so that he keeps trying and succeeds.

Generalities, however, are not always the answer. A specific suggestion sometimes is called for: "Try pushing on this side." "Try turning it that way." And often verbal suggestions are not enough. You help by doing a part of the job yourself, the tough part. The child can then cope with the remainder which is within his powers. "I'll start the button through the hole, then you can push it all the way through." "I'll begin the knot and then you can pull it tight."

Sometimes you have to do the whole job yourself. There is nothing wrong with that when a youngster is really at the end of his rope. You tie the bow. You open the door. You get the ball. Full and complete help, when called for, does not feed into a child's sense of autonomy but it does free him to move on ahead, unemotionally, into new situations better geared to his powers.

Some of us make a fetish of insisting that children do everything for themselves. We want them to work their own way out of their own messes, and to finish everything they have started. This rigidity is not the best technique for helping a child to feel strong. It can lead to too many tantrums. Some of us make a fetish of doing everything for children. We are too eager to ward off tears, too eager to ward off anger. We always jump in with maximum help, more than the youngster is asking for. The goal is flexibility. We must aim to give the right help at the right time.

COPING WITH TANTRUMS

No one method ends all tantrums. When they occur, it takes real finesse (and a lot of luck) to work your way through them. For one thing, the tantrums almost always embarrass us. Children can pick the darnedest places and times to blow their tops! Anger is hard enough to cope with privately but when the tantrums occur right out in the public eye, you need a lot of *savoir faire*.

You can build some calmness if you realize how universal and widespread tantrums are in the months around age two. We live only with our own children. We each tend to think that our child alone "loses his temper." Almost all children in this age range do. Some do more than others, and often these "some" have more frequent outbursts only because they are blessed with the gift of stronger feeling. Knowing that some tantrums are normal for this age lets us be more patient and tolerant. It keeps us more clearheaded, free to do whatever looks like the helpful thing to do.

Another complication in coping with tantrums is the old awe of habits. We forget that we are dealing only with a two-year-old. We project ahead to how horrible it would be if our child still had tantrums at twenty-two! We all know a few adults who are still power-crazy. And in America we don't like people who throw their weight around—the international bullies or little bullies in the neighborhood or in the family. We don't like dictators—dictators on a national scale or dictators

153

at the breakfast table. None of us wants his child to go on forever "acting like a two-year-old." But we mustn't forget that children don't want to stay two any more than we want them to. But, right now, they are two!

We must keep our eye on the child in front of us. We are not dealing with a grown-up—simply with a tyke who has lost control for reasons that make sense at this age. It doesn't help to "break the habit" of having a tantrum by squelching the child once and for all. If you are tempted, keep in mind that the adults who have a "hangover" of power seeking were almost always children who were squelched.

Often, of course, the problem is simply that we feel impotent, just as the child feels impotent. When we try to soothe or comfort him or help, frequently he flails out at us. The result is that we have a tantrum too. We scream at the child, or yank him, or come up with that "helpful" angry retort: "I'll give you something to cry about!"

A conflict of wills flares up over tantrums, as it is apt to flare up a hundred and one other times during the child's search for autonomy. The child's concern with power kindles our own smouldering need for power. Most of us were squelched a little more than necessary when we were young. Each of us still has some hankering for two-year-old bigness left over inside of us. Living with young children can sharpen this hankering and lead to a royal battle of wills.

We say "yes" and the child says "no." We request and he says "won't." We say "come"—and the child goes. The child's pint size and his obvious pigheadedness could just as easily touch off our sense of humor. He could just as easily challenge our tact and spur us to find a smart way of working around him. But too often our eyes get bloodshot. We don't see a little two-year-old toddling away from us or having a tantrum —we see an adversary! The child wants to feel big? We'll show

154

him who is big! We may well be showing *ourselves*, proving over again what should have been established a long time ago, when we were two.

No one magic technique soothes the wild beast. You usually have to play temper tantrums by ear. The basic fact is that the child momentarily has lost control of himself. He needs us to help him regain control. Certainly this argues against our becoming angry, too—then there is no one around to run the ship! It argues, too, against the common practice of scooping the child up and isolating him, to "cry it out" and get over his anger all by himself. Occasionally this may be the only thing to do. Generally, however, just our presence—as calm and as unupset as we can be—is an intangible yet very real help in itself. The simple fact that we are there, and not angry, gives the child a sense of direction that helps him get his anger under control.

Basically, you have to watch what is going on. At the very beginning of a tantrum, when anger is at its sharpest, you can generally do nothing but stand by. Watching, however, you usually can tell when it is safe to move in—to hold the child and soothe him, letting some strength and calmness flow from you to him. You can tell when it is possible to divert him. You seldom can reason with a child who is having a tantrum. He hears his own feelings of impotence much more clearly than he can hear any of your logical arguments. But any calm words—whatever comes to mind—sometimes help a youngster get back in control, if your timing is right.

Twos do recover from their tantrums. They express their feelings openly and directly but their anger is short-lived. Unlike adults, Twos do not sulk. Their whole day is not ruined. They have a wonderful capacity to bounce back and, almost without breaking their stride, to go right on with their search for bigness. We would do well to copy their ability to roll

155

with the punches. Children are down—and they are up again. We tend to stay upset by tantrums much longer than the little fellow who has had the outburst.

We stay upset possibly because we take tears too seriously. We read too much meaning into children's angry faces and their tight, clenched fists. A child having a tantrum makes quite a fuss but, translated, all the fuss means is: I want to be big! I want to feel strong! We may have to ride the tantrum out, giving what little comfort we can. But we can take our leads for the future from it. The child is showing us what matters to him. The next time we may be able to feed him power without all the noise and bother!

FOR INDEPENDENT STUDY

1. If your child is around two, or even if you are simply reading about temper tantrums, there is only one kind of additional reading you should do: Read something humorous about children. You will need all the sense of humor you can muster or borrow. Some of the chapters in *Please Don't Eat the Daisies*, by Jean Kerr (paperback edition by Crest Books, New York, 1959. 35¢) or the new book by the same author, *The Snake Has All the Lines* (New York: Doubleday, 1960) may buoy your spirits and do you more good than any academic literature.

What would you do?

Question 15 A five-year-old, going on six, wets his bed almost every single night. With whom do you tend to agree: *a*) Father says: "Let him alone. He'll outgrow it." *b*) Mother is fed up. She wants to punish the child—make him wash his own sheets or anything so he stops! *c*) Grandmother has read about an electrical device that wakes up a child when he starts to wet. She thinks the parents ought to try that. *d*) Even the adolescent in the family has an idea. She suggests doing what they do in school: Have an "honor roll" at home and put the child's name up on a family bulletin board with a big star every time he has a dry night.

accidents
and injuries

Chapter 18

From the end of the first year on through the sixth year (and later too, in fact), *accidents are the leading cause of death in children*. *Accidents*—falls, cuts, bumps, blows from falling objects—*are the leading cause of injuries*. This is hardly surprising, for young children are constantly exploring the possibilities of their own bodies; they are everlastingly on the go and into everything. But the statistics on death and injuries are sad news. And very complicating news.

When they most want to be free, these children need constant supervision. When they most want to be on their own, they need someone who will keep a close eye on them. Adults have to move in two conflicting directions: We must protect children because it is very clear that they are vulnerable to accidents; *and* we must free them because it is very clear that they are vulnerable to overprotection! Accidents can kill and injure physically; overprotection can kill the spirit and wound psychologically. Both are severe hazards.

158

TOO LITTLE ADULT SUPERVISION

The adult must stay loose, so to speak, as an athlete does, ready to move one way or the other. You have to be ready to leap in, when supervision is called for. You have to be ready to back out, when freedom is the need. Parents and teachers of young children need very quick footwork.

Many of us, understandably, are all too ready to turn young children loose. We give them all the rope they want (sometimes enough to hang themselves!). By the time a child is two, parents have had a long hard winter—nine months of pregnancy, twelve or fifteen or eighteen months of demanding physical care. Many a mother is at a very low ebb in her own spirits at the very time when the child starts to ride high.

One of the most physically exhausting periods is around the end of the first year, a few months before and a few months after. We say the child can crawl and walk. He *can* get around under his own steam, but he does not at all times. Of necessity, his mother lugs and hauls and carries. The child's legs get tired—he is not yet a hiker by any means. He goes along very slowly most of the while—he is hardly a sprinter. He *can* go along, but his mother is his auxiliary engine and she gets a very steady workout.

The child around two loves to climb but his mother is still the main derrick. She lifts her twenty-five-pound load a thousand times a day it seems—into bed; out of bed; up into the car; out of the car; up to the mirror; up into a chair; up and down, up and down, time and time again.

Mother's physical fatigue often combines with the blue feeling that she never has a moment to herself. Pregnancies are not just for nine months. The dependence of the infant makes pregnancy seem like a two- or three-year sentence. Not uncommonly, another child is conceived during this time. In

159

her low moments, whether she is again pregnant or not, a mother can feel as if her whole life and every waking minute in it goes to children. She loves her children but still has many moments of resentment against them—they ask too much and drain her dry. A mother can feel very glad when her two-year-old or three-year-old is out of her sight and out of her hair for a short while.

We all, of course, warn children about dangers, hoping that our words will go along with them, even if we do not. Often we yell and shout at them, hoping to pound the warnings in. And, after the event, we all complain: "Why didn't you look where you were going?" "Why didn't you stop and think for a second?" But children seldom carry with them our words of wisdom. We have to be Johnny-on-the-spot. An alert adult—not words—is the best protection against accidents with very young children.

These youngsters are here-and-now creatures. They do not yet have any great capacity to project ahead, to anticipate, to foresee, to imagine the consequences of their actions. They are still wrapped up in themselves. They move fast, and faster each day it seems, so they often do not see what lies a little bit ahead. Warnings will not keep them from running into the swings. Warnings will not keep them from tumbling over the rake. They need us, on hand, to be their safety engineers.

ADULTS AS SAFETY ENGINEERS AND GUARDS

We do the main part of our job as safety engineers very inconspicuously and in advance. We study the layout—of the living room, porch, playground, bathroom, everywhere—before the children arrive. Poisons are removed and locked up. Sharp, pointed tools and instruments are removed and locked up. Fans and heaters are completely out of the way—and their wires, too! Dangerous spots—where a child might fall

160

off or fall in or fall down—are fenced off, not with words but with honest-to-goodness fences. You guard especially against pools of water. Anything that might fall on a child is removed. Anything that could break under a child's weight is removed. Anything that might slip or slide or fall when a child uses it is removed. There is no point in saying "Don't" to the child. The hazard must say "Do" to us! We have to do whatever is necessary to create a safe environment in which a busy child, thinking primarily of himself, can operate with ease.

We do our best as safety engineers. Then we have to become guards. We cannot spot every danger in advance. Situations do not stay the same. The minute you put a moving child into them, you add a very unpredictable element. We must be alert and available, the way policemen are always on hand in crowds—"just in case." You may be sitting or talking with a friend but you never take your eyes off young children. You are ever-ready to move if you are responsible for one of these active, unpredictable youngsters. The only time you can completely forget them is when you know they are sound asleep. (It is good to check once in a while, even then.)

Young children are a lot of trouble—there is no getting away from that. They cost time and they cost energy all the while they are growing up. There is no way you can have a child without effort. Anyone who thinks he can be a parent without spending himself (and spending money!) is in for a sad awakening. Dependent, impulsive, busy children need a lot of supervision. The earlier you learn this lesson and accept it gracefully, the easier it is to face up to the realities of being a parent.

OVERPROTECTION

Some parents turn their children loose too casually. Others hold on too tightly. They read danger into situations where

161

no danger exists. They save their child from physical harm but, in so doing, expose them to psychological harm which can be every bit as crippling.

Overcontrol stems from very understandable causes, just as underprotection does. Facts that were real in other times, other situations, and with other children overpower the actual realities of the present moment. They make us mistake the child we have now for someone else. Not uncommonly, for example, we tend to overprotect the youngster whose older brother or sister has died or been injured or handicapped. We forget that now we have a new child, a different child, in a different setting, and with needs all his own. Not uncommonly we tend to be super-cautious with the child who once was seriously ill. We forget that the illness was last year—this is a new year. We tend to oversupervise the child who has some handicap. We see his one handicap and let that color our whole vision of the total child. He becomes a "handicap," not a child.

There is some temptation to cling to our last child. We become, not safety engineers or guards on hand "in case," but policemen with a prisoner in custody. We don't have our eyes on the child—we respond more to the feelings inside of ourselves. This is "our baby," although the baby may be showing in all of his behavior that he is growing up fast, and wants to.

There is some temptation too, to be overprotective of girls. We don't see them as they are in the under-six years, hardly aware that they belong to one sex or the other. A little girl is simply a busy, active human, feeling her oats and trying like all humans her age to build her body skills and achieve that satisfying sense of power. We look ahead—twenty years—and see instead a dainty young lady who ought to be a "lady."

This projection from one child to another, from one situation to another, from one time to another, is seldom useful. Instead, we must "read" the child who is right in front of us,

162

as we once did with self-demand feeding. Children "demand" their independence and power, just as clearly as they once demanded food. The trick is to be on the lookout for the signals the children are sending. These signals are a much more reliable guide than our memory of what some other child once did. They can tell us when to stand close by, and when to let the reins go a little.

LEARNING TO TAKE A CHANCE WITH CHILDREN

To some extent we probably all worry needlessly, too, about our first-born. You can chalk this up to inexperience. We have had no previous children to teach us how satisfying power and strength and independence are to this age. We do not realize what is at stake from the child's standpoint. Nor do we know what children can do. We underestimate their abilities. We are sure that they are climbing too high, sure they are running too fast, sure they are swinging higher than they should.

Our inexperience also blinds us to the fact that young children have a very real sense of caution within themselves. From two on, for example, children seldom climb higher than they feel they can comfortably go. At the right height for them, they stop of their own accord. They judge by how the rungs feel in their hands, how the steps feel under their feet, how far down the ground looks to their eyes. Young children are adventurous but they are cautious too. They cannot foresee a train of events that might flow in the future, but if they are not tearing around, they are very careful in their immediate surroundings—provided there are no tricks or gimmicks or hidden jokers they have no way of knowing about.

You have to learn to take some chances with children, just as you have to learn to be constantly alert. No degree of care on your part can wipe out the possibility of all accidents. There is bound to be some blood; and some tears. Life after

163

all has its dangers and its pains. Even if you could, you would not want to shield young children so completely from life that they stopped living.

When accidents happen to young children, they go back to being babies again. They want warmth and sympathy from you—not harsh, unfriendly reminders of how you told them "not to do that." They want whatever physical care they need. And they want to catch from you a sense that life is fun and worth living, in spite of all its hazards. Patched up in body and spirit, buoyed up by your proof that warmth and sympathy are always available, learning that life is bearable and well worth the pain, children bounce back from their misadventures and go right on adventuring.

FOR INDEPENDENT STUDY

1. Two governmental publications, differing in depth, are available: *Accidents and Children*, Folder No. 48 (1959) of the U.S. Children's Bureau is available from the Government Printing Office, Washington, D.C. (15¢). *Accidents in Childhood: Facts as a Basis for Prevention*, Technical Report Series No. 118 of the World Health Organization (1957) is available from the United Nations Bookstore, New York. The Metropolitan Life Insurance Company also has a top-notch free pamphlet which any of its local offices or agents will be glad to give you: *A Formula for Child Safety*.

What would you do?

Question 16 Your three-year-old has a habit of sucking her thumb and twirling her hair at nap and bedtime. About the only way you can stop her is to keep her hands securely under the covers. Sometimes even then she manages one way or the other to get her hand loose and suck her thumb. What is your inclination: *a*) Gently talk with her and urge her to try hard to stop of her own accord. *b*) Give up and let her suck. *c*) Do nothing until she falls asleep and then each time, religiously, go in and take her thumb out of her mouth. *d*) See if you can't find some way to make it impossible for her to get her hand loose.

from three
to six
-children at play

Chapter 19

If humans stayed forever wrapped up in an overwhelming desire for bigness and power, we would have a terrible world. Each citizen would be commander-in-chief of his own private army of the resistance. As a matter of fact, we probably wouldn't have a world at all. Parents would have stopped having children long ago!

Even with the best of understanding, youngsters who have independence as the one big thing on their minds can be mighty hard to live with. The search for a sense of autonomy does not go on and on, however (if a youngster has found what he has been looking for). It subsides and settles down into an important but more appropriate place in behavior. Each of us, even adults, still needs to feel important; we even have some moments when we don't mind in the least being the "big shot"—we relish these moments, in fact. But if we have had a good toddlerhood this need to be the all-powerful one is a momentary need. It is not the only thing we can think of.

The change from an obsession with power and bigness does not come overnight. A youngster does not go to bed one evening a bossy, overdetermined, resistant, touchy little fellow and wake up the next morning sweet and agreeable. Gradually his stubbornness flares up less frequently. Temper tantrums occur less often. The conflicts over owning and possessing do not arise every time children get together. "No" and "won't" increasingly take their rightful place alongside of many other more agreeable words.

By about the third birthday—a little before for some children and a little after for others—the healthy youngster knows that he is *someone*. He no longer has to prove it every whipstitch. He knows that he has a wealth of powers. He no longer has to make a public show of them, at least not on every occasion. Slowly, almost imperceptibly, the youngster once more in development begins to think and feel like a somewhat different kind of person. He begins to look for a new and different kind of satisfaction in his days. He judges the experiences of his life by a different kind of standard and, as he does, he becomes vulnerable to new and different dangers.

BUILDING ON THE PAST

Obvious physical changes which anyone can see often cause changes in behavior. The onset of crawling, walking, talking marked the beginning of the period of power seeking. Many physical changes start the years of adolescence on their way. Menopause in the life of a woman is another example of a physical change that triggers a new way of feeling and a different way of acting.

167

No such dramatic physical development happens around the third birthday. The child's new way of looking at himself and of looking at people and the life around him stems more from the consolidation and firming-up of all the growth that has been going on. In the first three years muscular development and coordination had been the single big grain. The three-, four- and five-year-old is still as active as ever, and very much concerned with extending his body skills. But he has laid the base. The gross movements are all there. Now his attention can go into perfecting some of the finer points of movement. Now, too, language development begins to emerge as the most prominent and steady gainer. Since he first sat up and crawled, two years or so ago, the child has been primarily a muscle man. From three on, his brain starts working over-time, too.

The child is no longer as easily distracted as once he was. His capacity to pay attention and to stick at a job has length-ened. His ability to project ahead and to think beyond the very present moment has increased. He can plan a little before leaping into action. Earlier the toddler was highly impulsive, quick to respond to whatever stimulus crossed his path. Every-thing was an irresistible challenge to him and to his body. The Three, the Four, the Five has more capacity to inhibit and to hold back his first and most immediate response.

A real shift in the center of power gradually takes place. When the child was searching for autonomy he wanted to feel big but the real power was in the things around the child. He saw sand—he had to feel it. The sand lured him on. He saw a cigarette butt—he had to pick it up. The butt was a magnet. The two-year-old saw chalk and he had to scribble with it or pound it. The two-year-old was given paint and paper. Quickly, impulsively, without restraint or forethought he smeared and splashed a splotch of paint in the middle of the paper. The sand, the paint, the chalk, the butt had the

168

power to drag the under-three child into manipulating them and to drag him into activity, whatever activity the material suggested.

As the change comes, around three, the power shifts. Youngsters begin to develop some control inside of themselves. The material no longer decides for them—splash, grab, smear, pound. Now the child has an idea. He is starting to cook up a plan of his own.

His beginning idea may be a good one or a bad one. That is not the crucial standard to apply now. What counts at this time is a simple, basic, new fact: *The child has the beginnings of an idea.* The time will come later when we and the child will both measure the worth of those ideas by how they square with reality and by how they apply to our work-a-day world. Right now the beauty of the idea is not its practicality but the fact that the child has it! The idea is at its best in his head. He is beginning to proceed in terms of some notion that makes sense *to him.* Up to year three the youngster has been a "strong man in the circus." Somewhere around his third birthday he seemingly changes his brand of cigarettes! He is becoming a "thinking man," too!

CHILD'S PLAY

At this very beginning stage of thinking, the young child never looks like Rodin's statue of "The Thinker." He doesn't sit and ponder. He doesn't stop and stare, hold his chin pensively and scratch his head. The young child has a distinctive style for his personal, private, puzzling processes. *He plays!* This is the way—through play—that three- and four- and five-year-olds use their beginning ability to have an idea, and express their beginning power to plan and organize.

Unfortunately, the word "play" presents some semantic difficulties. It has different meanings at different ages. Adults

169

play; we play golf and we play bridge. Adolescents play; they play football and basketball and baseball. School age children play; they play hide-and-seek and they play marbles and mumbledy-peg. All the ages after three and four and five "play" but they play games with fixed rules and regulations. They "play" with set and established ways of winning and losing. In baseball: Three strikes and you are out. In football: Four quarters and the game is over. In school age games: "96,97,98,99,100. Here I come, ready or not!" And adults play card games all "according to Hoyle."

This is *not* the young child's play.

Three- and four- and five-year-olds play everything according to *themselves*. The heck with Hoyle! The child makes up the rules. No outsider says what shall be done: "You are supposed to have five men on a side." No outsider says how the play shall be carried on: "You can't touch the other fellow below the hips." The child is beginning to think for himself. He must be the one who decides what will happen, when it will happen, and how.

The young child's play is not, however, wild and scattered. It has rules galore and the rules are very rigid ones. But the youngsters themselves make up the rules. Listen to "child's play": "I must be the baby and you must be the mother and I must be sick and you must be taking care of me." The rules are rigid *but* the children change them as they play. "This must be the fire-house." But a few minutes later or a day later that same big packing case "fire-house" *must be* the garage or store or filling station or the post office or an airplane.

The play that starts slowly before three, emerges sharply somewhere around three, stays uppermost as the dominant characteristic for a long span of time after three and is full of rules—but they are the children's own. All the regulations they think up are their way of putting their impress on life around them. Sand is no longer sand. Sand is a cake. Sand is a highway. Sand is a tunnel. Sand is a sea. Sand is whatever a child wants it to be. A tricycle is no longer a tricycle. A tricycle is a bus, taxi, ambulance, tow truck, fire engine, racer, boat. . . . A child is not a child. He is baby, doctor, policeman, digger, soldier, mother. . . . He is alive and he is dead. He is on horseback, he is the driver of his truck. Children are *beginning* to have an idea, and play, with its special child rules, is how they express that idea.

The word "play" raises one other complication, almost a moral issue. Adults play after work. We play in the evening or on weekends or holidays. We play on vacation. Adolescents and school-age children play after school or in recess, on Saturdays, in the summer. For all the later ages "play" is an escape from life. For the young child play is the whole of life. For the later ages, play is relaxation from work. For the young child play is his work. For the later ages, play is a change of pace. For the young child play is his steady pace—play is what he does all of the time, with everything around him. Play fills his working hours, play fills all his waking hours.

We think of certain activities as fitting neatly into particular times of life. Retirement seems just right for the elderly person. Getting a job is the appropriate activity for a young adult. The young married couple have a baby and begin their family; this "feels right" to all of us and we are glad. These activities jibe with the purposes of their age spans—after sixty-five, around twenty-one. Just so, child's play—his precious make-believe—fits exactly right into the age span from three to six. Play is how the young child should spend his time.

If "play" still seems like a confusing word for summing up the significant activity of three to six, call these the years of peak imagination. They become good years if children have the time, the freedom, the materials, the companionship, the support from adults to be what they are not, to do what they cannot. These become good years if children have ample

171

chance to pretend, to make-believe, to take the world as they meet it and to reshape it in terms of the ideas in their own heads.

A SENSE OF INITIATIVE

If you want to get more technical, you can describe these children as searching for a *sense of initiative*. This is another way of describing the satisfaction that matters most of all in this period—the satisfaction that means health for the child and nourishment for his continued growth. A sense of initiative wraps up three-, four- and five-year-olds, just as a sense of trust beautifully described the overriding concern of infancy, and a sense of autonomy so neatly said the dominant concern of the toddler and the two-year-old.

You do have to understand the special meaning of the word "initiative," however. When applied to three-, four- and five-year-olds the word does not have the standard meaning of ambition and energy and drive. The everyday definition of "initiative" calls to mind the men of the Junior Chamber of Commerce. Energetically they carry out well planned charity balls, paper collections, clean-up campaigns. These are men with "initiative," as we usually use the term. The only thing the child from three to six has in common with them is his energy! He bubbles and bustles with the best of them. He is still as much on the go as ever he was. But from this point on, the two part company.

The bright, shiny new ideas of young children, no matter how energetically and busily carried out, do not serve the community. They do not even always bring us any peace of mind! This is the time in development, for example, when the simple act of getting dressed becomes a major production. Threes and Fours and Fives cannot simply put on the clothes we lay out for them. They have their own ideas—and seldom

172

very good ones at that. None of the routines flow along now just as a matter of course. The child has to think about things he once took for granted—the glass he will drink from, the plate that is his favorite. Once he threw his weight around. When the child is seeking a sense of initiative, he seems to be casting his ballot on every issue—and to have no end of "favorite sons" (and enemies!). The choices seldom seem as important to us as they do to the children.

To understand the technical use of the word "initiative" and to understand the child who is seeking a sense of initiative, you must concentrate on the root in the word—*initial*. The beginning. The child is starting—*just starting*—to cook up a plan of his own. The idea will not necessarily lead to a picture that you can recognize, or to a building of blocks that you can give a name to, or to a game that will look familiar and that will make sense to you. The child is just beginning to think *but*—the big difference now—*he* has something in mind. He is no longer just manipulating materials. He is no longer just exploiting and exploring their use with the first reaction that comes to mind. Three to six is *beginning* to operate on a plan—even though we cannot always follow all the ins-and-outs of the plan or recognize the finished product when the child is done. But our knowing what is going on does not matter; the child has something in mind and this is what counts.

At times when adults are groping for something to do, a member of the group may say: "Why don't we go to a movie!" But sober thought soon reveals that the group has no car— there is no way to get to the movie. They have no money— they couldn't get in to the movie if they could get there. And no good movies are showing anyhow. Then we say: "Oh, well. It was an idea."

By the time we are grown up, our ideas are supposed to be good ideas. They should work out. They should be feasible

173

ideas. When adult ideas do not square with the world of reality we pass on quickly over them and move on to a new and better idea that does. But the young child is at the beginning of his thinking. When he has an idea—good, bad or indifferent—this is no light matter. Just having an idea makes the moment a good one. As these moments of ideas pile up in the years from three to six, the child gets what he is looking for —a satisfying sense of initiative. He is beginning to think. He is beginning to put all the brain power that has slowly been accumulating and all the body power that has been building up to *some* planned and purposeful use.

FOR INDEPENDENT STUDY

1. The Public Affairs pamphlet, *Three to Six: Your Child Starts To School,* by James L. Hymes, Jr. (25¢) discusses in more detail this age range. Much better than more reading, however, is to watch children. Whether you observe one child alone or a small group of children, you cannot miss seeing dramatic play. It goes on all the while, everywhere, almost every minute of the day. Dramatic play even occurs when children swing. If you can get close enough to hear what they are saying out loud to themselves, you are almost sure to hear words or sounds that indicate beyond a doubt that they are living some imaginative, pretend role. Run one spot check after another. Whenever you see three-, four- or five-year-olds, jot down what they are doing. Just be sure to get close enough so that you know what is really going on, not simply the surface show. Ninety-nine times out of a hundred, if the children are not hand-in-hand with an adult or eating or toileting or asleep, your records will show that they are making believe, playing some part, imagining something that is not really true.

174

What would you do?

Question 17 Your three-year-old is on the verge of becoming very pesky at mealtimes. She is getting fussy about a special glass she must have for her milk and a special plate for her dinner. What is your inclination: *a*) Before all this gets out of hand, and so that she doesn't become the center of the whole stage, make it plain that one glass or plate is as good as another and that she has to do what everyone else in the family does: Use the plate and glass in front of her without any fuss. *b*) Keep peace in the family. Let her have the plate and glass she wants, if it makes her happy. *c*) Give in once in a while but, every now and again, put your foot down so your three-year-old learns that she isn't a little princess who can have her way all of the time. *d*) Take turns so that everyone in the family has the chance to use the plate and glass the girl thinks are so special. This way your girl will get her turn but she will also see that she is not the only one in the family. Other people have some rights, too.

the two themes
in imagination

Chapter 20

Two persistent themes run throughout all the imaginative activity of children from three to six. Children either pretend that they are small, weak and dependent *or* they play a role that lets them be big, strong and bossy. As you watch them it becomes very clear: Youngsters are continuing in a new form —play—their old search for a sense of trust and their search for autonomy. They are still engaged in their main job of knowing themselves, of building their trust in others, of learning how to fit into this world in which they live. Their way of approaching these tasks changes, however. In the recent past, they threw their weight around. Now they have a different *m.o.* Their new *modus operandi* is to begin to use their brain power through play—pretending, imagining, making-believe. The road changes, but the new road brings children to the same old ends.

176

TAKING THE ROLE OF THE HELPLESS

Time after time children say: "I must be the baby." Then they set up the rules of their game so that the others look after them and care for them. They rig the rules so that the others are good to them and, in a sense, "love" them. Children say: "I must be tired and you must put me to bed." "I must be hungry and you must feed me." "I must be your little baby and you must hold me."

Many children play their self-chosen role right up to the hilt. When they "are" babies, they want a bottle to hold up to their lips. Often they suck. And children insist that there be water or milk in the bottle—they are sucking for real. When they "are" babies, some are not content to pretend to get into the baby carriage or into the play bed. They actually climb in, despite their big size. We have no word other than *play* to describe what young children do, but in no sense do they "play their roles"—they *live* them. They are not putting on a show or "just" pretending, as adults do. The children *are* babies, for the moment. Their play is for real; it makes up the truest moments of their day.

Boys play the role of babies as girls do. Given half a chance, three- and four-year-old boys as well as girls will play contentedly and with great absorption with dolls. They tuck their doll babies into bed. They fuss with the blankets. They puff up the pillow and kiss the "baby." In a thousand and one ways boys as well as girls are tender little mothers. As you watch, you cannot escape the feeling that the dolls are simply intermediaries. The children are giving themselves the love and comfort that they want.

House play and doll play are favorite imaginative activities of all young children, and of both sexes. Frequently children

177

also choose parts drawn from other times in life when protection and comfort are sure to be forthcoming. Four- and
five-year-olds have a special affinity for playing cowboys. One
prize role is to be shot, either wounded or dead. The child
lies stricken, helpless. All the others—the alive and strong and
able—must "do something" for him.

Three- and four-year-olds and older children love to play
"sick"; "I must be sick and you must be the doctor." This is
one play-way of saying: "Be good to me, as if I were a baby."
Children love to be captured and to be prisoners. When they
are locked up, captives, they cannot move (the way a baby
cannot move). With no freedom, the children feel small
again. Their "guards" often are not very gentle. Even when
the guards are bossy, the victims have a wonderful chance to
feel sorry for themselves.

In their dramatic play, children respond very eagerly to
differences in elevation. When they seek the chance to feel
small once more, nothing makes as good a play space as some
little nook or cove. If no natural cranny is available, the children create a homemade one. They build their special safe
and secure cubby holes under tables or chairs or stairways.
They haul out blankets or covers or sheets, anything they can
spread over two chairs or drape down from a table. Youngsters love at times to cut themselves off from this busy, demanding world and go back to some secluded hideaway.

All children at times choose the roles of the weak who must
be protected. Big five-year-olds do, and so do little girl Threes.
These roles of dependency are chosen most frequently when
the real world goes awry. Especially when a new baby enters
the home, or when some tension upsets the home, or when a
child is being pressured to act more grown-up than he comfortably can, this theme of littleness becomes paramount in
play. But a crisis is not needed to set off the theme. "I must
be the baby" (or a reasonable facsimile thereof) flows from

all children as a standard and healthy part of their growing up. Their real world may be swimming along or all messed up. But every child, quite normally, seeks now and again to create a new world where he can be sure to get a booster shot of love and tenderness and care.

THE HIGH AND THE MIGHTY

The same children just as often take on the role of the strong. They are *not* the baby—"I must be the mother!" Few moments delight three- and four- and five-year-olds more than when they have the chance to dress in grown-up clothes. Shoes with heels, old skirts, old hats, pocketbooks, all the discards from the adult wardrobe make wonderful toys. Dressed fit to kill, "mother" talks seriously on the play telephone. She shops ever so busily at the store. She energetically sweeps and cleans and cooks and washes clothes and irons them.

Exactly how else "mother" acts depends on who sets the role. When "I must be the baby," mother can be tender, sweet and kind. When "I must be the mother," she is apt to be a tougher mother than most children know in real life. Mother spanks. Mother issues orders and bosses people around. Mother insists and demands and commands. Mother punishes. These play mothers really act like "big Berthas" at times.

Four- and five-year-olds—children who go to school or whose older brothers and sisters do—sometimes play school. Teachers who watch this play are apt to wince. They hope that they are not as dictatorial as they often are portrayed. And they probably are not. Children's dramatic play is not a faithful reproduction of real life. It is a faithful reflection of the feelings children have inside of them.

Guns play a prominent part in dramatic activity. Many adults do their best to stop gun play. Some parents will not

179

buy toy guns for their children, and most teachers will not let youngsters bring guns to nursery school or kindergarten. Although the adults try hard, they seldom win. Prohibition is very hard to enforce. A child may not have a gun, but he can always find a block or a stick. If he cannot find a piece of wood, he always has his finger: "Bang! Bang! You're dead. I shot you." A gun—store-bought or homemade—truly gives a child his money's worth. The youngster can be shot by the gun—then he is the "baby type." Or he can shoot the gun and be the strong and potent one. Children's guns are neatly double-barreled.

Horses, those fierce and galloping beasts, are another favorite in children's play. The "horses" may be tricycles or, as often, simply the child's own two legs. The youngster slaps his thigh as if it were the horse's side and off he charges. When they are not on horseback, young children are sure to be flying planes, speeding along in trucks and cars, chugging like trains or skimming through the water in their boats. Anything that moves and symbolizes force—a fire engine, a steam shovel—becomes a child's vehicle to power.

"I must be the conductor and you must show me your tickets." "I must be the pilot and you must be the passengers." "I must be the driver." As you watch the child swing his steering wheel and as you listen to the noises he makes, you know that he is more than the driver. He is the car, the engine, and all of its 300 horsepower.

Just as they use nooks and crannies and facsimilies of caves to create their own sense of smallness, children turn to height to make themselves feel big. Especially when they are four and five, and quite sure of their physical powers, youngsters love to dramatize on top of a play house or high up on a piece of climbing apparatus. The climbing itself is fun but, at this time in development, added fun comes from being "captain" or "boss" and shouting down orders from on high.

180

If you are overly sensitive to good human relations, you shudder a little as you listen in on this child's play. The bosses are very bossy: "You men there. You dig, I tell you. Now get going and dig, you men." The child saying the words—it can be a boy or a girl—swaggers as if all his life he had only the example of slave drivers. The "men" he bosses—they can be boys or girls—meekly, mildly, humbly do as they are told (or, at least, their own individual interpretation of it!). They are acting little, and they look like little slaves.

Imaginary Playmates

Many three- and four-year-olds, not only those who have no brothers and sisters or those who have no chance to play with other children, invent imaginary playmates. We cannot see them, of course, but the children can. We cannot hear them, but the children can. These imaginary playmates have names. They must be fed. They must take their nap. Imaginary playmates can give adults a rough time. In our blindness we sometimes almost step on them; or we go off without them, or forget to set a place at the table for them. Our carelessness and neglect are not laughing matters to the child. Imaginary playmates are very real to the children who create them.

Every adult suspects at times that these imaginary playmates are the child's tricky devices for getting around the law or for manipulating adults. The friend—not the child!—wants another piece of candy. The friend—not the child!—cannot eat the spinach (so the child doesn't either—that wouldn't be polite). The friend—not the child!—broke the lamp or wet his pants or spilled the milk. We feel concerned and outwitted by these make-believe people. But imaginary playmates are not truly tricks for manipulating us. Like all aspects of dramatic play, imaginary companions are the child's means of manipulating his own feelings.

181

Back and forth the play goes. The child is little, the child is big. He is dependent and independent. Children turn on power and turn it off, the way we turn a tap or a faucet. They turn on weakness that invites love, the way we switch a light on and off.

Significantly, while all this is going on, during the years that start around three, children usually begin to slough off some of the thumb-sucking and blanket clutching and other baby comforters that have been so important to them. These supports gradually disappear, unless some unusual deprivation during infancy or harshness in the training period or some special crisis in life right now has heightened the need for them. Now the comforters are reserved for specific moments, when children are tired or sick or momentarily frightened and worried. Comforters are no longer apt to be the steady companions of the normally healthy child.

Healthy children have a new "equalizer." They have a new way of balancing out and coping with some of the injustices of life. They have a new device for insuring that they keep inside of themselves the right level of feeling—safe enough, strong enough. *Play* is now their equalizer. Play becomes the new "do-it-yourself" comforter. We are likely to say: "The children are 'just playing,' " but their play is a far, far cry from idle waste of time. Make-believe is how children put their ideas to work. *And* make-believe has deep emotional significance. With its persistent dual themes—"I must be little." "I must be big."—child's play is an ingenious safety valve, a device that works to make children feel comfortable inside and free to grow.

FOR INDEPENDENT STUDY

1. An old book, an English book, which may be very hard to find, is an excellent interpretation of young children's

play: *Imagination in Early Childhood,* by Ruth Griffiths (London: Kegan, Paul, Trench, Trubner and Co., Ltd., 1935). A much more recent and more available publication also does an excellent job of throwing light on the materials children use best when they play and on why they use the materials (and themselves) the way they do: *Understanding Children's Play,* by Ruth E. Hartley, Lawrence K. Frank and Robert M. Goldenson (New York: Columbia University Press, 1952).

2. Adults don't play the way children do but we have our grown-up counterpart of child's play: our day dreams and our imaginary conversations! If you can recall the way you have "played out in your head" some recent experiences when you wanted to feel either big or small, you will be able to appreciate more sensitively the two themes in children's imagination.

What would you do?

Question 18 You invite a five-year-old, a friend in your neighborhood, to have Saturday lunch with you as a special treat. He eats a good lunch. You give him a big piece of chocolate cake for dessert. But you can tell by looking at him that he would love to have a second piece of cake. What is your inclination: *a*) Offer him another piece. *b*) Give him a second piece if he can work up his courage to ask you for it. *c*) If he comes out and asks for it, give him a piece that he can take home with him to eat later. *d*) No matter what happens, don't give in. He had one big piece and another would just spoil his appetite.

imagination
and the intellect

Chapter 21

The specific content of children's imagination—the roles children take, the particular make-believe games they play—is very much determined by what the children know and have experienced. *Imagination is rooted in reality.* Strange as it sounds, the fantastic springs from the familiar.

Many people assume that the opposite is true. Fairy tales, for example, are often identified with the under-six age. The tales are imaginative, the children are imaginative—the two must somehow go together. Similarly, elves and witches, gnomes, leprechauns and cows that jump over the moon are believed to be "just right" for the child under six. These are fanciful creatures, young children themselves pretend to be people they are not—the two must be made for each other, or so some people think.

Pictures drawn for some young children's books, the illustrations on many of their toys, or wallpaper for their rooms frequently illustrate this misconception. If the artist is not thoroughly grounded in a knowledge of youngsters, he is apt to draw a chick with a high hat, a pair of spats, a cane, a big bow tie—with any fanciful elaboration so that the chick does not really look like a chick. Some people say: "That is a wonderful picture for young children. They are so imaginative!" But the tricky chick shows the artist's developed imagination —it does not help the young child to develop his own imagination.

So commonly, when we look at something drawn for young children, we *ooh* and *aah* and say: "That's cute." The illustration is not our style; therefore, it must be good for a child. But you can almost make a generalization: If you think something is "cute," that is the tip-off that it probably is not good for children under six.

FEET ON THE GROUND, HEAD IN THE CLOUDS

Under-six children are realists. They are concerned with the truth. This age is made up of hard-boiled detectives: They just want the facts! All their imagination stems from their very solid, down-to-earth concern with what actually is and what actually goes on. Three- to six-year-olds have their feet firmly on the ground. That is why they can and do so easily have their heads in the clouds!

This solid rooting in reality is apparent from even casual observation of children's play. The most frequent dramatic play centers around the activities that children know best— house play. Children take the roles that they have observed the most—baby, mother, father. They reproduce imaginatively the activities that have happened over and over in their lives —eating, shopping, driving, washing, cleaning. When youngsters seem to go far afield—playing cowboys, riding horses— they always are still tied to their best-known and most familiar sensations—being big and being little.

185

This rooting in reality becomes more apparent as you study local variations in children's play. Children of graduate students on many college campuses often play "writing dissertation"! The struggle for the Ph.D. has been the dominant experience in their households. Children in some mountain regions play "skinning the hog," reproducing in their way a very important and striking event in their local community. Some urban children at times have had as their most favorite dramatic activity, not cowboys and Indians or cops and robbers, but cops and strikers! Children reproduce imaginatively the sharpest reality they have known.

The exceedingly close relationship between what we know and what we can imagine ought to be apparent to all of us from our adult living. You must be thoroughly informed in the sciences, a top-notch expert, before you can have any bright new ideas about rockets and space travel. The chances are overwhelmingly against the rank amateur in the sciences coming up with an innovation in fuels or rocket design.

Only the highly skilled artist can crash through with the new ways of a Dali or a Picasso. The sheer beginner in art is much more apt to be completely traditional. He doesn't know enough to be able to break away. The more skilled and experienced a football coach is, the greater the likelihood that he will be able to dream up some totally new play or new formation. Despite all the "grandstand quarterbacks," the bright ideas do not come from the person who has never played the game.

The best writers are the ones who become the best experimenters with writing technique. Those thoroughly grounded in music stand the best chance of being original in that field. Imagination—the child's imagination, the adult's imagination —takes reality as its springboard. It modifies what is, it distorts what is, it exaggerates what is to create something new

186

that is not reality. But reality—truth, what actually happens —is always the base.

The more the child knows, then, the better foundation he has for imagination during these play years under six. He cannot imagine out of the blue. He cannot create out of nothing. *The richness of the child's imagination will depend on the wealth of experiences he has had, from infancy on.*

AN EARLY START FOR STIMULATION

Stimulation—the feeding of the senses which are the gateways to the brain—must begin early, at the very start of life. We all know that infants have physical needs. We are coming to see that they have emotional needs—to feel loved and safe. Children also thirst for mental stimulation. They do not grow if their physical and emotional needs are ignored. Neither do they grow if their senses are unchallenged and their brains are idle. We dare not ignore the child's hunger to taste and feel and smell and hear and see—and think!

Today stimulation is known to be so important that ways are being sought to stimulate even premature babies. In the past these children were thought to have only physical needs. Today many hospitals have developed techniques which safely allow a nurse to pat or stroke the premature infant in the incubator. This is an attempt to duplicate the stimulation that full-term babies receive inside of their mothers as the mother walks, bends, sits, and changes her position. Stimulation of the senses is recognized as important, even before a child has developed to his full first nine months.

After birth, even though babies cannot begin to understand our words, it is good that we talk to them while we nurse and bathe and dress them. During that brief playpen age, it is good to have the playpen near the kitchen or near the living

187

room, wherever Mother is. Mother's movements and her talking are a challenge to the child. They offer stimulation that he misses when he is isolated, away in his room, cut off from the sound of humans.

During the waking hours in the early months, it is good to change the baby's position so that he has a different view every now and again. And, quite apart from colic or restlessness, it is good for mothers to lift their babies and carry them and walk around the house. Youngsters need a "grand tour" for their intellectual development. They need to begin early to see the world, to smell new smells and to hear new sounds.

Mothers wisely hold their babies up to the window to look out and see the sights. The virtues of a ride in the carriage are not limited to a dose of fresh air. Children also get a dose of new ideas—the sun overhead, the clouds, leaves on the trees, the sound of horns honking, of people talking, of dogs barking and of brakes screeching.

We must play our role as "safety engineers" to make sure that the child in the crib and the playpen, and the crawler on the floor are not exposed to dangers. In particular, we must guard against objects so small they can be swallowed (everything goes into the mouth at first!), or so small that they can be stuffed up a nostril or into an ear. We must guard against things painted with toxic paints. But we must never become such overly cautious safety engineers that the child has only a bare, sterile world in which to live his early days. A vacuum threatens the child's intellectual growth, just as other dangers threaten his physical well-being.

Babies and toddlers are probably not aware of color differences. Whether an object is red or yellow or green or blue, or whether he meets a variety of color is probably not the crucial question at the beginning. But it is crucial that the child have something—many different things!—that he can hold and hear and suck and see. As early as possible, and continuously,

188

he needs the experiences of different sizes and textures and tastes and sounds and sights.

Confronting the child with new sense experiences must continue and expand as he becomes a walker and as he moves on into year two and year three. There is some temptation to think of these children as involved only in physical development, and to leave them alone too much. Our company grows in importance during these years. Children need us not only for our supervision and for our emotional support; they need to hear the words we say and the ideas we express (even if they don't understand them). A child needs to hear adult sounds. After all, he is headed toward adulthood.

There are virtues (and headaches as well!) in having young children join the family at mealtime, rather than always eating alone and then playing alone in their room. From the first year on, there are great virtues in looking at books and magazines with children. Reading does not begin at six! Children start to learn to read when they are one year old. Mother talks about the pictures. Baby pats the picture and soon starts to name what he sees—baby, milk, car, kitty. . . . The delight children get from this activity shows in the way they ask for stories again and again, always wanting "more, more . . . !" These early reading times are among the soundest supporting emotional experiences in a child's life. They are one of the best and most stimulating intellectual experiences.

WIDENING HORIZONS

Somewhere in the second year, certainly by the second birthday and from then on, children should "join the family and see the world!" *Young children are here-and-now youngsters.* They thrive on firsthand experiences. Every one of them is from Missouri—under-six is the true "show me" age. It's not that you take young children to Tahiti or Egypt or to the heart

189

of darkest Africa. Youngsters need first to know the sights and sounds and smells of their immediate environment, their neighborhood.

They need to pat a dog. They need to pat a horse and to pat a truck! They need to sniff the smoke from burning autumn leaves and sniff (and squash) a flower. They need to watch men digging and to see a steamshovel at work. They need to see a train, a boat, a plane, and they need to hear you talk about all these things as they watch and touch and smell.

Children thirst to use all of their senses. By adulthood we become more refined and restrained. We simply look and listen. Such passivity is never enough for the young child. Two gateways to the mind, the eyes and the ears, cannot do the job. The young child has to "know" things through his lips and his tongue and his fingers and through his nose. We say "cold." Any youngster can soon learn to say after us sounds that seem the same. Only the child who has picked up ice in his fingers and who has sucked ice and rubbed it on his cheek can begin to put meaning into those sounds. "Cold" is not simply a noise—it is an idea.

The full use of all the senses is the child's only way to learn. Just as we have to beware of giving children too little to think about, we must also guard against clamping down too soon on smelling, tasting, handling. The more children have a chance to feel the fuzzy and the smooth, to feel the heavy, the pointed, the rough and the sharp and the velvety, the more fully their thirst for stimulation is met.

When a child has early and continuous firsthand experiences, his imaginative play is rich. His backlog of satisfying tasting-feeling-smelling-hearing-seeing from his first three years makes the years from three to six more satisfying. He began to think earlier; he has more ideas now that he can put to work through his play.

190

FOR INDEPENDENT STUDY

1. There is a growing awareness of the social waste and danger stemming from the lack of stimulation in urban and rural slums. One book on the problem is *The Culturally Deprived Child,* by Frank Riessman (New York: Harper and Row, 1962). But many a young child, not in a slum, lives his days understimulated, seeing and knowing less than he could. *Young Minds Need Something To Grown On,* by Murial Ward (Evanston, Ill.: Row, Peterson, 1957) not only has an excellent title which puts the case for first-hand challenge and stimulation very beautifully; it is a sound and specific and helpful book as well. Although it was written primarily for teachers in nursery schools, parents of young children and kindergarten teachers will get help from it, too.

What would you do?

Question 19 One five-year-old in a Sunday School group is always picking on smaller children, bullying them and hitting them, especially when he thinks no one is looking. What is your inclination: *a*) Ignore it. Children have to learn to work out their own quarrels and to take care of themselves. *b*) Make it perfectly plain that bullying is not a good way to act. Ask the child, for example: "How would you like it if I picked on you all the time?" *c*) If you possibly can, move the child to a group of larger children so that he cannot get away with his bullying. *d*) Encourage the other children to hit him back whenever he starts anything. Explain to them that bullies almost always are cowards at heart.

191

obstacles
to play

Chapter 22

Our country, more than any in the world, ought to prize children's play. We are a nation of innovators. We are forever cooking up a new idea—a better car, an ingenious way to preserve food, a new and different kind of textile. We are not bound by tradition but pride ourselves on our ability to dream up a better mousetrap. Our creative artists—composers, writers, poets, painters, sculptors—do not always hold a high place in our culture. But we do pay handsomely for imagination in merchandising, in production, in advertising, and in every aspect of the business world.

PLAY PAYS OFF

We ought to be thilled with the years of childhood when youngsters are not stuck in a rut—the years when they dream and constantly create the new. Their play from three to six is such excellent practice for inventive and innovating behavior in the years ahead.

192

We in America are very concerned at present about whether our children work hard enough, study hard enough, and demand enough of themselves. We are very conscious of the need for "high standards." Strange as it sounds at first, child's play has a direct contribution to make to this need. Few ages *work* as hard as these play children. Playtime is drill time in attention span. Playtime is drill time in absorption. Playtime is drill time in taking on a job and sticking to it. When young children play the air is not filled with laughter and silly giggles. Three-, four- and five-year-olds are intensely serious about their play. Their earnestness fits into our present national mood. We ought to be very pleased that children so young work so hard at their tasks.

Children's play is practice in invention; it is practice in hard work; and it has a third virtue which ought to have some appeal to us: It is not expensive! Most of the "things" that children need for their play are dirt cheap. Of course, you can spend a fortune if you want to. And youngsters prod you to spend. But the toys and equipment that best support imagination at this age are not elaborate or fancy. The essence of children's play is that the youngsters build their own meanings and ideas into whatever is at hand. The children themselves are the "toy manufacturers." You don't really have to spend much cash for finished products which have the details worked out.

At three and four and five years of age, the best play equipment is *unstructured.* The toy or the equipment has no one set purpose, no one set use. Children are free to use the material in any way suggested by the ideas in their own minds. Boards, boxes, barrels, blocks, sand, paint, clay, wheel toys— these are "unstructured." Simple dolls, dress-up clothing, kitchen pots and pans, empty cereal boxes and cans, simple toy telephones and cash registers—all these let the child's imagination take over. A block of wood can be an iron; it can

193

be a car, a fire engine, a building in a sand city. It does not cost much money to stimulate a child's imagination.

The three points above are the legal case for children's play. A fourth point—more simple, more human—should also be very compelling: *Children love to play!* It is their all-consuming passion. They "vote" for play every single chance they get. The "people's choice" should carry some weight with Americans.

Unfortunately, although the cards are stacked in its favor, play is not very popular with us. We have misconceptions about how to stimulate it. Once it flowers, we tolerate it but we try to end it as soon as we can. We want young children to "get down to business"—*our* business. We can't believe that play, *their* business, is important.

A WEAK BASE OF EXPERIENCES

So far as stimulating the imagination is concerned, we seldom take the time to give our children enough firsthand experiences. We provide them with a very weak base for their special kind of child-thinking.

One reason for the dearth of stimulation may be that we fail to realize how rarified our home life has become. Our homes today are simply housing centers—bedroom, dining room, kitchen and bath. No production goes on within them. Fathers "go somewhere" to "do something"—to an office, to a factory, to the city. Mothers are not growing food or processing it—they buy it ready-made. We all try to move to "nice" neighborhoods but the residential areas of our cities and suburbs are not "nice" for children's thinking. Too little real life goes on in them. It takes steady effort to build back into children's experience what once was there automatically within the home and the immediate neighborhood.

194

To satisfy their thirst for stimulation, to give children something to "chew on," we have to take our youngsters to see people at work and machines in action. Three- and four- and five-year-olds need to see the ships on the river, the trucks at the terminal, busses at the depot and trains in the railroad station. They should walk through a field of corn and a field of squash; they should see a cow barn and a chicken house. They need to visit an honest-to-goodness bakery and a saw mill and a factory. Not enough of us take the time—or make the time—to give young children these firsthand, mind-stretching, sense-stimulating experiences.

Once they are on the spot, children ought to climb up into the cab of a locomotive or sit in the cockpit of a plane. They need to ride on a tractor, to sit behind the steering wheel of a truck. If we do take our children to see things for themselves firsthand, we are apt to become overly cautious: "Don't get too close." "Don't touch." But young children must get close to the heart of things. Seeing—at a distance—is not believing, for them.

Most recently a new hazard has arisen to rob children of the firsthand experiences they need—T.V.! T.V. may be good, bad or indifferent for adults, adolescents and school-age children. At its very best, T.V. is a waste of time for children under six. Frequently, it is a hazard. Yet there is reason to believe that television is our nation's number one baby-sitter —for babies, for Twos, Threes, Fours and Fives.

Babies in cribs, babies in carriages, children in playpens, toddlers and older young children stare quite willingly at T.V. —there is no question about that. But their staring is a symptom of their thirst for stimulation. It is not the best means for satisfying it. T.V. moves too fast for young children. Youngsters hang on by their teeth, trying to catch up to the action. T.V. deals almost always with events that are too far removed from children's experiences. The show goes over their heads and produces a booming confusion, rather than any solid knowing.

Worst of all, television has a screen, 21 inches or some other size. That screen curtains children off from reality. Under-six youngsters need the real McCoy, not a long-distance shot of it. The best show for a young child is a real horse he can pat, whose breath he can see, whose hoofs he can hear, whose wet nose he can feel, whose true size he can grasp. This—the real *anything*—is a child's "spectacular."

Even if we don't nourish well their senses and their minds during the early years, children play and imagine. The urge to get the beginnings of an idea is so strong that it cannot be stopped. The children do the best they can; but when they have a weak base of experience, their imagination is limited. They cannot "feel" their roles with strong reality. And certain stereotyped roles—cowboys, shooting—repeat themselves over and over again.

PLAYING DOWN CHILDREN'S PLAY

When the imagination is going on, for better or worse, too often we again fail to play a constructive role. The main trouble is that we are too eager to press our reality down on children. We don't want them to be three or four or five— we wish they were nine years old. We like their paintings best when they "look like something." We nag them to "tell us a story" about what they have painted. Somehow we only feel comfortable with children's dramatic play when we recognize what is going on. In school we try to get children to act out "Billy Goats Gruff" or "Little Red Riding Hood" or any tale where *we* know the plot. But this kind of dramatization is not good dramatic play for young children. The idea has to be in *their* heads—not ours.

We tend to leap in to stop children's play when we think it isn't "nice." A child spanks her doll; we have a compulsion to teach that she shouldn't spank, not even a doll! Two children are playing house and a third wants to join them. The two say: "Go away. We're married. You can't play with us." We have to set the record straight—they are not really married and they shouldn't be so exclusive!

Day in and day out, we interrupt children's play as if nothing was going on: "They are *just* playing." We minimize the significance of children's activities, and youngsters catch our impatience. Our attitude weakens their sense of their own worth, just as a man would feel less significant if his boss felt he was "just selling," or as a woman would feel less worthy if her husband felt she was "just a housewife."

WE ARE HARDEST ON OUR FIVES

Our intolerance toward play and our impatience to get this imaginative time in development over and done with reaches the fever point as children near age five. Most of us put up with make-believe when children are three and four. From five on, all we can think of is getting them ready for school, getting them ready to read. We try to change the children. It seldom occurs to us to change the school so that it gets ready for children as they are, and as they have to be for health.

The time for learning to read hangs like a black cloud over the fifth year of life. It shouldn't. Reading is a very important skill. Anyone is handicapped today unless he can read, loves to read, and does read. But learning to read should never be a problem to children. They will want to read, when the right time comes, as much as we could ever want them to. From their standpoint, reading is a magnificent way to feel powerful. Once a child learns to read he is no longer a baby. He does

197

not have to go around begging everyone: "Read it to me." "Show me where it says so-and-so." "Read me the funnies." Knowing how to read is a great source of strength. It lifts up the child, exactly as his new skills of walking and talking did earlier. We don't have to break our necks to "sell" reading to children.

We worry needlessly about reading and, because we worry, we jump the gun! So often we mess up the teaching of reading the way earlier we needlessly complicated toilet training, training in property rights, and in eating habits. Just as we produce too many children who resist food and who resist sleep, we turn out too many who resist reading. We plug away and plug away. Struggling through year five and year six, we finally teach children how to read. And then, all the rest of their lives, too many of them read as little as possible! They read the funny sheets, yes. Comic books, yes. *Life* with its pictures. *The Reader's Digest*, condensed and simple and abbreviated. The headlines, maybe.

America's peculiar reading problem is that our people know how to read, but they don't! One main reason for this is simply our impatience. We spoil reading. We spoil play. We rob Peter and we rob Paul. We take away a solid joy children could know when they are seven and eight; we take away a solid joy they could know when they are five.

Children who go to kindergarten are apt to suffer the most from our impatience with play and our compulsiveness to have Fives "get down to business." Most kindergarten children spend much too much time sitting, coloring silly pictures in workbooks, doing fruitless exercises that presumably are designed to "get them ready to read." They line up too much; they keep quiet too much while the teacher talks too much; they "play" games the teacher organizes, all presumably to "get them ready for first grade." Fives in kindergarten get too

198

many of their ideas from books and words and have too few firsthand experiences. They get feeble ideas as a result.

The pressures on children at home are apt to be more subtle but no less real. Youngsters sense what their parents want. And we all seem to want our five-year-olds to read or to be ready to read at the crack of six. We sparkle when a child asks us a word. We beam when he tries to write his own name. Our faces light up when he colors in the workbook we bought at the five-and-ten or the supermarket. Almost everyone seems sure that his Five is ready to read. There is much reason to doubt this, but no reason at all to doubt that *we* are ready to have them read. We are so ready we are almost overripe!

A child cannot skip being five, not without paying some price. He cannot skip the extended chance he needs to play and make-believe and imagine, not without paying some price. Dimly he feels that there must be something wrong with him the way he is. By being impatient with play, we lessen children's chances to have the beginnings of an idea and we take away their emotional equalizers. Tragically, in our hurry to rush through these play years we build a less sturdy intellectual and emotional base on which reading and other reality experiences must later be built, when the time is right for them.

FOR INDEPENDENT STUDY

1. Sometimes adults feel a little unsure of themselves, uncertain about how to stimulate children's play and about the materials young children can use. Several excellent books offer a tremendous richness of ideas: *All Children Want To Learn,* by Lorene K. Fox, Peggy Brogan and Annie Louise Butler (New York: The Grolier Society, 1954) and *The Complete Book of Children's Play,* by Ruth

E. Hartley and Robert M. Goldenson (New York: Crowell, 1957) are the newest books. But the materials range from a good paperback—*How to Play With Your Child,* by A. Arnold (New York: Ballantine, 1955, 25¢)—to the whole set of books: *Childcraft* (Chicago: Field Enterprises Educational Corporation).

2. *Before The Child Reads,* by James L. Hymes, Jr. (Evanston, Ill.: Row, Peterson, 1958) is a brief book for both parents and teachers which states in fuller detail the case for providing rich experiences for five-year-olds so that this year becomes a time for learning, even though it is not for most children the time for learning to read. So, too, does *Fostering Intellectual Development in Young Children,* by Kenneth D. Wann *et al.* (New York: T. C. Bureau of Publications, 1962).

What would you do?

Question 20 You have been shopping with your three-year-old. As he hurries to get into the car to go home he accidentally drops the worn-out old teddy bear that he always carries with him wherever he goes. What is your inclination: *a)* Pretend you didn't see it and go along. If later the child misses his teddy, point out that he lost it, after all, and once something is lost it is gone forever. *b)* Pretend you didn't see it and go along. If later your child makes a fuss, you can always buy him another—and maybe he won't even notice that the teddy is gone. *c)* Unobserved by your child, scoop up the teddy and take it along in case he should ask for it but don't say anything until he does. *d)* Tell him that he has dropped his teddy and point it out to him.

200

teaching children about sex (or anything!)

Chapter 23

In infancy and toddlerhood we do such a beautiful job of teaching children their native tongue that we can use that teaching as a model for how to proceed in other areas of instruction during the training period. In the three, four, five-year-old age span there is a similar "success story" that we can pattern after and use as a guide in teaching children to read (or teaching them anything). The bright spot is how we teach our children about sex.

Many children, somewhere in the three to six age span, want to know about their own bodies and how they operate. They want to know where babies come from. Similarly in this age span, but especially when children are five, they ask questions about words and symbols. There are direct parallels between how to proceed in sex education and how to proceed in teaching reading.

201

EDUCATING FROM THE START OF LIFE

The first important point to recognize is that in both areas these questions are not the true beginnings of education. Every child has been exposed to sex education almost since birth. Every child has inevitably been exposed to reading since the day he was born. At three, four and five (with sex education), and at five and six (with reading education), we do some teaching a little bit more openly, a little bit more self-consciously. We say some words, we give some information. But this stage of the game is only one more step in a continuous process of education.

The infant's early exploration of his body is a part of his sex education. The young child's continuous experiences with urination and defecation is a part of his sex education. The fact that the child lives with a mother and father, who look and act distinctively like a woman and a man, is a part of his sex education. Teaching about sex does not begin on some one momentous day when suddenly, and grimly, you start to *teach*. No matter when the first question comes, a lot of sex education has already taken place.

The same continuous process has gone on in the teaching of reading. A youngster must be able to use words, to know the meaning of words, to know the real objects that words stand for, before he can make any great progress with the printed page. You teach your child to read—you make a start —the very first time you talk to him and every time you talk to him. You teach reading—you make a start—every time your child handles an object and gets its feel through his senses, from the first rattle and teething ring, on. You actively teach your child to read whenever you take him on a trip with you, beginning with the first walk in the baby carriage, right

202

on through those car rides to the store and to the post office and to the bank.

In a most significant way, you teach your child to read every time you read! Whenever you look at a newspaper, whenever you open a letter, whenever you glance at your shopping list, you are teaching reading—and you have done all this constantly ever since your child was one day old. The process of identification goes on. You are a reader—your child wants to be like you. He wants to become a reader, too.

Obviously also, you have been teaching your child to read every time you have read to him. Every bedtime story has been a reading lesson, just as every dressing time and bath time and toileting time was a silent lesson in sex education.

There is one-year-old teaching of reading. There is two-year-old teaching of reading, three-year-old teaching of reading, just as there is five-year-old and six-year-old teaching of reading (and one-year-old sex education and sixteen-year-old sex education). No one year in the process is more important than any other. No one year ought to make us more jittery and tense and worried than any other. Good teaching always proceeds in a simple, natural, easy way. You do what seems right at the time.

THE "OPEN DOOR" POLICY

A second important point to recognize is that you never teach sex or reading or anything "once and for all." All learning takes a long time, unless you are teaching some exceedingly limited and simple idea. Facts and attitudes and skills sink into us very slowly. We need to live with them for a while before they truly become a part of us. As we live with them, new questions arise. We come back to ask again, and get more help.

203

If you give a good answer to your child's question at age three about where babies come from, you will have to give the same good answer over again many times when he is still three and at later ages. Your six-year-old will ask you. Even adolescents come back with new aspects of the old question that occur to them for the first time.

This quality applies just as much to the teaching of reading. No one "learns" to read when he is five. No one "learns" to read in first grade. The most children can do is to make a five-year-old gain and a six-year-old gain. For a long time to come, they will be back again and again to find out still more about reading. So much of the pressure that we bring to bear on our five-year-olds in particular (and the pressure most six-year-olds feel in first grade) stems from the misconception that we must get the job "over and done with." This simply is not possible.

What *is* possible and important is to make a good start, one that satisfies the child. Then the door is open. He feels free to come back. He knows where he can get answers and where he can get help. Life is repetitive. Basic questions arise again and again. Your youngster will come back for more *if* the beginning was pleasing to him.

The child's sense of satisfaction is crucial for good learning. Anger, fear, worry, tension are roadblocks—for adults, as well as for children. When we feel anxious we say: "I got all mixed up." "I couldn't pay attention." "I couldn't concentrate." Our unpleasant feelings botch up our thinking. In contrast, satisfaction and contentment keep us loose. We think better; we learn better.

In sex education these complicating emotions are stirred up when young children are punished or sharply and harshly stopped from exploring their bodies and showing interest in their urination and bowel movements. Then it is hard for

204

them to raise questions about reproduction. They feel "naughty" for wanting to know what they want to know.

In sex education the child takes the early lead. In reading, the shoe is on the other foot. We don't stop children, we push them ahead of themselves. But either way a youngster is flooded with emotions that complicate his learning. He senses that something is not right with what he feels and wants to do. He gets tight inside. A task that could be so easy becomes difficult. A child gets "all mixed up."

In reading and in sex education (in *all* education), we must have confidence that the right time will come. Children ask their questions about sex when they are three or four or five for a very obvious reason: Children are surrounded by themselves! They are surrounded by the two sexes. They are surrounded by the fact of reproduction, both human and animal. Naturally, inescapably, as their power to think matures, their desire to know about body functions and reproduction also develops.

So too, all children living in any kind of standard urban, suburban or rural home are surrounded by reading. There is no hiding place from the mail and books and magazines and newspapers that come into a home. Children cannot miss the advertisements on the roads and in stores, the posters and billboards that are everywhere. Youngsters are engulfed by street signs, notices, labels, every place they turn. Naturally, inescapably, as the power to think about these symbols develops, children can hardly escape having the desire to learn to read.

TAKING YOUR LEAD FROM CHILDREN

We tend to hold back on our teaching about sex. If only we could bring a little of this reticence to the teaching of reading,

205

instead of being overeager and overanxious! But good teaching is neither too early nor too late. You teach when the time is right.

Almost universally, somewhere around three or four or five, children ask the question: "Where do babies come from?" It is a simple question with a simple answer: "Babies grow inside their mothers." Almost universally around four or five or six, children ask parallel simple questions about reading with equally simple answers: "Show me how to write my name." "Where does it say *stop*." "How do you make an *S*?"

All you have to do in either case is to answer the child's question. And stay available! In sex education three- and four- and five-year-olds often say, "Oh," and go about their business when you have answered their question. They only want to know a little at the moment, and your answer satisfies them. They will come back for more at some later time. With reading, most fours and fives and sixes also want to know only a little: "This is your name." "This says *stop*." "This is how you make an *S*." Your answer satisfies them. If you don't make a production out of it, they will come back for more.

We worry that sex will prove so fascinating that, once children start asking, they will never stop. But it is a mistake to ignore the child's questions about sex. It would be as great a mistake—one we seldom make!—to enroll the child in a course in biology! We worry that reading will prove so unappealing that, once children start asking, we often try to tell them everything at once. We never ignore their opening questions but we do err often by immediately enrolling them in a life course in reading! Both worries are groundless. The child gives us our leads on what we should do next.

Some children want to know more, right on the spot. They bounce right back with another question. Almost universally, all children ask the same question about reproduction: "How does the baby get out?" Children know about their urination

206

and their bowel movements. They are beginning to make connections in their mind. They are really asking: "Do all products of the body come out the same way?" Here is another simple, logical question with a very simple answer: "There is a special opening for the baby to come through." You take your lead from what the child wants to know. This is the wise process to follow with reading, too.

TIME FOR IDEAS TO SINK IN

Children live with your answers. They mull them over in their minds. Initially they are sure to have some misconceptions but these easily get straightened out when the children come back to ask for clarification. So it is with reading: Children make mistakes when they start. Very commonly, five-year-olds write letters backwards or upside down. They "read" signs and words— "That says so-and-so"—but they are wrong. This exploration is a basic part of learning. Don't take these early "errors" too seriously, any more than you take seriously the "errors" children make in their make-believe play when they think they are babies and really they are not. As long as the door is open and as long as the child is surrounded by sex or reading (or anything), there is no cause for alarm.

Generally children have to grow to be five or six or seven before they have the power to think up the next, more technical and complicated kind of question: "How does the baby get inside its mother?" But if you have laid a good base of understanding to build upon, this is still a very simple question with a very simple answer: "You know that boys and men have a penis. Girls and women have a vagina. The two fit together. A cell (or a seed or a sperm) from the father's body meets a cell (or a seed or an egg) from the mother's body . . ."

Generally children have to grow more before they have the

207

power to think up the technical questions about reading. Most children are not full of these questions in first grade, and very seldom in kindergarten. Usually it is not until second and sometimes third grade that their brains have matured enough to enable them to pitch into reading with any great vigor.

You make a three-year-old start when the child is three: a five-year-old start when the child is five; a six-year-old start when the child is six. As long as your timing is right—you don't tell the child less than he wants to know and you don't tell him more than he wants to know—he will always come back for more.

THE ART OF PACING

Some three-, four- and five-year-olds do not ask where babies come from. There can be many reasons why. Regardless of the reasons, the wise procedure to follow is clear. Since you are aware that most children usually want to know around this time, you expose your child to situations which make it easy for him to raise the question. You might take your youngster to visit a mother who has just had a baby. You might read him a story about babies. There is even nothing very wrong with being forward and asking the direct question: "Do you know where babies come from?"

There is a technical name for this process: *pacing*. You get a little ahead of your child. You open up opportunities for him. Call what you do *baiting*, if you will. The process is identical with what fishermen do. You throw out your baited line where you think the fish ought to be. From then on, it is up to the fish. The fish may bite. The child may ask. What happens depends entirely on how hungry the fish is and on *how ready the child is*.

You bait and you pace with reading too, if your child has shown no interest. Around year five and year six, you make doubly sure that he is exposed to books, to signs and to writing. This is a prize time to read a lot to children. (It is a prize time for you to read adult books, too!) A child can't ask about reading if he sees very little of it around him. You pace your child and make it easy for him to take the next step in his development. But you must have the decency to wait until the child takes that step! He has to nibble at the bait. He has to respond. A child can't read if he isn't "hungry."

Children differ. We all know they do. They differ in size, weight, hair color, and in every imaginable characteristic. Because they differ, you have to allow some reasonable leeway. Most children ask about sex when they are three or four. This means that some children will ask when they are two. Others —just as normal, just as healthy, just as bright—will not really care until they are five, six or seven years of age. Most children have a strong interest in reading when they are late Sixes or Sevens. You have to allow some leeway here, too. A few children will want to know a lot about reading when they are five. Others—just as normal, just as healthy, just as bright— don't get really excited about reading until they are late Sevens, even eight years of age.

With sex, as with reading, there is no special virtue in being an early bloomer, nor is there any special harm in being a late bloomer. A head-start because we pressure them does not mean that children stay a year or so ahead. A somewhat later start because children are slow growers does not mean that they stay forever a year or so behind. Children always catch up and function at whatever level their normal power lets them operate. By age sixteen you cannot tell which children entered puberty a little early or a little late. By third grade you cannot tell who began to read at the crack of dawn and who began a little later. The only time that is "right" to start is the time that is right for each individual child.

No matter how many questions the young child asks about

sex, he does not suddenly become sex crazy. When he has the answers he wants, he goes back to his total life. *He plays!* Play is the continuing big task of these early years.

No matter how many signs a five-year-old gives you that indicate he wants to know about reading, this does not suddenly transform him into a sedentary scholar. When he has the answers that satisfy him, he goes back to his total life. *He plays!* Play is the paramount pattern in the three-year-old's life, in the four-year-old's life, in the five-year-old's life. These children are on their way toward the time when reality and structure, when words and symbols, when success and achievement, will be tremendously important. But our job is to live with them as they are *now*. Tomorrow is another day.

FOR INDEPENDENT STUDY

1. If you don't feel completely at ease talking with children about sex, either of two inexpensive bookets will be of great help to you: *How To Tell Your Child About Sex*, by James L. Hymes, Jr. (New York: Public Affairs Committee, 1949. 25¢), or *What To Tell Your Child About Sex*, by the Child Study Association (New York: Permabooks, 1959, 35¢). The former sticks to children under eight; the latter covers a wider age range. The first draws a better parallel between sex education and all teaching; the latter gives more specific help on exactly what to say when youngsters ask their questions.

2. Similarly, there are inexpensive pamphlet materials that explain the process of teaching children to read, materials written for parents rather than teachers. The following are all helpful: *Janie Learns To Read* (Washington: National Education Association, 1954. 50¢); *Reading Is Fun*, by Roma Gans (New York: Teachers College Bureau of Pub-

lications, 1949. 60¢); and *Ways You Can Help Your Child With Reading*, by Sally L. Casey (Evanston: Row, Peterson, 1950). There are also full-length books, *Your Child's Reading Today*, by Josette Frank (Garden City: Doubleday, 1954), *Helping Your Child Improve His Reading*, by Ruth Strang (New York: Dutton, 1962), and Scott, Foresman—the publisher of one set of basic readers used in some schools—has published its own book for parents explaining to them how *Your Child Learns To Read*, by A. Sterl Artley (Chicago: Scott, Foresman, 1953).

What would you do?

Question 21 A five-year-old goes to a private kindergarten that has a low wooden fence around its playground, with a gate for the children and parents to come through. One morning the child almost begs her father to lift her over the fence instead of coming in the usual way through the gate. If you were the father, what would be your inclination: *a*) Give in and lift her over. *b*) Explain that a rule is a rule, and that the rule is that children and parents must come through the gate. *c*) Change the conversation and divert her so that she puts her mind on something else. *d*) Remind her of the rule but tell her you are willing to break it, if she wants you to. Give her the responsibility for making the choice.

the social development of young children

chapter 24

Most people are not as fully aware as they should be of how deeply young children need "mothering"—the tenderness and gentleness and enjoyment and understanding that a loving parent can give. But most of us are over-sold on mothers! It is hard for us to believe that the child under six needs anyone else. Actually, *friends are as important to the young child as they are to us.*

The capacity to have a friend, and the need to have a friend, do not develop at the very end of this under-six period. A deep concern with age mates comes to full flowering in the three-, four- and five-year-old span. And, of course, the roots of this concern go down in the earlier years.

Parents sense this social drive when they say about their young child: "He needs someone to play with." The tone, however, is apt to minimize and underestimate the need. We say the words as if companions will keep the child busy or

212

"out of harm's way" or out of *our* way. Friends do all of these things. But these reasons are not the fundamental ones that explain why a child needs "someone to play with." Friends make possible the fullest utilization of the three-, four- and five-year-old's resources and offer the fullest challenge to his human capabilities. The young child with a friend uses himself to the fullest. He gives all he has to give. The child alone, with only his mother, is coasting. Mother-love, basic as it is, is not enough nor is a friend simply a luxury.

THE SOCIAL DIRECTION OF GROWTH

The human child is a social creature. His sociality is a quality of the utmost significance. If it were not for this deep-seated social urge, disciplining a child so that he could live in society would be an almost insuperable job. Fortunately, children want to live with others and need to live with others. They have built into them a very special supersensitivity to all those things that make living with humans possible. The whole direction of their growth—their internal maturation—is toward the ways of acting that make human society possible.

We usually say: Competition is the law of life. Competition has its place but there is much more reason to believe that *cooperation is the law of life.* We each have a due regard for our own survival but we have an equally strong, if not stronger, concern with working and living with others. People are not our competitors. They are not our enemies; or opponents, or adversaries. The healthy human looks on people as allies, friends on his side. Quite early he wants to relate himself as closely as possible to them.

Babies show their social side early. The very first post-natal changes that become apparent are in the area of social development. In the first month, for example, most children typi-

213

cally begin to smile, either on their own or in response to an adult's voice or approach. As early as the second month of life the child's first sound-making apart from crying emerges, and this is basically a social response. The baby produces his little vowel sounds on his own *and* in response to the stimulation of people who talk to him. Baby begins to "talk back," not argumentatively but in a pleasing, social, conversational way.

Throughout the first year the baby continues in many ways to show his special enjoyment of people. His smiles continue when mother is around. His whole body wiggles in anticipation of mother picking him up. He relaxes and is content when mother holds him. The baby's excitement and eager appetite for "Peek-a-boo" and "Bye-Bye" make it very clear that he thinks people are fun.

We often go to great lengths to have a play room "just for the baby." We learn too late and to our sorrow that the baby is most content in whatever room we are in! The fact is: Children are not good hermits. They simply love to be around people.

Somewhere around the middle of the first year these babies who have been so social—eager to be picked up by anyone, responsive to anyone—suddenly seem to turn anti-social. They shrink back from people whom they do not see every day. Even fathers, to their deep consternation, find sometimes that their own babies cry when they approach. This behavior may look like backsliding. Actually it is all to the good. The children have grown enough in six months or so to be able to distinguish between strangers and familiars. They are not turning antisocial. If you are not well-known to the child, your best bet at this time is to back up to him. You make a gradual approach and his very strong social urge will soon assert itself. He will take the lead, tugging at you. Then you are all set.

PARALLEL PLAY

With such an eagerness for people inside of them, and with a background of so many satisfying experiences with mothering in their first year, it should surprise no one that, during the second year, children continue to respond very selectively to people. If need be, you can hurry the toddler past a lamp post or past a car. You have real trouble hurrying him past other children. Eighteen-month-olds, twenty-four-month-olds—all children around two years of age—gravitate toward other children as if the children were a magnet.

At this time children typically engage in what is called *parallel play.* They want to do the same thing that the others are doing and play close, but not too close, to their age-mates. Their paths stay parallel, as railroad tracks are parallel. The children are not really "together" but they find solace and satisfaction in knowing that someone else their size is around.

This parallel play brings children into occasional contacts with each other. The "tracks" do not always stay a fixed distance apart. Having had their eyes on each other, the children now and again "collide," filled with curiosity to find out more about these other humans and what they are like.

Their initial social interminglings are what you would expect: very fumbling, awkward, beginner's attempts. It is not uncommon for children to pull hair at this time. They are not angry. They are not hostile. They simply want to know: "Does the hair come out?" "What happens when you grab a handful?" Children pull with a look of intense curiosity on their faces. Often the victim does not mind but adults leap into the fray. Our expressions are seldom as calm as the "pullee's." We easily mistake social curiosity for aggression—or perhaps we want children to be perfect to begin with!

215

The Fights at Home

Children poke at each other's eyes. They poke into each other's ears. They put a finger in the other fellow's mouth. Despite tears—"victims" cry sometimes and the explorer occasionally gets hurt—the children come back for more. We can all thank heaven: People are fascinating!

Parallel play has its share of other conflicts. Arguments and fights over property flare up almost always at this age. These "parallel players" are very possessive people. They want what they have, they want what they own, *and* they want what they see! A tug-of-war is a frequent occurrence. As children get older, their arguments are more apt to be conflicts of wills. One child wants to do something one way; another child has his own ideas. Around two, however, the fights are likely to be over things.

Fights—no matter what the cause—are most apt to flourish at home. This is one of life's sad facts. We think home ought to be "Home, Sweet Home." Actually, it is one of the best battlegrounds. Siblings get in each other's hair (and many other things!) a thousand times a day it seems, and nine hundred and ninety-nine of these times come when we are cooking supper or have our hands full in some other way with no time to play referee.

The arguments and conflicts between siblings should not surprise or disturb us as much as they do. For all of its countless virtues, home is less than the perfect place to raise children! Mixing different ages with their varying interests is always a hard job, and space at home is always so limited, especially on rainy days, but even when the sun is shining, youngsters are caged up and almost sure to get in each other's way from time to time.

The noise of these fights is almost always worse than the

216

fight itself. In a way the battles are a compliment to homes rather than a criticism; nor are they necessarily a sign that something is wrong. Children feel a lot freer to show how they feel, because they feel "at home." The noises (of anger, of resentment, of jealousy) come out in the open. In settings where the children are not so secure, the same feelings exist but they often stay hidden. Nor are the quarrels (if they really don't take place one thousand times a day) necessarily bad. In children's living these sibling arguments are often only sparring matches. They are not really the "feature bout." Because the children do feel safe, they try out their social techniques—of attack, of defense—on each other. Underneath the noise of battle, there is often basic good feeling. After all, we only fight with people we care about!

There is seldom much point in really trying to referee the matches. Even the Supreme Court would have difficulty coming through with equitable decisions. When children have lost their sense of humor, the best approach is to try to keep yours. Young children don't bear grudges. If you can patch things up so everyone feels he has a fair shake, life goes rolling on again—until the next fight starts!

MORE COOPERATIVE PLAY

The process of becoming an able social being, one who can give and take, is a long, slow process. Social development calls for a great deal of experimentation. It means going down a great many dead-end streets. It means trying out wrong approaches and gradually sloughing them off. Children are social but, at the same time, young children are highly egocentric. These two equally strong forces have to be blended comfortably and that takes a lot of time—for growing and for gaining experience.

By three years of age or so, most children engage less in

217

parallel play and more in what might be called *integrated play*. They are less apt simply to remain side by side using the same material but each will proceed in his own way. From three on, the chances are that children will be working together on some common and shared activity: playing house, or playing fireman, or playing train, each with his part in the total endeavor.

Parallel play does not suddenly stop at any one time, however. Even three-, four- and five-year-olds stay to some extent within themselves. One evidence of this is the common form of speech in these years called the *collective monologue*. The children are playing together; they talk "together." But what one says does not necessarily follow up on what the other fellow has said. One child is quiet while another fellow talks. When the first child's turn comes, he responds to his own inner train of thought rather than to what has just been said. Thinking goes along on parallel tracks when the children play together.

In their social development, as in every other phase of their growing, children differ. Some have a much stronger, much earlier appetite for friends—they are in the middle of things from the earliest possible moment. Other youngsters need more time to stand on the sidelines and watch before they make their social debut. Still others may never want to join the three-, four- or five-year-old counterpart of Rotary! They are quite content and comfortable to spend a lot of their time alone. We have to respect each child's individual style.

The so-called "shy child" tends to make us nervous. This is especially true today. Most of us would like to make our youngster a little "organization man" at the earliest possible moment. But children have to set their own pace in their social advances as in everything else. You seldom help a child to feel comfortable with people by pushing him into closer relation ships before he is ready, or by feeling dissatisfied and worrying over his personal way of making social approaches.

Sometimes, of course, past experiences make a child stay aloof and uncomfortably so. He is alone, not because that is his easy natural way, but because he feels unusually unsure of himself. Almost always, the best way to help is to begin at the beginning: Children move into their sureness with age-mates on the basis of their feeling sure with us. The best way of ending this uncomfortable shyness is a very indirect one. You don't force or lure or shame the child who is feeling uncertain into playing with others. Let him have experiences with you that are fun. When he feels safe with you, he will move out to feel safe with others, in his own good time—and in the way that fits him best: bold or quiet, a leader or a follower.

From three to six, sex distinctions are usually not too important. The chances are that boys will play with boys and that girls will play with girls. But very frequently the sex lines are crossed and children think nothing of it. A strong preference for the same sex—little gangs of boys, little cliques of girls— is four or five or six years off in development. Now a child is a child. His sex matters less than what he can do. The active children will probably run together. The climbers will probably climb together. The quieter children—they can be of either sex—will probably play quietly together.

YOUNG CHILDREN CLUSTER IN SMALL GROUPS

When they are on their own, free to choose, you never see large numbers of three-, four-, or five-year-olds playing together. Two is company, three is company, but four and five are a crowd. And larger numbers seem to children like a howling mob. A kindergarten group of five-year-olds may have twenty children in it but you will never see these twenty, voluntarily on their own, come together for anything! Young children cannot tolerate large numbers. They are still much too egocentric. Crowds call for more submerging of themselves and their ideas than they can healthfully take. Twenty children can be in one group; ten or twenty can use the same park playground. But young children need the freedom to cluster—two together or three together is their natural style. A group of twenty must really be about eight groups in one.

In a nursery school group of four-year-olds—a large group of Fours, sixteen children let us say—youngsters know who is absent and who is present, sometimes before the teacher does! Even though children have to keep their distance from all but a few, people are so important to them that they keep track of who is missing and who is on hand.

Often by three, almost always by four, children have their special friends. Out of all those available they choose one or two to whom they are very close. These are their pals, the youngsters with whom they do their playing and spend their time. Such friendship groups, however, are not firmly closed circles. A child drops out, a new youngster joins. There is change and, at the same time, steadiness and constancy to these early friendships. Children do not play with "just anyone." In groups their associations are not simply "by chance" —who ever happens to be standing near or happens to be around. By age three or age four the strong social drive within children makes them select, out of all the possible people, one or two they like the most.

Having a friend makes the whole day better for a child, just as it does for us. To be a friend makes the child feel better, just as we feel better when we are friends. Their faces light up at the sight of a friend. Their life steps up when the friend is around.

Children do not discard their mothers. They still care deeply about them. At times Threes, Fours and Fives need mother more than anyone else. But mother no longer has the sole place in the sun. She has a solid place but it is one in a widening circle of humans. Young children do not cut off the old; they branch out to include the new.

FOR INDEPENDENT STUDY

1. The idea that there is a social direction to development, that humans are made for each other rather than bent on eliminating each other, flies in the face of many of our common everyday assumptions. You ought to read more about this idea than can be covered in the brief space available here. The best material is a very brief book, *On Being Human*, by Ashley Montagu (New York: Schuman, 1951), or the larger book which elaborates on the same theme, *The Direction Of Human Development*, by Ashley Montagu (New York: Harper, 1955).

2. Almost every standard book on growth and development gives a full picture of the social growth of young children. *Brothers and Sisters*, by Edith G. Neisser (New York: Harper, 1951) goes into more detail on the specific question of the relationships among children within the family. *Your Child And Other People*, by Rhoda W. Bacmeister (Boston: Little Brown, 1950) is specifically for parents and full of wise suggestions about young children at home, in school and in the community.

What would you do?

Question 22 A five-year-old in a private kindergarten has just discovered that he can squirt water by pressing his finger against the nozzle on a drinking fountain. The water sprays up on the wall and on the floor. If you were the teacher, what

221

would be your inclination: *a*) Let him. What is the harm? School ought to be a place where children can experiment, and a little water never hurt anything. *b*) Stop it the very minute it starts, and give the youngster the devil! Make him clean up the mess he has made, too. *c*) Tell the boy that he shouldn't do it and tell him why. But if he wants to very much, don't make an issue out of it and make him unhappy, just so long as he cleans up afterwards. *d*) By all means, stop the activity with no hesitancies and no apologies but with no anger either. Be sure it doesn't go on, and be sure too that the boy knows why it shouldn't go on.

group living
for
young children

Chapter 25

Children under six years of age are often called "pre-school children." This is a misleading term because it suggests that these youngsters are not yet ready for school and for group living. Actually most three-, four- and five-year-olds are "school age." Most of them are as ready for school as they will be when they are six.

The intellectual needs of the child from three to six demand constant stimulation and exposure to mind-stretching first-hand experiences. Their continuing need to extend their body mastery calls for challenging equipment, for space and time and freedom to use the equipment. Their social and emotional development calls for a maximum opportunity to be with friends their own age—not in helter-skelter aimless play but in a free yet carefully planned setting under skilled guidance. And these children very much need, for their growth, an opportunity for comfortable separation from their home for a brief part of the day. The needs of children from three to six

223

are so varied and so specialized that it is the rare home which alone and unaided can provide all that these children need for good living.

The shortage of good nursery schools and good kindergartens—the complete absence of such facilities in many places—is one of the greatest hazards to three-, four- and five-year-olds. As a nation, we are not using the tools which could mean more satisfying and more healthy living for our young children. You can call these youngsters "pre-school" only if you mean that we do not have the schools we need for them.

A GREAT TIME LAG

The first *private* kindergarten was established in America in 1855—more than 100 years ago. The first *public* kindergarten in America was established in 1873, almost 100 years ago. In all the time that has elapsed since, we have succeeded in creating only enough public kindergartens for less than half of our five-year-olds. In some states, of course, almost 100% of the Fives have a public school which they may attend. In others, after one hundred years, there isn't a single public school kindergarten! And in many states only a small percentage of Fives have a school. These are usually the children who live in the wealthier cities and wealthier suburbs. The rest of the Fives, perhaps already at a disadvantage in other ways, have no school.

The nursery school situation is markedly worse. The first nursery schools—schools for three- and four-year-olds—were established in America at the end of World War I, around 1918 and 1919. More than forty years have gone by. We still have no public nursery schools anywhere! A few nursery schools receive public funds because they are part of a university or part of a research program, or because they exist for some special purpose. Overwhelmingly, however, the only chil-

224

dren who go to nursery school are those youngsters whose parents are wealthy enough to be able to afford paying tuition.

The statistics on the numbers of schools give only the quantitative picture. Qualitatively, the nursery school-kindergarten story is even more dreary. Almost all of our public kindergartens are severely overcrowded. Fives need a warm relationship with their teacher. They are still dependent children, despite their major areas of independence. They are active children. Since they are at the very beginning of their social growth, they need to talk and they need to work in small clusters. They need firsthand experiences. Having relatively short attention spans, they need the freedom to change their activities often. For all these reasons, Fives must have a very special class size.

The exact number in a good kindergarten group is hard to specify but, in general, twenty to twenty-five children should be tops! And for Fives, this number is *not* small class size. For this age, twenty to twenty-five is a large kindergarten. Twenty to twenty-five means that the group is bursting at the seams with about as many children as can be brought together in one room, no matter how many teachers there are, without running the risk of harm. Only the most privileged suburbs in America hold to this maximum number today. Teachers feel they are lucky if they have *only* thirty children, Many teachers try to work with forty, fifty or sixty children. But the question isn't whether the teacher is lucky or unlucky. The child is the one who matters. There are definite hazards to children when class size mounts far above twenty.

Of course kindergarten is not the only grade level that is swamped today, but large class size presents a much more severe hazard to five-year-olds than to junior- or senior-high youngsters, or to college students. Large numbers—much more than twenty—hit unusually hard, and with devastating effect, at almost everything that matters to the young child.

225

Crowds are never desirable but their impact is not as severe once children are more self-confident, more able to separate themselves easily from home, more able to deal with symbols and verbalisms, more able to learn just from books or from words, and less active, less in need of firsthand experience.

America's panic about reading has also damaged the quality of kindergartens. About forty-one percent of our five-year-olds go to public school kindergartens but many of them are kindergartens in name only. Actually, they are first grades—and not very good first grades at that! The children stay seated too long. They spend wasted hours on workbooks. They take far too few trips and use far too few other excellent tools for learning—blocks, paints, clay, dramatic and imaginative activities.

Fives are play children. They learn through their play. At their age, play is the appropriate means a school should use to produce sound, sturdy, healthy, competent children. Desks, books, pencils, paper are standard school means toward this end at older ages. Unfortunately, these are the means we all remember best. There is tremendous pressure on the kindergarten today for conformity—to look like the rest of the school and for teachers to use the same teaching means with Fives that they would use with fifteen-year-olds. Our five-year-olds are learning less than they could; they are living much less well than they should.

The same low quality exists in the nursery school field. Here all schools are private. In many states, although not all, private nursery schools must meet some minimum standards. But private education, especially at the nursery school level, usually means "operating on a shoestring." Too frequently, nursery schools have untrained teachers who are paid low salaries and who work with too little equipment and less understanding in groups that are too large. The nursery school field as a whole has two peaks. Some schools are excellent.

They represent the best education available at any level. But many schools are terrible. There is not much middle ground.

The parent who wants to buy nursery education for his child must remember the warning: *Caveat emptor!* Let the buyer beware! You must be sure to investigate carefully before choosing your school. And be prepared to spend a lot of money. Good schools cost a lot of money. Colleges demonstrate this. Colleges need gifts and heavy endowment or tax support and must still charge a high tuition. The inescapable fact is that good private education is very expensive. It is almost impossible to buy it through tuition alone, at the nursery school, kindergarten or at any level.

THE ARGUMENTS AGAINST GROUP-LIVING FOR YOUNG CHILDREN

Almost every university nursery school has a long waiting list, sometimes several hundred names. Many parents realize that their children need more than they alone can give them between the ages of three and six. But we have not yet—after 100 years—reached the point of agreement among most parents and most citizens that we must provide good facilities for three-, four- and five-year-olds at public expense, with state aid and local taxation. Many factors stand in the way.

One obstacle is our dislike of taxes. Many communities could afford public nursery schools and better public kindergartens. Their citizens have the money but prefer to spend it privately, for private good. Many people think it is right that nursery schools and kindergartens should remain the privilege of the lucky few who can afford them.

Right now we are busily engaged in extending education upward. There is tremendous concern about the establishment of junior colleges, community colleges, more state col-

227

leges and state universities. There is no corresponding push to extend education downward. We have schools in America for 100% of our six-year-olds and we are standing pat on that.

Many people think of three-, four- and five-year-olds only as "young." They have no awareness of how able these children are, how ready they are for ideas, how ready for some experiences of separation and independence.

Many adults think of schools for children under six only as places for "social adjustment." They peg nursery school and kindergarten as good for the only child or for the child who lives in a neighborhood where he has no playmates. Such children do have special social needs. But *all* children three to six have social needs, and social adjustment is not the sole goal of good nurseries and kindergartens. Young children—all of them—need ideas as well. They have an intellect that needs nourishing and a body that needs challenge.

The most common notion is that "young children need their mothers." All children do, of course. But the time when children needed *only* their mothers was much earlier in development; in infancy and the first year and the second. Three-, four- and five-year-olds cannot stand permanent separation from their mothers, but neither do they thrive on complete separation from the stimulation of companions their own age, from the challenge of materials, the opportunity for independence. By age three, children have many needs.

Some say the home alone should meet all these needs, as well as the need for love and security. A few homes can do the total job. (No one urges that nursery school and kindergarten attendance be compulsory, only that we have enough schools for all children who need the experience.) We often fail to recognize both how keen the young child's needs are and how much family living has changed. A mother may be a devoted "teacher" but it is very hard for the apartment-house dweller, the suburbanite, the farm family, to provide the companionship, the equipment, the space, the time, the experiences that young children must have to make their best growth.

Men in particular (bachelors most of all!) are apt to say that mothers who send their children to nursery school or kindergarten "just want to get rid of their kids!" Almost all mothers do want to "get rid" of their children—not forever, but for some small part of the day. This should be no surprise. Nor is it realistic to think that mothers who are at home with their three-, four- and five-year-olds are with their children all of the time, ever-loving, every minute of the day. Mothers are busy people. They hold many jobs. They are mothers but they are wives, too—and purchasing agents, housekeepers, social secretaries, laundresses, citizens, etc. Most mothers whose young children go to school for a part of the day find that they are more able to "mother" because they have had a little free time to get some of their other chores done. They love their children more and enjoy them more because of the brief separation.

FAMILY TIES: STRONGER OR WEAKER?

Other people fear that nursery school and kindergarten will weaken family ties and lessen the influence of the family. The reverse is more apt to be true. Good nursery schools and kindergartens strengthen families. They are primarily schools for children but they are schools for parents as well. Parents and teachers confer frequently in good schools. There are parents' meetings that center around the common problems faced by mothers and fathers of young children. The skills of the parent do not grow rusty when a child under six goes to school. Family skills become keener, sharper. The home, as a center where children can find understanding, becomes stronger.

Parents are free to visit good schools often, too. They have the chance to see their children in comparison with others.

229

Such observation is very reassuring. We often worry needlessly about our youngsters and fret over quite normal behavior. Nursery school and kindergarten observation also alerts parents. Sometimes we hope for the best and assume that children will "outgrow" all their difficulties when actually the children need special help. Good nursery schools and kindergartens are a family's DEW line—a special Distant Early Warning system. They can protect families and children, like our radar in the far North which warns us when trouble is in the offing.

Co-ops—A Promising Development

Because good nursery schools are so expensive and so scarce, one special kind of school has come into being. This is the cooperative nursery school. A co-op is a do-it-yourself school. Co-ops hire a topnotch teacher and the teacher is paid in cash. Tuition must cover this cost, but parents pay for much of the rest of their child's education through their own personal services. Parents serve as unpaid assistant teachers, as the equipment constructors, housekeepers, secretaries, as the unpaid workers for whatever other jobs need doing to create a good school. Parents are at cooperative nursery schools almost every day. They have to be. There could be no school without their personal participation. Parents in co-ops spend some cash but, most of all, they spend themselves.

Co-operative nursery schools came into being as one creative solution to the sheer economics of education. They have a very important by-product, however. Inevitably, co-ops give parents many guided firsthand experiences with children—their own and other children. Co-op parents read a great deal about children. They meet constantly to talk about education and children. The co-op is a demanding school but parents prize it for the growth it brings them as parents and as people.

230

GROUP LIVING FOR YOUNG CHILDREN

WHEN GOOD SCHOOLS ARE NOT AVAILABLE

Co-operative nursery schools, of course, do not fit into every family's way of life, and we are a long way from having the public nursery schools and good public kindergartens that we need. For the present, most families have no alternative but to work very hard and very self-consciously to provide the experiences that their children need. Almost all parents of young children face exactly the same situation as parents who live in the few communities which have closed their schools to avoid integration. The children have no school to go to, the home must try to do the whole job.

Parents of a three-, four- or five-year-old are wise to invite a friend of their child's to have lunch with him occasionally and to encourage their child to accept invitations in return. Eating away from home is an important beginning experience in separation. Parents are wise who take their child (and a friend or two) on short excursions to expose the children to new ideas. Parents must use public library facilities extensively so that their children do not miss out on the exciting world of young children's literature. They must build their own collection of children's records so their youngsters have some exposure to good music. They must make certain to have paints and clay and blocks on hand in sufficient quantity so children can express the ideas that are flowing in to them. Wise parents must work out cooperative arrangements with other parents so small groups of children—two or three—can have the time and space and equipment to play together regularly.

When schools do not exist, adults need to work extra hard and very conscientiously to make sure that homes and communities become educative. Otherwise, these years of three and four and five become waste years when children's minds and bodies are simply idle.

231

FOR INDEPENDENT STUDY

1. Because there is such a tremendous need for consumer education in nursery education to protect parents from buying a bad school for their three- and four-year-olds, you ought to know about *Some Ways Of Distinguishing a Good Nursery School* (National Association for Nursery Education, 155 E. Ohio, Room 200, Chicago, Illinois. 5¢). This little sheet ought to be distributed by some group—churches or the PTA or the school board—in every community. The price drops to 3¢ each in orders of 50 or more.

2. A book is available which does something of the same job for parents whose children are starting to kindergarten: *Kindergarten—Your Child's Big Step*, by Minnie Berson (New York: Dutton, 1959).

3. If cooperative nursery schools interest you, The National Association for Nursery Education publishes a complete bibliography listing the many very helpful booklets produced by individual co-ops. The major book in the field is *Parent Cooperative Nursery Schools*, by Katherine Whiteside Taylor (New York: Teachers College Bureau of Publications, 1954).

4. Churches frequently attempt to help meet the need for more group living facilities for young children by establishing week-day church-sponsored schools. The need, the procedures and the problems are well set forth in *Through The Week: Church Sponsored Nursery Schools and Kindergartens* (Nashville: Board of Education of the Methodist Church, 1956). Two good books are *Growing and Learning in the Kindergarten* (1959) by Mamie W. Heinz, and

232

Nursery-Kindergarten Weekday Education in the Church
(1960) by Josephine Newberry (Richmond: John Knox
Press).

What would you do?

Question 23 For the first time ever, your four-year-old
pops out of bed at night and comes into your room saying she
is "scared." What is your inclination: *a*) Be a little tough.
You know there is nothing in the room that could scare her.
Put her straight back to bed so you nip this business of "being
scared" in the bud before it gets out of hand. *b*) Let her climb
into bed with you and spend the night so she doesn't have to
go back to that scary room again. *c*) Gently, but firmly, point
out that she is a big girl now and that there is nothing to be
afraid of in the room. One way or another, but nicely, get her
back into her bed and see that she stays there. *d*) Give in to
her fear, even though there really is nothing unusual in her
room. Go back with her, sit by her bed, rub her back, stay with
her until she falls asleep again.

children's fears

Chapter 26

Young children have many scary moments. They are so small, living like dachshunds in a world of Great Danes. Or like the smallest foreign car, surrounded on the superhighway by tremendous diesel trucks.

For all of their great strides in coordination, young children are still slow movers. The world seems to race by them. They are the pedestrians caught in the middle of the street in rush hour traffic. Young children are also always the newcomers. Adults have had a long time to get used to the sounds and movements and sights of this world. Children are taken by surprise much more than the rest of us.

The barber shop is a good symbol of how easily frightened the young child is. To adults a haircut is the most ordinary routine imaginable. The barber shop chair is harmless and unforbidding, not a cause for alarm. Yet probably more tears are shed, more screams are screamed by children in the barber shop, than in any other single location in the community.

234

It can be hard for any of us to put ourselves in the child's place and to know how this very commonplace operation looks to him—the strange man with tremendous hands—the boost up onto a high perch. A strange voice close to his ears. The confinement of a white robe suddenly surrounding him. The sharp scissors and the buzzing clippers! Adults never worry what happens to the hair that is cut. We never shudder about whether the man will know when to stop cutting. To us a haircut is "just a haircut." To a child it holds elements of terror!

THE PROGRESSION IN CHILDREN'S FEARS

Up to about age three children meet, in the most everyday circumstances, no end of noises that seem loud and that come unexpectedly. In what are to us simple run-of-the-mill settings, little children suddenly come upon strange and unfamiliar objects and people. All these intense and unpredictable happenings can be upsetting. Babies and toddlers live in a haunted house. We know the wind is banging the shutters; we expect the noise. Little children often are taken off guard and are frightened.

Around three—not on the birthday, of course, but somewhere in that age range—these specific fears usually lessen somewhat. Children have grown. They know their way around a bit more. They are less apt to be troubled by the specific event which takes place before their very eyes or which bangs away at their ears. They trade in their old fears, only to take on a new set! Now children begin to be frightened by things that never happened to them and that are not likely ever to happen.

This strange kind of "progress" is similar to the development around six months of age when children, who earlier accepted anyone, momentarily became shy and afraid. They had grown. They could see what they had not seen before—that faces look different, that not all faces are the same. Around three children again "progress." Now they have more power to begin to have an idea. The result? The dark suddenly seems forbidding. With much more active imaginations, children fill in the dark with creatures who are not there. Earlier the dark was just the dark. Now who can tell what is in there? Fear increases but the children are making progress. They are beginning to have ideas.

Three, Fours and Fives begin to be troubled by robbers and ghosts and kidnappers—villains the youngsters do not meet face-to-face but conjure up in their active minds. The prospect of wild animals—bears, in particular—frightens children, even though they have had no experiences at all with such animals and are not likely to. Formerly these children slept the "sleep of the innocent." Around year four, and especially when they are five, children are apt to wake up crying, terrified by nightmares and bad dreams—and this is progress!

The younger children are, the more they are realists. Or perhaps babies and toddlers simply do not know enough to be afraid. As they grow older, children become pessimists, ready to believe the worst. In one experiment, children under two were seldom troubled by a harmless snake. They were even attracted to it. From three or so, however, the same harmless snake began to seem threatening.

DELIBERATELY INSTILLING FEARS IS FOOLISH

In civilized life, fear is usually not a very useful emotion. It does give us greater strength, greater speed, greater endurance. When we are frightened, we can yell louder, hold on tighter and pull harder. The extra boost of power which fear summons up within us would serve us well in the jungle where survival might depend on speed of escape or strength in battle.

236

Occasionally in city and suburban life, spurts of strength help. More frequently in our complicated civilized world, we must think our way out of difficult situations. Puzzling, rather than panic, is our salvation.

There seems little point, therefore, in deliberately making children afraid. You can make no case at all for purposefully frightening them as a means of control. The common threats —"If you are not good, the bogey man will get you." "If you do that again, I'll call the policeman"—serve no constructive purpose. Children fill their own worlds with enough frightening images. We do not need to add scary people to the population.

You can make no case whatsoever for the most prevalent threat of all: "If you do that again, I won't love you." "I'll leave you." "I'll give you away." Sometimes we say these very words. More often we say something else but our obvious anger and irritation shout this threat at children and it truly terrifies. Our steady love—no matter what a child does he can always count on us—is his single strongest bulwark against fear. If we desert him, or threaten to, then the whole world becomes frightening. No child can cope with this life all on his own.

We do want to build *caution* into our youngsters. We want to help them become aware of hazards. They need to know, clear-headedly, how to cope with the dangers that arise in their lives. But building caution is done on a very specific basis. You give wise instructions as particular incidents and events approach. Certainly, too, caution can only be built through calmness and a quiet approach. You cannot scream and shout caution into youngsters.

MAKING LIFE LESS TERRIFYING

Even when we do not instill them, fears infect children. It does not help to minimize these fears or to brush them off lightly. You don't help fears to go away by pretending that they do not exist, or by insisting, cold-heartedly, that they "should" not exist. You seldom help children by a sales talk: "That's nothing to be afraid of." Or by a pep talk: "You're not afraid of a little thing like that." At the moment, the child *is* afraid. Almost always it is better to let youngsters show their fears and come right out and say they are afraid. Once a fear is expressed, it becomes a little more manageable. "Out of sight, out of mind" does not apply to children's fears.

The trouble is: We fear fear itself. *We* become afraid that our child will build a bad habit of being scared. Instead of doing the simple, decent, comforting thing that could so easily help him over a difficult moment, we push the youngster away. We make him face, alone and unaided, the danger he sees. None of us wants his child to be a coward, but we have to learn that courage is not built by piling up moments of weakness. Courage grows as a child steadily feels moments of strength.

So often, all a child needs is a little boost. When he is afraid, he needs our support—not a rebuff or empty words. He needs a hand, a lap, an arm, our company, *us* to give him the strength he does not have. You stay with your child for a few extra minutes until his fears settle down. You let him hold your hand or cling to your side, instead of pushing him away. The helpful thing to do comes so easily and naturally, once we get over our own fear that our child will build a "bad habit."

Wartime studies of the bombings of cities show clearly that children can take almost any experience so long as they have the support of their parents. Without their parents, war was terrifying. Without parents, everyday life can be terrifying. When we separate ourselves from our children—not necessarily by distance but because we hold back our support—fears mount, rather than lessen.

238

We are wise, too, when we anticipate the times that may upset children. Almost anything hurts more when it comes as a surprise. Visits to the dentist, visits to the doctor, the time for a shot, and especially when children have to go to the hospital for essential medical care, are all times when the danger of fear and upset are present.

One way of lessening fear is to approach the coming event gradually. Many wise dentists, for example, never "do anything" to a child on the first visit. They consider the time spent in getting to know the youngster and in letting him explore the chair, the instruments, and the room, to be time wisely invested. So many of us adults stay away from dentists (and doctors) not because of lack of time or money but because we still carry with us fears from childhood when someone did not take the time to help us feel just a little bit safe and at ease.

Hospital surgery that involves the separation of children from their mothers is always more safely done after year six. When medical needs must take precedence over psychological needs, wise doctors are glad to spend whatever time it takes to initiate a child slowly into his hospital experience. They take the time to let the child know them. They encourage children to visit the hospital and to see the room where they will stay. They let a youngster get acquainted with his nurse.

Stories about forthcoming events help to build familiarity and to lessen dread. There are good books through which children can learn about going to the doctor, getting a shot, going to the hospital, to the dentist, etc. Make-believe play is another great aid in preventing fears and in lessening their impact after the event. Children frequently play "hospital" or "doctor" or "barber shop," before the event so they have a safe picture they can cling to in their minds, or afterwards, draining off some of the fear by letting it come out in the open.

FEARS, NOT TEARS, ARE THE TARGET

Mother's presence is another excellent way of lessening fear. Children may cry more in the dentist's office or the doctor's office if mother is present. This does not mean that they are frightened more. Quite the contrary. Mother's presence means that children feel free to show their fear, free to find an outlet for it. We tend to back away from tears. Many adults say that the children are "all right" just so long as their mothers are not around. The chances are that the children are really doubly frightened. They are afraid of what they fear *and* they are afraid to show their fear.

A few hospitals, realizing this, make it possible for mother to come right along with her sick child. The two room together. Mother frequently does many of the routine nursing jobs, instead of an unknown busy nurse. The support of mother's presence lessens the fear within the child. The youngster may cry more—in the hospital, in the dentist's office or the doctor's office—but he is frightened less. The goal isn't to stop tears, but to stop fears.

Nursery schools, kindergartens and first grades—all involved in separating children from their parents—would do well to follow the procedures that wise hospitals have found so good. Teachers are usually in a great hurry to get rid of parents, but many a child could take the beginning days of school in his stride, without fear, if we made the process more gradual and more safe. Schools are wise (and sensitive) if they let children visit ahead of time with their mothers to get the lay of the land; if they begin with short sessions, so a youngster dips in to get a satisfying taste; if they begin with only a small part of the group at once, so a child does not feel lost in the crowd; and if they let mothers stay as long as the children need them.

At school, on the street, in the hospital, anywhere, some

240

children do not cry. They reveal their fear by the tenseness of their bodies, by the high pitch of their voices, sometimes by a change in their skin color, and often by a change in activity —either more quiet or more intense. Other children show their fear by vigorous and insistent over denial that they are afraid. Sometimes youngsters show their fear by a continuous playing-out in imagination, a concentration in make-believe on some event or happening. The child is always better off if he finds some way of letting out his fear—through words or tears or play—than if he has to push fear further down deep inside of him.

Specific fears are not too serious. There are ways of overcoming them. One of the best is to give the child the know-how to handle the situation. The child who can flip on a light switch and end the dark is master of the dark. The adult who knows how to pick up a snake and who knows which snakes are dangerous is master of snakes. The swimmer does not fear the water—he knows how to cope with it. Skills and understanding, sympathetically and gradually built up, are the best antidotes for fear.

Skills can help the child who is shy because he does not know what to do with people, for example. A few specific lessons in how to play "tea party" or how to build a town with blocks or how to play "store" can sometimes build confidence. A few gentle instructions in how to pat a dog, or the facts—calmly told—about why we have thunder and lightning can often do the trick of ending needless specific fears.

The time to be concerned is not when a child has a fear—this we can easily help him cope with. We must be concerned when fear has a child. Too often, all the little fears that have been instilled, or ignored, or made light of, pile up within a youngster so that he becomes afraid—not of dogs, not of lightning—but of life. A child becomes less adventuresome, less curious, less at ease in this world than a comfortable person

241

ought to be. There is no one specific remedy for this pervasive fear. The general direction, however, is clear: First a child must feel safe with us. We are the beginnings of his life. Once he is completely sure of our love, he is in a better position to venture out.

FOR INDEPENDENT STUDY

1. *Fears Of Children,* by Helen Ross (Chicago: Science Research Associates, 1951. 60¢) is an excellent pamphlet. In one specific area *Doctors, Hospitals, Nurses and Children* (New York: Child Study Association, 1957. 50¢) is outstanding. So, too, is the Association's *Children and the Threat of Nuclear War,* by Sibylle Escalona (1962; 40¢).

2. For a further discussion of the business of helping children get off to a good start in school, the pamphlet available free from the Equitable Life Assurance Society, *Looking Forward To School* (1956) is helpful. Vassar College has also produced a most sensitive film, *Starting Nursery School* (16 mm. sound. Available from the New York University Film Library, 26 Washington Place, New York).

3. Among the books for children which have been specifically written to prepare them for experiences which might prove frightening are: *A Visit To The Doctor, A Visit To The Hospital,* and *A Visit To The Dentist,* all Wonder Books available in supermarkets, drug stores, etc.; *Johnny Goes To The Hospital,* by Josephine Abbott Sever (Boston: Houghton Mifflin, 1953) and *Inside The Hospital,* by Helen B. Radler (444 E. 68th St., Society of Memorial Center, New York, 1955) and *All About An Operation,* by Helen B. Radler (New York: Society of Memorial Center, 1956). In

a different area of possible fear there is *Switch On The Night*, R. Bradbury (New York: Pantheon, 1955).

4. One of the best ways to develop an acceptance of the reality of children's fears is to make a list of your own fears: of the dark, of examinations, of snakes, of speaking in public. What can you remember of how your own fears started? Make a list too of fears you have overcome. Try to recall what helped you get over them. Recall also, if you can, any efforts well-intentioned people made to help you overcome your fears, but which didn't work.

What would you do?

Question 24 One four-year-old in a nursery school has been "trike crazy." For several weeks the minute the group goes out of doors he heads for a tricycle, rides one as fast as he can go, swerves and stops sharply, and turns corners on two wheels. He doesn't use any of the other equipment but spends all his time on his beloved tricycle. What is your inclination: *a*) Let him alone; he seems fine. *b*) Encourage him to use the blocks and the sandbox and climbing apparatus so he has some wider experiences, but don't insist. *c*) Make a bargain with him. Let him play with the tricycle for part of the outdoor time if he will try some of the other equipment for the rest of the time. *d*) For a few days keep all the tricycles in the storage closet so the youngster has no choice but to widen his interests.

fathering
and mothering

Chapter 27

The child under six needs good mothering. But mother herself is only one member of the family team and she is not the only one involved in mothering. To keep the record straight: Young children need "fathering," too!

There was a time—it seems to be disappearing—when fathers washed their hands of the whole business of raising young children. They turned the job over to their wives and saved themselves for later. That *later* time was always indefinable: "When the child is old enough to reason." "When he (or she) is old enough so that we can do things together" and sometimes "later" never arrived at all.

There was a time—it seems to be disappearing too—when mothers saved fathers. Men were the trump card in discipline. They were the ultimate threat, the court of last resort. "You just wait until your father gets home" hung like a black cloud over a child's head. Father's footsteps sounded much like the roll of thunder, the forewarning of an approaching storm.

244

These two special roles played a dirty trick on fathers—and a dirty trick on children, too. Everyone can be glad that most men today no longer save themselves or let themselves be saved. More and more fathers pitch in from the very start and play a full and continuous role in raising their children.

Good "mothering," of course, includes good fathering. Women are not the only ones who can be gentle with young-sters. They are not the only ones who can show sympathy and tenderness. They are not the only ones who can do the many kind and friendly things that let a young child feel safe, well cared for, and protected. Mothers are not the only ones who can laugh with their children, play with them, and get an honest-to-goodness kick out of the million and one things young children do that are humorous, appealing and fun. Fathers, fully as much as mothers, create an atmosphere of good humor and enjoyment in the home, an atmosphere of peace and pleasure.

FATHERS ARE PLAYING A MORE ACTIVE ROLE

Almost inevitably, the way we live today, fathers are away during the day. Monday through Friday they are not around for lunch. They do not share in the intimacies of a shopping tour or supervise the morning play time. But increasingly now, at the start of the day and at the end, on weekends and holidays, men do not "save themselves." They use the time they have with their children to make up for what their daily work forces them to miss.

Fathers can, and do, feed their babies. They burp them and hold them and comfort them when they are teething or col-icky or just a little upset. Fathers can, and do, help their youngsters dress in the morning and undress at night. Fathers can, and do, take over bath-time and turn it into a time for washing away, not only dirt but cares. They often are in charge

245

of bedtime, the prize time in the day. Bedtime is the time of intimacy, of one-to-one, face-to-face personal relationships. Bedtime can be the day's leisurely time. Many a father is an expert at reading the bedtime story. He is the "authority" when the most unexpected questions come up and the most unexpected conversations start. Bedtime can be the time above all for relaxed closeness between parent and child. Fathers, more and more, share in it.

Fortunately attitudes have changed, and men run no risk of seeming effeminate if they push the baby carriage on Saturday or Sunday. They no longer feel strange if they take their toddler for a walk or if—with a three- or four- or five-year-old in hand —they set out to watch a steam shovel digging, a truck unloading, or a steamroller smoothing out new asphalt. Children today have some of their most pleasing excursions holding on to the hand of those big strong "Daddies" who are the experts on the outside world.

Everyone gains from this male participation. Mothers get a break—and mothers need one! The woman who is dog-tired physically or ground down emotionally cannot give her young child the laugh and the lift that youngsters need. Children gain, too. They learn that two people love them. Where love is involved, "the more the merrier." The more young children know that a lot of people feel good about them, the better they feel about themselves.

Fathers gain most of all, however. Doing things with children is work. Like all work it has its irritating moments. Managing children confronts anyone with problems that call for hard thinking. But doing things that bring children pleasure is one of the satisfying experiences for adults. *We give*—that is *our* need in life. A child must get—that is his rightful stage in development. We give—our patience, our strength, our knowledge, our time—and we feel better for the giving. An adult must "put out" to have the sense of really being alive.

246

Fathers gain immeasurably in understanding, too. When you are in on the beginnings of behavior, it is a lot easier to be smart about later behavior. Coming in late on growth, knowing nothing of its origins, makes it almost impossible to do the intelligent thing. Fathers are lucky (and fathers get smarter) who have had some part in weaning, in toilet training, in the early development of language, in the beginnings of their child's social interests, in the first questions that children ask, in their child's initial eagerness to explore this fascinating world. Such men have a much better background for coping with all the later "puzzlers" that arise in family living: reading, homework, responsibilities, allowances, dating, driving a car, choosing friends, selecting a college, etc. They have a basis for knowing what their own child is like. They have a basis for knowing the fundamental trends in development. They have a basis for faith in their youngsters and in growth. They know what a child can do and what a child needs; they know what is beyond a child and what truly hurts him.

SUMMIT CONFERENCES—FAMILY STYLE

Men who "feel like a father" play a very important behind-the-scenes role in raising children. In families the real "children's hour" comes after the youngsters are in bed. This is the time when adults talk together, and go over what happened during the day to build some guidelines for the future. Mothers, making decisions right and left and on the spur of the moment, need to "see the movies of the game." They need the chance to go back over the day again, and to test their solutions on a fresh person who wasn't involved in each incident.

A child easily gets torn to pieces when he plays his mother against his father, getting the answer he wants from one or the other, wheedling until he gets his way. Mothers and fathers must present a united front. Without this family consistency, a youngster can feel quite lost. He may seem to be getting "the breaks," because he always wins, but such a child loses what matters most of all to him: a clear sense of direction, a feeling of certainty and solidity, the safe sense of knowing what he can and cannot do.

Consistency is very important, but no child gains if he meets only pigheadedness and stubbornness from his parents. A sense of justice and a sense of right are much more important than simply holding the line forever. We don't help our children when, in the name of consistency, we plod the same foolish rut until everyone drops from exhaustion and nobody wins. We have to give the best of our hearts and the best of our heads to our children—this matters more than blindly "fighting it out on this line if it takes all summer."

To do this more sensitive job, mothers and fathers need to talk things over together. They need to pool their ideas and viewpoints. They have to develop the best ways of proceeding by merging the best that the two together can develop. This pooled thinking sometimes reinforces the old approaches. Sometimes it develops a new consistency, a new line of strength that can be solidly held because it represents the best judgments of both. A child is lucky—a family is lucky—when the "board of directors" can meet so that solutions do not have to be found by one harried executive alone.

Talking things over is not a sign of failure or an indication that mother cannot do her job. Raising a child alone and unaided is a hard task. Too many new developments come each day. Too many unexpected and novel situations arise. Children were meant to have two parents. Two heads are clearly better than one. The late evening conferences about children are a healthy situation in good family life. They are not a mark of crisis, but clear proof that mothers and fathers are doing what they are supposed to do. When everyone is so completely sure that what he is doing is right, and never feels puzzled or any need to talk over what has gone on, the chances are that thinking has stopped.

HOME IS WHERE A MAN IS

The gains from these summit meetings can be many. Sometimes fathers—versed in the world of production and bustle—can see with more appreciation than a mother can, a child's efforts at independence, a child's expression of will and determination. Sometimes mothers—more experienced with their individual children—can soften a father's competitive urges and a father's concern for perfection and achievement. Not infrequently, mothers are hard on their girls and pushovers for their sons. In reverse, men sometimes expect the world of their boys and are soft-headed where their little daughters are concerned. Raising children calls for justice all around. Each youngster must get his full share of what he needs when he needs it. Two minds working together often mean a fairer shake for everyone.

Two minds. Two pairs of hands. Two pairs of feet. Two differing voices and sets of muscles and two differing pairs of eyes. A child's life is richer when, from the beginning, he has the benefit of both a masculine and a feminine approach to the world. A dual outlook within the home is especially important today because so much of the child's outside world is a woman's world.

Men disappear from our communities during the daytime hours. Men have disappeared from our elementary schools. Men have never existed in our nursery schools and kindergartens or in our church schools for the youngest children. The "hand that rocks the cradle" can be the only hand both boys and girls know outside the home until they become adolescents. Children of both sexes need to feel a hairy hand,

249

a more muscular hand, a bigger hand, a calloused hand. Home is the one place today where they can have this opportunity.

Little boys, especially, need to do things with their fathers. The boys' job is to grow up as men. They can do this only if they grow up with men around them. Little girls, no less, need men. In fact, they have a double need. Their job is to grow up so they can live with men. They must be steadily building in their minds an image of what men are like. And they need this image so they can bounce back from it and find their own role as women. They must live with men, and they must live as women. To know what they are and to know what they are not, they need a man around the house.

There is one important qualification, however: Boys and girls need a happy man, a willing man. Children need a father in good humor who can become an attractive image, not a grouchy and repelling one. You cannot pass a law and make fathers enjoy their children, any more than you can pass a law that forces mothers to be glad they are with their youngsters. The time spent with children, minutes ticking by, is not the crucial thing. What counts, always, is the quality of relationships.

Most fathers lead a hectic life today. Their world outside is fiercely competitive. They are under unrelenting pressure to achieve and to produce. Men battle traffic to get to work, battle for a parking place, battle on the job. We all see the toll this life takes in ulcers, heart attacks, in the earlier deaths of men—and in straight fatigue!

Father's role in the family must be geared to father's feelings, not to routine or regularity as if a father were a machine. Mothers have moments when they can hardly stand the sight of their children. So, too, men have their times of exhaustion, irritation, and of mounting worries. At these times a lively, demanding child may be the last thing in the world a father needs.

250

Mothers probably always serve as "coach" of the family team. They have to develop a feeling for when to send in the first team and when to call on the reserves. They have to know who the fresh player is, and which one is at the end of his rope. They have to make the decision to save one player for the game coming up, keeping him on the sidelines now so that he can build up reserve of strength. The art of good family living lies in flexibility, not plodding consistency. The challenge is to make sure that a child gets the best of each of us at any one time.

FOR INDEPENDENT STUDY

1. Every father (or anyone who thinks he may some day be a father) ought to read *Father's Day Comes Once A Year . . . And Then It Always Rains,* by Harold H. Martin (New York: Putnam, 1960). You are bound to laugh, and you may even learn something. If you want to be more serious, invest 25¢ in *Making The Grade As Dad,* by Walter and Edith Neisser (New York: Public Affairs Committee, 1950) or, better still, read *Fathers Are Parents Too,* by Spurgeon English and Constance Foster (New York: Putnam, 1951).

2. One book is available telling of a man's experiences as a nursery school teacher, his own reactions and the reactions of the children: *Father To The Child,* by Everett Ostrovsky (New York: Putnam, 1959).

What would you do?

Question 25 A father has just seeded a new lawn in front of the house. He has put up a string fence to keep people off the lawn. His five-year-old starts to climb under the string and

251

run across the lawn. The father says in no uncertain terms: "Stop! Don't go across the lawn. That's what the fence is for —to keep people off. The grass has to send its roots down and grow strong before any of us can walk on it. You stay off until I tell you that it is all right to walk on the grass. Until then I don't want you to step on this new lawn for any reason." With whom do you tend to side: *a*) A neighbor thinks: "Good for him! That is clear-cut and definite, with no two ways about it." *b*) His wife thinks: "Oh, dear. He sounds so stern! Doesn't he know that young children need love, not severity?" *c*) Grandmother thinks the whole thing is a tempest in a teapot. Why shouldn't the boy go across the lawn? What difference will it make? *d*) Grandfather doesn't object basically to what the father has done but he thinks: "He could have been more polite. He could have said 'Please'."

discipline
–what is it?

Chapter 28

Disciplining the young child is the most important job that parents have to do. For the sake of all of us, it is imperative during these beginning years that a child begin to learn the right ways to act, the decent things to do, the appropriate ways of responding so that we can have a good world in which to live.

A child cannot learn all of his discipline by the time he is six. He can only make a start. Every adult is still in the process of learning. Every day even we discover new and better ways that make it more possible for humans to inhabit some piece of earth together, whether that piece of earth be a metropolitan urban area or the globe itself. Learning discipline is a never-ending process but the start is very important. If a child does not make a good start, the chances are overwhelming that he will never learn the rules for getting along in our society.

The causes of delinquency are many, but one thing is com-

253

pletely clear· Delinquency does not erupt suddenly, out of the blue, with no roots in a child's past. No matter what the specific factors may be in any one delinquent's case, the causes always began operating in early childhood. The under-six years are the time to begin to make a law-abiding citizen, a considerate and useful member of society; or they can be the time when the seeds of rebellion and destruction are sown.

CHILDREN WANT LIMITS

Discipline is as important to the child as it is to all of us. To be undisciplined sounds so free, so gay. In contrast, discipline sounds like a blocking, stopping, nasty kind of action. It suggests the unhappy, frustrating parts of early growing up. The child who knows no discipline ought to be having the time of his young life. Actually, such a child is never happy in the least. Equally important, the child who is wisely disciplined is not frustrated or upset. Discipline brings contentment to children, as well as safety to our world.

A youngster who goes along during these early years never knowing what is right and wrong, never knowing what he should do and what he should not, has a terrible time. In a literal sense, he is lost. He feels the same gnawing unhappiness inside of him that we do when we get off on the wrong road on an automobile trip. If we have no map, no signposts to guide us, no markers, no one to tell us whether to go straight ahead or turn right or left or go back, we worry and feel unsettled and depressed. This is exactly the plight of the young child who knows no discipline.

Knowing no limits, he is full of fears. He sails, like Columbus, on a completely uncharted ocean. Such a youngster never knows when the sky will fall or when he will come to the edge of the world. His freedom from discipline sounds as if he shouldn't have a worry in the world. In fact, his every moment

254

is filled with worry. Lack of discipline is not the prize way to build confidence and inner peace.

Most important, the youngster who knows no discipline feels no love. He has been left on his own, ignored, "free" to do whatever he wishes. As far as the child can see, no one cares. This is the most troubling sensation of all. The big people *must* care, and they must show that they care. Weak attempts at discipline are equally bad. The youngster who wins every argument, who knows only flabby discipline—and can always get around it—becomes too big and too strong for his own good. He hasn't won anything.

From the standpoint of society and from the standpoint of the child, discipline is exceedingly important in these early years. But don't let its great importance lure you into doing foolish things. Disciplining a child is a tricky business. You have to think, hard and long, about what you really want in discipline, and about the best ways of achieving your ends. Sometimes we get so excited about discipline that we rush without thinking and grasp for anything "that works."

Discipline means that a child learns right from wrong; good from bad; the decent, the kind, the gentle, the thoughtful from the indecent and cruel and hurting—*and that he acts on what he knows because he believes in it*. These are not simple lessons to teach; not the kind you can beat into a child.

Children are born egocentric, thinking only of themselves. The task of discipline is to help them change so they become able to think of the other fellow, too. At birth children act quite unsocially. The whole world revolves around their belly button. The task of discipline is to help children change so they become able to live with others, as well as to live with themselves.

When children are born, their emotions have the upper hand. They cannot yet think—they are completely impulsive. They want what they want when they want it—because *they*

255

want it! The task of discipline is to help children change so they become rational, more able to think before they act, less driven exclusively by their own impulses and their own personal wants and desires.

At birth these creatures are in the grasp of two broad emotions: pain and pleasure. This is their world, the sole springboard for their action. What hurts *them*, what pleases *them*, is all that matters. The task of discipline is to help children change so they begin to feel concern, not only for what pleases or pains them, but also for what hurts and helps their fellow humans. The task of discipline is to help children change so they broaden their emotional range to include more shades of feeling: annoyance, irritation, dismay, desolation, contentment, gaiety, joy, ecstasy. Only people who develop a full range of emotions can control their feelings. Only people who have a full range of feelings can live well in human society. The initial, personal, massive black-or-white sensations are too oversimplified for decent living.

DISCIPLINE—AMERICAN STYLE

Teaching the kind of discipline "that works" to help children change in these fundamental ways is a tremendous job. It is an especially complicated job in our country. We are not a police state. We do not have a Gestapo. We have no Storm Troopers or spies or informers in every house and at every corner, in every school and office and factory. We do have a police force, to be sure. But in a democracy each man essentially is his own policeman. We do the right thing because we believe in the right, not because "big brother" watches over our shoulder every single minute and makes us be good.

There are occasional situations in which straight obedience is called for. We do what the policeman says because he says it. In the Armed Forces, ours is just to do or die—we jump when the command is snapped. In a traffic jam, we obey the officer's signal. In crisis or martial law, we simply do as we are told. Our discipline must include the capacity for this kind of obedience. But blind obedience to outside commands is not the central core of democratic discipline. The rare times when blind obedience is needed are highly exceptional. Ninety-nine times out of one hundred no policeman is around except the one that we all have to learn to carry inside of us. We are on our own. No one makes us be good. We are good because we have learned to believe that the right is the better path to follow. Discipline in a democracy must be internalized.

A police state can count on its machine guns and bayonets to change adults. Its citizens are good because of the ever lurking danger that someone will catch them if they are bad. In a free country "there is no one here but us chickens." We can, if we want to, "get away with it." The task we face in discipline is to help children change so they do not want to get away with murder or with anything else. Our children must prefer the good and not need continuously to be pushed into it. Our strongest police force—the force that marks our country off from Russia or Red China or from any dictatorial state—is *conscience*, our developed sense of caring. The means of discipline that we use must be carefully chosen to fit this unique and more difficult job. We must be everlastingly sure that our means do not defeat the end that we want.

Today, more than ever, we face an additional challenge in teaching discipline. We live in a very changing world. Nothing stays put very long. Problems are not solved, once and for all. Answers are not found today that will hold for all time. Individual families are constantly on the move. Geographically we go back and forth from one end of the country to the other. Economically and socially there is also tremendous change and mobility. Every daily headline features a new crisis unheard of in yesterday's edition. This continuous, never-stopping emergence of new situations creates a special character for the kind of discipline we teach.

Today, for all people everywhere, but for America in particular, a child cannot simply memorize his discipline. Yesterday's specific answers can become as outdated as the horse and buggy or the DC-3. Today's young children will live to see the year 2001. They will spend their lives in an unpredictable, unimaginable twenty-first century. We must discipline today so that they are prepared for that unforeseeable tomorrow.

Change today touches all countries but it is a special challenge to America. We welcome change. We are glad for progress. We do not resist the new nor do we cling blindly to the *status quo* as dictatorial countries must. Our children, more than many children in the world, must have within them broad basic concepts which can serve as guides to action in new situations. Our discipline must not be made up of little pat specifics, doomed to be outdated, outmoded and obsolescent. The techniques of discipline that we use must be geared to build flexibility rather than rigidity.

We have another distinctive characteristic. Ours is the "land of the free and the home of the brave." Our way of teaching discipline must be consistent with these qualities of our country. We are not a lock step people. We are not a formal, stuffy people. We are well-behaved. We want our children to be well-behaved. But we cannot have a discipline that spoils our relaxed and cheerful, our friendly free-and-easy, gait.

We believe in discipline—any sane person must! But we also believe that any one of us has the right to look the other fellow straight in the eye. We don't bow down. We don't scrape and kneel and humble ourselves before the high and mighty. Each of us, with faith in himself and respect for his dignity, is "high and mighty."

We believe in discipline—any sane person must! But we

also believe in differences. Our discipline cannot mean conformity. It cannot mean that we must all think alike or worship alike or dress alike. We live by the rule of the majority *and* by respect for the minority. Unlike the bossy countries of the world, we have to find ways of making discipline a creative force rather than a crushing weight. No part of America has any stake in a discipline that squelches.

We believe in discipline—any sane person must! But we also believe in rebellion. We have to. Our country was founded in rebellion. Our great gains in every area have come because we are revolutionaries at heart. We are not lawbreakers and we do not want our children to be law-breakers. But we do question. We do prod. We do examine. We do continuously challenge past ways of doing everything because we restlessly search for better ways—in government, in business, in the sciences, in healing, in art, in our homes and in our communities. The way we discipline must never curb this "divine dissatisfaction" within our children.

Persuading a child to join the human race—helping him to grow as a human and to grow so he can live with humans—is the big overall task of these beginning years. Some countries have an easy job. They can simply clamp on their discipline. Our task is infinitely more difficult. We face a delicate job that calls for sensitivity and thinking. We must believe in discipline, yet never become so naively infatuated with it that we plunge ahead blindly, with a heavy hand, blundering—and losing what we seek.

FOR INDEPENDENT STUDY

1. Many books have been written to help us all sharpen our awareness of the ideals and aspirations that are America. *Living Ideas In America,* by Henry Steele Commager, editor

Discipline—What Is It?

(New York: Harper, 1951) is called "a storehouse of eloquent expressions of American ideas and institutions." It, or a similar book, *A Treasury Of Democracy*, by Norman Cousins, editor (New York: Coward-McCann, 1942) is well worth reading as you think about the problem of how to discipline a child.

What would you do?

Question 26 Two five-year-olds are chasing another five-year-old in a friendly game. The boy being chased suddenly stops and says: "It's not fair! It's three against two!" The chasers stop and listen very seriously. Then the boy says: "It ought to be two against three!" With that the game goes right on as it had been. What is your inclination: *a*) Stop the children and explain that there are really only three of them: "It's two against one." *b*) Don't do anything at the time but later, when the children are not running, bring the three together and explain the correct mathematics. *c*) Just keep your mouth shut. There is no need to do anything. *d*) This isn't a question of mathematics but of ethics. Stop the children and talk just a little to them about fairness and having even sides.

discipline
–how do you
do it?

Chapter 29

Everyone must find his own comfortable way of disciplining children. If you try to "follow the book" when the book doesn't jibe with your own common sense, you are headed for trouble. And your child is headed for trouble, too.

Human relationships between parent and child, and teacher and child, must be grounded on a solid bedrock of confidence. Whatever we do must flow easily from deep inner convictions. If the adult is torn every time some incident arises—Should I do this? Should I do that?—a youngster gets nothing but uncertainty. If an adult stews and frets after every decision—Oh dear! Did I do the right thing?—a youngster senses nothing but unsureness.

At any one moment the best thing to do is whatever seems the best thing to do. Your feelings, your instincts, what makes sense to *you*, are the very best guides to follow.

This does not mean that the good parent always knows exactly what to do. A good parent is a parent who puzzles

261

(and this same quality is the mark of a good teacher). Not beset by doubts, but puzzling. At any one moment you have to act and do the best you can. But don't expect to have no questions in your mind, no little doubts. Only the very stupid are so very sure—about children or anything!

Similarly, doing what comes naturally does not mean that you must go on, forever and ever, always doing the same thing. At the time, you have to do what looks best. But adults can change. There is no need to get stuck in a rut. It is true that young children get much of their security from knowing that life has routines and a number of certainties. The child, a newcomer, finds comfort in regularity and in knowing that some events happen over and over, in the same time and the same way, and with the same results. In addition, repetition and regularity are real aids to learning. If life has no steady over-and-over quality to it, if everything is new and everything happens only once, a child cannot learn. But never think that consistency and routine are the only virtues in adult-child relationships.

Consistency is one virtue. But so is justice. And sensitivity. And flexibility. On the spot, an adult has to *do* something. Later, smart adults think about what they did and lay plans for the next time. The surest thing you can know is that there always will be a "next time." When consistency and regularity and "naturalness" bring only insensitivity, piled up day after day, no one gains.

MANY TECHNIQUES OF DISCIPLINING

You must be very careful not to fall into one inviting trap: It is easy to believe that discipline and punishment are the same thing. They are not. *Discipline* sums up our broad goals for the child as a member of society. *Punishment* is only one of many teaching techniques you can use to achieve these broad ends—and the trickiest, hardest-to-use-well technique of all!

The *silent forces* of maturation and identification are also techniques to help children change. These two operate constantly, sixty seconds to the minute, sixty minutes to the hour: 1) Children change as they grow; 2) Children change as they watch what you do, and try to do what you do because they want to please you. The fact that you say nothing does not mean that you do nothing. Even when you keep quiet, these silent forces persistently and powerfully move the child to change.

By and large, if you can feel comfortable about it, it is much better to rely on maturation and identification as your means of discipline *whenever children are acting their age.*

The way they act at that age may not be the way you want them to act forever. All children do some things which are "naughty but nice." The acts are "naughty" in that they trouble us a bit. They are "nice" in that the behavior is logical and necessary, a healthful expression of the child's normal growth at the time. Babies wet and babies burp. These acts are "naughty but nice." Toddlers and walkers knock over tables, tear magazines, and break things. Two-year-olds are stubborn at times, and possessive, and they sometimes pull hair. These are "naughty but nice."

Twos and Threes hit with their fists when they quarrel, and they sometimes bite and kick. Fours and Fives are much less physical in their attacks but much more verbal. They may even spit at each other when they are really angry. The chances are that they will call each other names. "Naughty"? Yes, but from a developmental standpoint, "nice." Fours and Fives are making progress. They are doing what they have to do at this stage in their growth.

Fours and Fives also sometimes call people names. They may even call an adult "stupid" or "stinker" or "do-do." The

263

children are not angry; they are testing out what words can do and testing out themselves. Naughty, to be sure! But none of this age-level behavior lasts forever. And now, while these children are growing more and more "talky," they are holding on to their fists and to their feet a lot better. They are not hitting and kicking nearly as much as they used to. You have to think of their words as typical age-level language; as such, they are just a bit "nice."

The more easygoing you can be, accepting what children do because they are the age they are, the more good you will do. Your tolerance, however, does *not* mean that you do nothing to discipline the children. It simply means that, at this point, you are relying more on your *silent forces*. You know that the children will change as they grow (if you keep them healthy). You know that if you don't call people names (or spit or kick or burp!), the children are bound to identify with you.

CHANNELING BEHAVIOR

We all have different degrees of tolerance and each of us has to be true to himself. You may well decide to take some overt action about some of this age-level behavior. One good technique is to *channel* the child's activities. You don't dam them up. You stop the activity momentarily, only to divert it to a channel where the same kind of behavior can go on, but where it will be safer or easier to live with.

Your toddler cannot tear up your prize issue of *Holiday*, for example, but perhaps he can rip yesterday's newspaper to shreds. Your Four cannot say "stinky" any more—*that* drives you crazy. But perhaps he can call people "scalawags" if he has to use a name. Your Three cannot bounce on the sofa— that is completely out of bounds. But out-of-doors he can jump and run to his heart's content. You think fast and come up with some bright idea that lets you and your child live

264

through the moment, and so that no one's nerves get too frayed. You cope creatively with the behavior, rather than try to talk the child out of himself by explicit teaching (or "knock his brains out" or knock him out of his stage of growing).

If the child's act is a natural one for *him*—the kind all children do when they are about his age because they are his age—your best bet (if you can feel right about it) is to have a gentle touch. Children grow strong only when they are allowed to be themselves. Active, forceful discipline seems to say to a youngster: "You're no good the way you are." The tough approach "works"—for the moment, but it threatens a child's whole sense of self-respect and it is not a good base for lasting discipline.

Good discipline, then, at times is very easygoing. It tolerates a lot that children do, confident that they will outgrow it. This tolerance is not an impatient nose-holding, with a silent prayer: "Please, dear God. Make them grow up fast." Your tolerance expresses a real gladness that children are children. It is your way of showing your deep sense of satisfaction that you have the child you do. You can feel this way only if you know that you are not being lazy, or sloppy, or overly casual. You are working all the time to help children change but you are working silently. You are counting on time—time to grow —and you are counting on your good relationships—your child's love for you and his urge to be like you.

SPECIFIC, OVERT DISCIPLINE IS IMPORTANT, TOO

Good discipline, however, is no one single approach. Some of us are too hard-boiled. We are not easy and good-natured enough with our children. But you can make the opposite mistake as easily. You can assume that everything that children do stems from their being the age they are. You can assume that no matter what they do, "children will be children." Such a one-track mind is not the way to good discipline.

Sometimes children need your firmness. Sometimes they need you to point out explicitly the right way to act. Sometimes they need you to draw a clear line so they know exactly how far they can go.

Your sense of timing is very important here. There is no point in drawing a line for the child who is too young. There is no point in saying "No" when a child's whole body makes him fight you. *But when you think your child is ready to learn, your big job is to teach him.* Never hesitate to be a little easygoing when tolerance is called for. Never back away from drawing a firm line when firmness and directness seem the right approach.

Being firm, however, does not mean being angry. Being firm does not mean being harsh. By all odds, the best way of explicity teaching children discipline is the same as the best way of explicitly teaching children reading or arithmetic or science or history. You talk with them. You don't have to bang their heads against the wall. You show them. You don't have to scream at them. You explain. You don't have to stick pins in them. Overwhelmingly, ninety-nine times out of one hundred, explicit teaching is talking whether you are teaching discipline or anything!

The talking way is the slow way. You never teach any lesson the first time around. No teacher does. You make a little dent. The next time the same situation arises, you make a bigger dent. Slowly, gradually, your reasons sink in. Slowly, gradually, because you make sense, your reasons become a part of the child. But you have to expect that talking-teaching will take time. All teaching does.

Not that you talk to the wind, or talk just for the sake of talking. Your firmness, your conviction that the child is ready to begin to learn, your sureness that what you are teaching is right, show in your behavior. You are serious. You are direct.

266

You get the child's attention and you say what you have to say directly to him. You don't shout your message as he runs away. You don't mumble it because he isn't listening anyhow. You say what you have to say so that a child can hear and begin to understand. You say it so that he senses from your whole manner that you are teaching him something of real importance.

You have your reasons and your reasons make sense. You are firm and clear and direct in explaining your reasons. But don't expect reasons alone to carry the day. Nor can you expect words alone—no matter how logical they are—to control the child's behavior the first time you say them (or the second or the fifth). Young children are not yet that verbal. Their own command of language is not yet that strong; their ability to respond to other people's language is weaker still.

Words Plus Action

Say what you have to say and then back up your words with appropriate action. If it is time to come in, say so and say why *and* come in with the child. If it is time to put toys away, start to put them away with the child. If it is time to get into the car, you get in the car with the child. If a youngster has climbed too high, bring him down while you are talking and explaining why. If a youngster is using a tool he should not use, take the tool away while you are telling him why you must. Young children respond to clear words and to firm action. The older the child, the more your words alone can do the job. With toddlers, three-year-olds, Fours and sometimes even with Fives it takes both words and deeds for real communication.

One urgent bit of advice: Don't ever let yourself say or feel: "What can you do with them?" Don't ever get in the position where you despair and give up. Children sense all too easily

267

when they are the boss, and this frightens them. Whenever an adult stops being an adult—"I just don't know what I am going to do!"—the child is completely at loose ends. Every child needs a strong adult. That is the only way he can feel strong himself.

Whenever you feel buffaloed, as if your back is up against the wall, take stock and think. Look again at what is happening. You may be trying to teach something that is over the child's head. If that seems so, a better solution is to rely more on your silent forces to change him. Your best bet is to tolerate what your child is doing for a while, and to accept the behavior as a natural part of his growing up. If this is your decision, your child will sense that you have arrived at it out of strength. You have thought, and you have decided. Such tolerance has a very different effect on the child than if he feels he has you backed up into a corner. In one case he is the boss—that is no good. In another case, you have decided. Your child will feel your confidence.

As you puzzle, you may come to feel that your child misbehaves because he very desperately wants something from you: more love, more attention, more of your time and your interest, more freedom. His way of getting what he wants leaves a lot to be desired. But, puzzling, you realize that his "mixed up" ways of acting come because he so deeply desires something. Don't minimize these basic needs of children. Don't ever say: "He *just* wants someone to notice him. He *just* wants someone to pay attention to him. He is *just* trying to show off and prove how big he is." When a child is hungry —starving!—for one of life's basic satisfactions, that is not the time for discipline at all. You will get much better behavior from your child if you do notice him and *do* pay attention and *do* help him feel big. Not once, but time after time after time. You are dealing with a famished child, not one who has worked up a pale feeble little appetite. You have to work hard and long to meet a child's needs; but once needs are met, children's behavior greatly improves.

Punishment

As you puzzle, you may equally well conclude that punishment is in order. Punishment (or rewards—they are both cut from the same cloth) is a valid teaching method. It simply is a very tricky one. Punishment is at its best for teaching some one specific lesson. You cannot punish a child into being generous. You cannot punish a child into being thoughtful or considerate. These broader goals come only through maturation, through identification, and through your persistently talking to make a good case for them. You *can* punish your child so that he learns to do or not to do some one specific act. Sometimes this is important.

Punishment (or a reward) is best for teaching quickly. Occasionally specific learnings cannot wait for words to sink in. Too much is at stake. You need to make your point immediately about staying away from a door (one specific door), about not crossing a street (one specific street), about not touching a machine (one specific machine).

You won't go wrong if your best judgment tells you that punishment is needed to get some one point over and to get the point over quickly. You don't have to back away from punishment when it seems to you the right thing to do. Your child won't like it and his tears will tell you so but this shouldn't surprise you. There is no reason on the face of the earth why a child should like to be punished, and no reason why he shouldn't express his dislike. You can't expect a child who is punished to grin and say: "Thank you." You have to learn to live with some tears. They won't kill the child and they won't kill you.

Beware, however, of leaping to the conclusion that every-

269

thing is a specific, and that everything must be learned at once. It is all too easy to let a punishing way become our total way. A youngster can live with an occasional tear. He cannot live well if he thinks that nothing he ever does pleases us. He cannot live well if harshness meets him at every turn, or if everything that comes naturally to him seems wrong to us. When we turn to punishment too often, we undercut and undermine our silent forces for discipline. We stop growth and we stop identification. We build resistance so that our words, when we use them, do not sink in.

This is one of the reasons why punishment is such a tricky technique. The younger the child the more you run the risk of seeming very active indeed but actually accomplishing nothing good. The closer the child is to the years when a sense of trust is so dominantly important, the more we take our "life in our hands" when we turn to punishment. Adults are bigger and stronger—and all of us are a little impatient. Punishment rolls so easily off our tongues and slides so easily off our hands. But too much of the loudest discipline can drown out the softest.

Punishment is tricky, too, because you must constantly adjust the dose. Rewards hold this same hazard. You must really hurt a child or really please him, otherwise your punishment or reward has no impact. When you rely too steadily on either of these techniques, you soon find that the cost of living constantly rises. What worked yesterday has no purchasing power today. You find yourself caught in a constant spiral and you never know for sure what it really takes to carry the day. This "inflationary" characteristic of punishment (and reward) is one of its most baffling elements. You really have to be skilled to use punishment effectively; it isn't the kind of technique you can use well off-hand.

But no one way of disciplining is *always* right. No one way is wrong. The "best" way fits the particular child in the particular situation—and it fits you. It takes a nice mixture of all the ways of teaching (a sensitive mixture) to produce a child who wants to be good; to produce a child who can be good and still have some of the revolutionary left inside of him; to help a child change so that he can live well in our free America and in that unpredictable future all of today's children face.

FOR INDEPENDENT STUDY

1. More books and pamphlets have been written about discipline than you can shake a stick at. If reading could solve the problem, discipline is one we certainly would have licked! By and large we go on our merry way despite all the advice of the "experts." Among the best pamphlets are the following: A *Guide To Better Discipline*, by Othilda Krug and Helen L. Beck (Chicago: Science Research Associates. 60¢); *Back To What Woodshed*, by Justine Wise Polier (New York: Public Affairs Committee. 25¢); *Discipline* by James L. Hymes, Jr. (New York: Teachers College Bureau of Publications. 60¢); *The Controversial Problem of Discipline*, by Katherine M. Wolf (New York: Child Study Association. 30¢); *The Why and How of Discipline*, by Aline B. Auerbach (New York: Child Study Association. 40¢). Two books may also interest you: *Understanding Your Child*, by James L. Hymes, Jr. (Englewood Cliffs, N.J.: Prentice-Hall, 1952) offers a framework to give parents and teachers flexibility in responding to the particular demands of varying discipline situations; *These Well-Adjusted Children*, by Grace Langdon and Irving Stout (New York: John Day, 1951) is a report for parents on ways others have found of producing healthy and yet well-behaved youngsters.

271

What would you do?

Question 27 Two five-year-olds are watching a cement mixer unload its cement at a new house under construction. One youngster asks the driver of the truck: "Where does all this cement come from?" The driver is very busy with all his various responsibilities but he does reply good-naturedly: "Oh, I just push a little button and presto, the truck gets filled with cement." With whom do you tend to side: *a*) One adult thinks the children shouldn't bother the man; he is busy enough as it is without answering foolish questions. *b*) Another adult is pleased that the driver is so good-natured; she thinks that young children need experiences like this with friendly and interested men. *c*) Another adult thinks: "That's a fine way to bring up stupid children." *d*) Still another adult is pleased because she knows how imaginative young children are—she likes the driver's touch of whimsy.

when something goes wrong

Chapter 30

When you stop and think about it, it is almost a miracle that every child does not have something psychologically wrong with him most of the time! The conditions under which most of us raise our children are a far cry from being perfect soil in which to grow healthy specimens.

A WORLD OF CHANGE

We live in a world of crisis, of little wars and the ever-present threat of big war. National and international events usually do not directly touch young children, but they do hit every one of us. To some extent the tension in the air and the uncertainty about what each morning's headline will bring make each of us less placid, less calm, less confident than we could otherwise be.

Other upheavals all around us are more prosaic but perhaps more upsetting to children. One, right on our doorstep, is our

273

moving about. We would be lost without our moving vans. In 1957-58 twelve million children moved, at least from one house to another. One million children moved from one of the main geographical areas of our country to another; another two million moved from one state to another; another two million moved from one county to another within the same state.

Many of the moving vans have carried families to "suburbia." Between 1950 and 1956 our suburbs grew nearly three times as fast as the total population of the United States, and over six times as fast as the population of cities. We move to the suburbs largely for the sake of our children—but the move is never an unmixed blessing.

The shift from one house to another has a different impact on the child under-six from that on older children. Youngsters over six have to leave their friends and school, their most familiar world, behind them. Younger children take their familiar world along with them: their doll, their bed, their mother and father. But for all children, moves can be upsetting (as well as challenging). Younger children are more apt to feel the impact of moving through its effect on their parents. Adults go through the exhausting physical effort and the upsetting psychological process of sending down new roots. At the time of a move it is difficult for parents to give young children the steadiness, patience and time that they need.

Constant moving about has one direct impact on your children. Families are less apt to have grandparents right next door. In "suburbia," when father leaves in the morning to go somewhere to do some mysterious work someplace, mother is left doubly alone with the children. An experienced old hand is not likely to be available to give her tips and guidance and assistance as she does her job.

Many specialists think that the total community is taking

the place of "grandmother," in an unhealthy way. Families with no deep roots seem to look around them for their leads on what to do and what not to do with their children. We try to "keep up with the Jones's" in cars, T.V., and the beauty of our lawns. We keep up with the Jones's in raising our children, too. Our certainties lie less within ourselves or in our own family's established ways. With so many of us new in our communities we keep looking over our shoulder to find out: "How are we doing?" Such nervous checking can lead to a lot of added pressure on children. Our youngsters compete for us. They carry our colors. We anxiously want them to be the best, for our sake, instead of wanting them to be comfortable, for their sake.

The absence of grandparents and other close relatives has a special impact on the three million mothers-of-children-under-six who are working. This startling statistic has one meaning if "kissing kin" live with the family and can take over the care of the young child. It has a more frightening significance when grandmother is 3,000 miles away, and the family has no blood ties in its new community.

CHANGE WITHIN OUR FAMILIES

There is great change and mobility too, within our families. Not too long ago a woman's life could be summed up in the old German expression: *Kirche, kinder, kueche*—church, children, cooking. Today women are much more highly educated. Women are playing a role as co-equals with men, partners in raising the family, and full citizens in our communities. Men, on the other hand, are sharing in tasks that were traditionally the woman's: shopping, washing and drying the clothes, cleaning the house. You might say that women are becoming more like men, and men are becoming more like women. Our

275

sex roles—what a man is supposed to to do, what a woman is supposed to do—are changing. This change creates major uncertainties as to how people should act.

One statistic reflects the many changes that have taken place within the home. In 1958, 11% of our families with children under eighteen were broken by death, divorce, or separation. There never are, of course, statistics on the number of families that stay together but unhappily—the so-called "whole families" whose internal security has been shot full of holes!

Another statistic is revelant here. Since 1948 our child population in the ten- to seventeen-year-old age span increased about 25%. In the same ten-year period, 1948-1958, juvenile delinquency increased almost 120%. No single factor is the cause of delinquency; but the incidence of delinquency does reflect all of the many factors which have had an upsetting effect on family life and on the capacity of families (and also of schools and churches and communities) to do their job of raising healthy children.

The many changes in our total way of living are paralleled by great changes in our way of raising children. One fact must be recognized at the beginning: Now, as in the past, we do almost nothing to prepare our youth for parenthood. Everyone starts as a rank amateur! We begin from scratch, as mothers and fathers. We are thrown on our own, to fumble and bumble and find our own way.

Almost the only help any of us has in raising children is our memory of how we ourselves were raised. In recent years this has been a most inadequate guide. The reason is obvious: The rules have changed! Knowledge about children has vastly increased. New insights are available which did not exist when we ourselves were children. Many a parent is caught between his dim memory of the "right" thing to do and what "the book" says. More complicating still: The books keep changing their minds as still newer ideas are uncovered.

Even in the most stable society with fixed rules of procedure, the absence of any preparation ought to mean that inevitably parents would make many mistakes. In a time of upheaval, lack of preparation is especially worrisome. Large numbers of conscientious mothers and fathers, trying to do a good job, find themselves at sea. One question is frequently asked, almost in despair: "What are you supposed to do?" Sometimes the same question underlies the angry, frustrated statement: "You're not supposed to hit them," but what are you supposed to do? At one time parents *knew* the answer, for better or worse. In fact, they didn't know there was any question! Parents did what was done to them. Today many parents feel that their hands are tied. The "old ways" of raising children are gone; the "new ways" are not the least bit clear.

Add all the social changes to the changes within family life, and mix these together with the changes in child rearing. It is a miracle that as many children turn out as well as they do!

It is a miracle—largely the *miracle of growth!* Children want to grow, they have to grow. Given half a chance, children want to grow like us, they have to grow like us. Fortunately, children do not need perfection in order to mature. They have within them a vibrant vigorous life force which is on our side. We can make a lot of mistakes—and we all do! —but the child's urge to grow covers up for us. Unless we trample on it and block and squelch it, the whole momentum of development carries youngsters in a reasonably good direction.

We have cause for reassurance, but not for complacency. Our efforts *and* the child's growth carry most youngsters along to a reasonable degree of maturity. However, about 10% of

277

our children will be so seriously hurt in the process that they will have to spend some time in a mental institution. And a much higher per cent—no one knows exactly how high—will be slightly wounded. They will not need hospitalization but they will never feel the peace inside of them that a healthy person should.

We probably never will be able to ward off all ills. We have not been able to wipe out physical illness through innoculations and immunizations and other public health measures. But much of this sickness can be prevented, *and* that which we cannot prevent we can spot early and correct early. Using our knowledge of how a child grows, of what a child needs, of what fosters health and threatens development, we can keep these problems from getting out of hand. Unhappiness—dissatisfaction with one's self, lack of trust in others—is not inevitable.

A STITCH IN TIME

We have learned to work closely with our doctors on physical ills. We take children for frequent check-ups. We have no hesitancy about telephoning when we think something might be wrong. A slight elevation in temperature, a slight loss of appetite, a slight change in energy or skin color—any one of these visible signs is enough to send us to the phone or to the doctor's office for advice. We feel no shame about asking for help. The fact that our child may have "picked up something" is no reflection on our skill as parents. We recognize that the air is full of germs, and that no one is immune.

We must build this same easy acceptance of the need for expert help in the area of behavior. In this world of upheaval it can be just as easy for a child to "pick up something" that can affect his feelings. The air is every bit as full of germs that attack the psychological system as it is full of those that

278

weaken the physical body. All on our own, unaided, not even the best of us can completely protect our children. The wise parent does not attempt to do the whole job of producing good behavior by himself, any more than he attempts to cure all physical ills.

There are experts who can help with behavior, just as there are experts who can help with colds, fevers and broken bones. Anyone who has any doubts about whether his child is acting healthfully—whether he feels right about himself, whether he feels right about other people—ought to check with his doctor. The specialty of the physician is the child's body, but your physician is the best person to begin with. If he finds no physical cause, he can put you in touch with other specialists— psychologists and psychiatrists—who have, as their professional field, the whole realm of behavior.

There is a shortage of such experts in every community. Our country is desperately short of "healers": those who heal the body, as well as those who heal behavior. But the greatest shortage is one of attitude. Today we postpone asking for help, just as we used to postpone going to the dentist. We wait until the tooth hurts—we wait until the child obviously hurts. It makes so much more sense to act on two old adages: *An ounce of prevention is worth a pound of cure,* and *It is better to be safe than sorry.* We never wait until our child is desperately ill to call the doctor. We try to nip the sickness in the bud. This must be our approach with behavior, too.

SIGNS OF TROUBLE

The early signs of distress in children are not too hard to spot. We ought to turn easily for help and advice *whenever a child seems to be acting differently from other children his own age.* The doctor may well say: "There is nothing wrong. This is simply your child's special style, his special way." But

279

the time to check is *whenever your child seems a little out of line with all the others.*

Some of us have had more than one child. Our knowledge of how our other children grew is one guide. All of us see our child in comparison with others, on the street and in the store, in nursery school and kindergarten, in church groups. Whenever you think your child is not acting his age, don't hesitate. Check with your doctor. If you find yourself feeling: "He's acting like a little baby" or "He's acting like a two-year-old" something may be out of kilter. In our world it is a miracle when things go right, not when something is wrong.

A second very simple sign can alert us to the fact that a youngster may be in trouble: *Whenever you feel weighed down by your child's behavior,* check to see if something is wrong. Being a parent is not an easy job. But being a parent should not be so difficult that every day is torture. Every day, to be sure, in every household there are minor upsets: a few tears, a squabble or two. Family life does not take place in Never-Never Land, where all is sweetness and light. Adults and children, children and children, have their fair share of minor battles. But if you think that full-scale war is being waged, don't delay in checking. Something may be wrong.

By and large, youngsters should be fun to live with. By and large, youngsters should be easy to live with. Our feet may be tired, our backs may ache, but the good times should far outweigh the bad! As you look back on a day, you will be able to remember the few crises that you had to solve one way or another. Most of all, you should be able to remember some laughs and a lot of smiles, much good humor, a lot of pleasant and pleasing companionship and solid mutual satisfaction. If you and your child are almost always lined up on opposite sides of the fence, something may well be "rotten in Denmark."

One thing is certain: The time to check is when children

280

are young. The longer youngsters live with their problems, the harder the problems are to solve. We tend to be optimistic. We want to hope that children will "outgrow" their bad behavior. Children do outgrow a lot of it. But they never outgrow deep jealousy or deep fears or deep shyness. They don't outgrow a hunger for love, a hunger for bigness, a hunger for attention. These hungers are like our hunger for food. If we miss a meal, we are emptier when the next mealtime comes around. If we miss the next meal, we are famished. Our hungers don't just disappear. They get worse with each succeeding hour.

An early check-up may bring great peace of mind. Someone who really knows children's behavior may be able to say to you: "Don't worry. The behavior will pass, just give it time. Your child will outgrow the way he is acting." An early check-up may bring you and your child another kind of peace if someone who knows children says: "This youngster looks starved to me. Let's work together to begin filling him up." Either way, you can't go wrong. The only "wrong" thing is to assume blithely that children don't have problems. They do. But we can help them to be solved.

FOR INDEPENDENT STUDY

1. The recent White House Conferences have each produced excellent "chart books" picturing the social trends that especially affect children. One is *Children and Youth: A Graphic Presentation*. Children's Bureau Publication #363 (Washington: Government Printing Office, 1957. 50¢). This brings up-to-date the figures compiled for the mid-century conference. The second book is *Children in a Changing World: A Book of Charts* (Washington: White House Conference on Children and Youth, 1960). The

story of these trends is also told in text in *The Nation's Children: The Family and Social Change*, by Eli Ginzberg, editor (New York: Columbia University Press, 1960).

2. Several inexpensive pamphlets for both parents and teachers are useful when something goes wrong: *Some Special Problems of Children Aged 2-5 Years*, by Nina Ridenour and Isabel Johnson (1947; 30¢); *Teacher Listen: The Children Speak*, by James L. Hymes, Jr. (1949; 25¢); and *Why Children Misbehave*, by Charles Leonard (60¢). All are available from the National Association for Mental Health, New York, N.Y. and probably also from your state, city or county mental health society. One professional book is exceedingly provocative and well worth the time of anyone eager to pursue this area in depth: *The Aggressive Child*, by Fritz Redl and David Wineman (Glencoe, Ill.: Free Press, 1957). This brings together two books under one cover: *Children Who Hate* and *Controls From Within*.

3. Everyone should know the guidance facilities that are available in his own community. Make a survey of your town or city or county. What public child guidance facilities are available, and how long is their waiting list? How many child psychiatrists and psychologists are in private practice? You may be shocked at the scarcity of healing facilities. One way of doing something about the shortage is to join your local association for mental health.

4. Some of our troubles with child rearing could be reduced if boys and girls in high schools had the chance to study children and how they grow and develop. Preparation for good parenthood ought to be one of the "musts" in the general education of all of our youngsters. Find out whether the high school in your community offers any help in this field. If it does, find out whether it offers only a brief unit on child care, whether all the information comes from

books, and whether boys as well as girls have the chance to study children. Sometimes this field gets pegged as "Home Ec" and only girls take it—and very briefly at that. You might also want to look at one of the many excellent books available for use in high schools: *Learning About Children*, by Rebekah M. Shuey, Elizabeth L. Woods and Esther Mason (Philadelphia: Lippincott, 1958).

What would you do?

Question 28 A five-year-old has a temper tantrum almost every time he cannot have his way. With whom do you tend to agree: *a*) Father thinks it is time for someone to lay down the law and make it perfectly clear that the child cannot scream and fuss the way he does. He argues for a good spanking the next time the child blows his top. *b*) Grandfather is rather pleased with the boy's behavior. He takes the temper as a sign that the boy "has some guts" and "stands up for his rights." *c*) Mother isn't too troubled. She is sure the child will outgrow his tantrums when he gets a little older. *d*) A neighbor thinks that the way to handle the situation is to let the child "just cry it out." She suggests that the next time he has a tantrum everyone walk away and leave him and pay no attention whatsoever.

teaching values to children

Chapter 31

Childhood is popularly regarded as a "time of innocence." We like to think that little children do not yet know the cheap ways, the shallow ways, that guide so much of adult behavior. It is true that youngsters are born with open minds. But quite early in the under-six years, for better or worse, taste begins to develop: a taste for the decent, a taste for the gentle, the humane, and the fair, *or* a taste for their unattractive opposites. The teaching of values goes on almost from birth. Young children are busily learning, all of the time, what to think is good and true and beautiful; they are busily learning what to consider bad and false and ugly. The values children learn are more important by far than any facts or skills they acquire, for values determine what we do with our skills and how we use our facts.

The fact that very young children learn values is quite clear in the area of prejudice. By the time children are six, most who are Negro have somehow already learned in a vague way that their skin is black and that black is not as good a color as white. Most white children, by the time they are six, have already been taught that they are white, the "superior" color.

By six most children have an awareness of the religious group to which they belong. They cannot, of course, begin to spell out the doctrinal differences that mark them off from others. They do know, in a dim way, that some groups are considered better than others. They know whether theirs is one of the "good" groups or not. Similarly, children often vaguely know their national origin and whether, in a particular neighborhood, theirs is a "good" national origin or one not so good.

Young children are not "the innocents." They are well on their way toward carrying within them feelings of false self-esteem or of false and needless self-hate. They have been taught what to value—or, at least, a "good" beginning has been made.

EXPERIENCE IS THE BEST TEACHER

Few of us set out to teach prejudice. In the under-six years we do often try to teach some of the real virtues of life. Unfortunately, we usually try to teach children their morals verbally. Young children's books that carry some lofty message are almost sure to be best-sellers. The moral of the story —manners are nice; honesty is the best policy; be kind to dumb animals—catches the adult's eye. The moral is less apt to catch the child's eye and very unlikely to influence his behavior. Morality cannot be built by words alone. Young children are not verbal enough themselves to be greatly impressed by what we say. If our timing is just right, capping and reinforcing some incident in the child's life, our words make a dent. Most of the time, however, our "talky" instruction and our general exhortations have little power to build character, to affect feelings, to establish values, to determine behavior.

Nor can morality be taught in some separate place or only on some one day. Children are learning what to prize and how to act on Monday, Tuesday, Wednesday, Thursday, Friday, Saturday, Sunday—and in kitchen, living room and bath. The lessons that become a part of the child are those that occur and reoccur, over and over and over again.

Children learn much more from what *we* do than from what we say. They pick up their prejudices—in race relations, in all human relations, in art, in music—from all the living that surrounds them. "Little pitchers have big ears," and those ears (and eyes and pores) absorb the values of the home. Children soak up our ways of acting and feeling, just as they soak up our fears and the speech in the air that they breathe.

Children learn much more from what *they* do than what we say. The lessons that cut deepest are not those that strike their ear drums. The lessons to worry about or feel good about are those which children practice with their muscles. Youngsters learn the life they live—the life that surrounds them and their own daily deeds.

It is scary to realize how early in life basic values begin to be formed. It should scare us! Everyone who is a parent or a teacher is under a tremendous obligation to confront children with the best—the fairest, the most decent—way in which to live. We cannot sell children a bill of goods that we ourselves have not bought. The first job is not to get them to be "good." *We* have to be "good"—then we have it made. Our doing must come first. This is what children remember. They are learning even when we have no notion at all that we are teaching.

286

Some Very Dubious Lessons

Unthinkingly, we sometimes teach quite bad lessons. Many a child under six, for example, is openly exposed to bribery and payola. We buy our way out of our difficulties with him. The child gets very explicit lessons in the overriding power of money in our society. He is paid off, if not in cold cash, with other kinds of bribes. "Eat your cereal, and you will see the pretty picture at the bottom of the bowl." "Be a good boy, and I will bring you back a present." "Stop causing all the trouble you are causing, and I will buy you some gum." Youngsters begin to learn a very low morality, a far cry from discovering that virtue is its own reward.

Children have many direct experiences in learning that might makes right. Unthinkingly again, we are the villains. Sometimes we even spank a child and say, while we spank: "I'll teach you not to hit other people!" More often, we simply throw our weight around. We are bigger and we have the upper hand. The child has to do what we want him to do, willy-nilly. He is yanked and hauled, with no consideration for his side of the story. The child bows, not to law or to any inherent justice; he bows to superior force, and stores up inside of him a lesson he can use later when he is the bigger one.

Not infrequently, *we* bow and give in to a show of strength. Tears may be a child's big guns. Or we retreat because of his threats and verbal assaults: "I hate you. You're the worst mommy in the world." Quite young, some children learn that they can cajole or wear down the opposition. Children harp and plead and storm, alternating between appeals and complaints, until we surrender to keep some peace in the family. Law does not carry the day. Appeasement does. The lessons of their daily life say to some children: There is always a way

287

out. There is always someone you can reach. Everyone has his price.

We have to develop very critical ears to hear ourselves as children hear us. We need very critical eyes to see ourselves as children see us. The nursery school teacher, for example, says: "We don't throw sand. We don't push. We wait for our turn." Listen, and this sounds like a good lesson in conformity. When in Rome, do as the Romans do—because the Romans do it. It sounds like the kind of lesson that led the German people to go along with the extremes of the Nazis: "We don't like the Jews." Is this the lesson that we really want to teach? The good lesson is a very simple one: Sand in the eye hurts; pushing is dangerous; shoving in ahead isn't fair. Unless we think carefully, we teach very bad by-products that ride along on our words and deeds.

We are putting more and more emphasis on school grades. Today some parents even want report cards on their kindergarten children! What are we teaching through this great emphasis on grades and through the two-dollar bills we give children for their A's? Learn so you can get an A, or learn to love learning? And which lesson do we really want to get over? Off-handedly at home, without thinking, we say that "we jewed him down on the price" or that "the nigger in the parking lot took care of my car" or that "the wop who runs the shoe store fixed my heel." Are these the overtones that we want children to hear?

In kindergartens and in other grades in school, how do we want our children to stand and to walk? At ease and quite informally, or lined up, two by two, in lock step and quiet? Which is the American way? How much freedom of choice do we want our children to experience? Should they all do the same thing at the same time or should there be room for the "minority of one"? Should children have the right to change

288

their mind, or must they always stick at what they have started until they are through? Which is the American way?

GOOD FEELINGS LEAD TO GOOD VALUES

It is frightening to realize how early in life values begin to be learned. This early start has its reassuring side, too. We must be sure not to miss it. For one thing, the fact that children start early and learn through deeds—what we do, what they do—means that in the long run they will probably have about the same values and ideals and standards that we have. We all have our faults. Our children are bound to have many of them. But we have our virtues, too. Inevitably our children will pick up some of those. We are not angels, but we are not devils either.

Once you have a child you take on a new obligation to live as decently as you can, all of the time. But we each can have confidence that what we give to our children, as we are when we are our honest selves, is not too bad. We mustn't become stilted and scared lest we do the wrong thing. Children need humans, not teaching machines. We can be less than perfect. At the same time, because we have children, we can try to grow and improve.

An early start means a long life ahead. Attitudes begin to be formed early but this does not mean that they are set, once and for all. Fortunately for all of us, in a child's long life, many people play a part. We each backstop the other. At home, mother's virtues supplement father's. No one of us has to be perfection, neatly packaged all in one. Increasingly, children begin to learn from each other. If they are fortunate enough to have teachers they really like, they identify with them as well as with other adults outside the home. Learning values goes on all through life. The learning doesn't begin

289

after six ("when children are old enough to understand"), but the job isn't over and done with by year six, either.

This time-perspective can be reassuring to us. We must apply it to our children, too. Often, as a part of their natural growth, youngsters say words that do not represent the point at which we want them to stop in their growth. Two four-year-olds are playing, for example, and a third child wants to join them. "Go away. You're a Catholic. You can't play with us!" If you forget how the years stretch out ahead, you can easily take children's words too seriously. With some time-perspective you can relax and ask yourself: Is this really prejudice? Or simply a four-year-old testing out the power of words, as all four-year-olds do? (Especially when the poor excluded child isn't Catholic!)

Quite normally, children are more clannish and cliqueish at times than we want them ultimately to be. Their social development at the moment will not let them be otherwise. Children may be rougher on animals and pets than we want them ultimately to be. Their curiosity and impulsiveness and bad coordination will not let them be otherwise. At any one time they may love the comics more than we wish they would. Or, later, be more in love with rock-and-roll than with "good" music.

A time-perspective lets you not only hear the words a child says—it lets you see the child who is saying them. It lets you bring a little sense of humor and a little tolerance to what the child does because you understand where he is now in his growth. The clear melody, pounding rhythm, and deadly repetition of the T.V. commercial jingle may be right for him now. The child won't stay pegged at this level of musical taste, unless that is all the music you know, too. He won't stay with the comics forever, unless that is all the reading you do. He won't use words to hurt, unless that is your style.

In teaching values (or reading or discipline or sex or any-

290

thing!), what counts most is keeping open the channels for growth. The child whose own needs are met stays free to learn. The child who has respect for himself is always in a position to respect others eventually. The child who has a satisfying sense of his own bigness carries within him no need to rise up over the dead bodies of others.

The child who feels unloved and unsure, who is not sold on his own worth, is the child who cannot learn. He will not be able to use well the years that stretch out ahead. He will always be pulled back to the empty years of his own childhood. Such a child may well have to hate, and have to hurt, and have to fight what decent people want. Irrationally and emotionally, he will respond not to lessons he sees all around but to his dissatisfied feelings within.

We must create the best world we can for our children—in our living rooms and classrooms and communities. But most important of all: We must be sure children stay free to grow and free to learn. We can help children get off to a good start in learning sound values in the years under six, not by what we say to them, but through how we live with them and let them live. If we treat young children decently, they will go on after six continuing to learn as they grow, and to grow as they learn.

FOR INDEPENDENT STUDY

1. A *Primer For Parents: Educating Our Children For Good Human Relations*, by Mary Ellen Goodman (New York: Anti-Defamation League of B'nai B'rith, 1959. 40¢), *Prejudice And Your Child*, by Kenneth Clark (Boston: Beacon Press, 1955), and *Race Awareness in Young Children*, by Mary Ellen Goodman (Cambridge: Addison-Wesley, 1952), are well worth reading at this time. Covering a broader area of values, *Consider The Children—How They*

Grow, by E. Manwell and Sophia Fahs (Boston: Beacon Press, 1951) is also highly pertinent. *And* if by any chance you do not know the stunning collection of photos brought together by the Museum of Modern Art under the leadership of Edward Steichen, *The Family of Man,* (New York: Simon and Schuster, 1955) this chapter gives you a wonderful excuse to give yourself a thrill. The book is also available in a paperback edition, published by Maco, New York, 1955. $1.00.

What would you do?

Question 29 A girl who is not yet five shows a great interest in reading. She sits with books and tries to figure out words. She is always asking her mother to tell her words she does not know. When you ride with her in a car she can tell you almost every traffic sign along the way. With whom do you tend to side: *a*) Father thinks they should try to get the girl into first grade and skip kindergarten. *b*) Mother doesn't want to do anything special, except to see that the girl has lots of books and, of course, to answer all her questions whenever she asks them. *c*) Grandfather is troubled about such early reading. He thinks the parents ought to insist that the girl play more with other children, be outdoors as much as possible, and stay away from books. *d*) Grandmother is sure that if a child starts to read so early she will be out of step all through school. She hopes the parents will divert the girl from reading and get her interested in other things.

on to years six, seven and eight

Chapter 32

This book draws to a close now that the child is approaching his sixth birthday. A book has to end somewhere but, frankly, the end of year five is a bad stopping point!

It is true that we act as if the beginning of year six were a major dividing line. Presumably the child under six is one kind of child; six-year-olds and older are another kind. Under six they are simply "pre-schoolers." When they are six, we draw a deep breath—*They are school-age!*—and life suddenly takes on a more serious cast. This sharp division does not square with the facts of growth and development.

There is a purely artificial, man-made fence between Fives and Sixes: Sixes go to "first grade." Actually, some children are starting "fifth grade" when they are six. They went to their first grade at age two; their second grade at age three; their third grade at age four; their fourth grade at age five. Now that they are six they move ahead into one more year of their schooling. The so-called "first grade" is not a super-special year, not one that ought to differ markedly from any year that has gone before. Year six is one more year of school, just as year six is one more year of life.

HISTORICAL RATHER THAN PSYCHOLOGICAL FACTS

The abrupt transition that we generally make between school and the "pre-school" days stems from factors in our history, rather than from our knowledge of children. The cleavage began in the "pre-scientific" days before there was any serious study of children, and before we had much basis for knowing what helps children and what hurts them. It goes back to a time when only a small handful of youngsters went to school at all: the children of the wealthy, the privileged, professional people, and intellectually ambitious parents— children who showed through their behavior that they were ready for formal schooling.

The cleavage goes back to the time when schooling was thought of in a very narrow and limited way. School taught the "Three R's"—nothing else! In those days we knew so much less about the whole integration of human functioning. We simply were not aware of the constant merging within the human of the physical, intellectual, social and emotional components. In addition, on the one hand, life was simpler; there were fewer demands on the citizen; one had to know much less in order to live. On the other hand, life outside of school was much more instructive. Children got a real education working beside their parents, learning the basic skills of hunting, fishing, sewing, cooking, of farming and of a trade, and by being a part of a busy family.

Today's living is vastly different; our knowledge of how to produce a healthy human is vastly greater. Yet we carry along with us, in the knapsack of traditional practice, the old notion

294

that there is a sharp dividing line between school-age and pre-school children. Actually, without our realizing it, we have modified and worsened the old tradition. We identify "school age" today with age six. Originally, under the special conditions described above, many a child was seven or eight before he went to his first grade to begin formal schooling. For one thing there were not as many schools; going to school meant traveling some distance (and not by school bus!). Fewer laws governed school attendance and those laws were not vigorously enforced.

This older age for beginning formal school work is reflected in the laws that are still on the books today. Nowhere in America is there any law which requires children to go to school at age six! Almost all of our six-year-olds do. Most parents assume they must. But compulsory education does not begin anywhere until age seven. In some states it is not compulsory for a child to go until he is eight. In practice we have lowered our school entrance age. Unfortunately we have not modified our notion of what first grade should be like.

There is a lot of evidence that even the special handful who once were the only ones to go to school were not thrilled by their schools' strict and formal and "sitting" ways. The freer, more open, more rugged life of those early days must have been a major therapeutic force equalizing life for those children. But today, first grades are dealing with younger children and they take everyone's child—not only the child from a privileged home or the occasional youngster who shows some unusual academic gift or is a fast grower. Our program in first grades tends to be as "Three-R-centered" as ever—and some people seem to want it to become more so!

Americans tend to think that European schools are tougher, with higher standards, and that they demand more of their youngsters. We worry about the American school and wonder

295

if it somehow is "soft." Comparisons are always difficult. Many European countries, for example, are more stiff and formal than we are, and are trying to produce a somewhat different kind of citizen. And many European countries are highly critical of their own schools; they look at what we do admiringly and criticize themselves for being insensitive and behind the times in their understanding of children.

It is worth noting, however, that at least some British schools and some schools in other European countries begin formal education more gradually than we do and are actually more sensitive than we are to what Sixes and Sevens are like. The English have their so-called "infant schools." The term sounds strange because we use the word "infant" in a different sense. The infant schools in England cover what we would call nursery, kindergarten and primary education. They are less apt to have an artificial break at age six, suddenly demanding more sitting, verbalization, and symbolic learning from children. The dividing line comes more frequently after infant school—at age seven and more commonly at age eight. In other European countries the counterparts of our public schools also tend to begin their formal emphasis on the Three R's at seven or eight, rather than at the stroke of six. This time schedule ties in better with how children develop. Six is not a good dividing line for most children.

Asking the Right Question

The question, of course, is not: When are children old enough to go to school? You can answer that question flatly: *Most children are ready for school at age three.* Certainly almost all are ready by age four. Very close to 100% are ready for school by age five. The question is: What kind of a school will children go to, when they are ready? A three-year-old can do beautifully in a school that is geared to three-year-olds. A six-year-old can be miserable in a school geared to eight-year-olds.

Neither is the question: Can children sit at age six? Or can they keep quiet at age six? Or can they work in workbooks at age six? Or can they begin to learn to read? Children are malleable. If we start much, much too early the answer becomes a flat *no*. There is some age when, no matter how much pressure we apply, the achievement demanded is utterly beyond the child's capacity, but we seldom miss the mark that completely. The usual child in a sitting-reading first grade can, with a struggle and by paying a price, do what is expected of him, or at least a part of it. The real question is: What does this sharp cleavage and abrupt dividing line in the experiences of children do to the children themselves? We have to look not only at what happens to the learning but at what happens to the child! Many first grades with "tough" standards fail as many as 25% of their children; the demands are simply beyond these youngsters. But how the "successful" 75% learn to feel about themselves, about people, about learning and about life should also concern us.

America is in a rush. Our country is always in a hurry about everything. Through the years we have pushed children to begin school younger and younger. This could be an exciting development *if*, along with it, we were willing to fit our schools to the children who actually came. We have seldom been this smart or sensitive. Younger children come to school but to the same old school—geared as it was originally, for the few, for older children, for very special and limited goals.

Most communities let their children enter first grade if they will be six by October or November or December or by January 1. Some communities let children enter first grade if they are five years and four months old in September. All these children are ready for school—there is no question about that. But is their school ready for them? That is the big question.

THE SIMILARITIES ARE MUCH GREATER
THAN THE DIFFERENCES

Sixes are almost identical with five-year-olds. They show only one obvious, clear-cut, special new characteristic. Around six, children start to lose their front baby teeth! From the standpoint of how we treat these children, this difference is completely inconsequential. It couldn't matter less!

Six-year-olds are every bit as active as five-year-olds. They are very wrapped up, as under-six children are, in developing mastery of their bodies. Perfecting skills of climbing, running, riding, balancing, of using their hands and fingers, matters just as much to Sixes as it does to three-, four- and five-year-olds. But don't peg this concern as "physical education" or relegate it to a fifteen-minute recess time. Body mastery is how all these children build their pictures of themselves as able, competent people: *big* people. A sense of autonomy is of fundamental importance now, just as it was when the children were younger.

We often say to six-year-olds: "Oh! You're big now! You're going to school." These children want desperately to feel big. Whether they get a full dose of this healthy feeling depends on the help their school gives them, not on our cheery words. In the crucial area of body mastery, many first and second graders have only a recess time—and no challenging equipment with which to test and expand their skills. Too often they have only a bare and barren playground where they can race around and "let off steam." Six- and seven-year-olds do let off steam in recess time but they would have less need for safety valves if, throughout the whole day, we recognized what these children are like and put less pressure on them.

Six-year-olds are every bit as full of make-believe as they were at three or four or five. They do not suddenly become

298

old sobersides on their sixth birthday. Watch them, once school is out. Instantaneously, wholeheartedly, they *play*. On their own they never play the games which call for choosing sides, or following the other fellows' rules, or games with a winner and a loser. They play with their own games of make-believe. For sturdy emotional and intellectual growth, these children still need a full chance to pretend. We don't help them as much as we could when we push this most important business of their lives off into the after-school hours.

The dramatic play of older Fives, Sixes, Sevens, Eights differs from the dramatic play of Threes, Fours, Fives. The older the child the more he wants realistic props: an iron that really heats, a doll that really wets, a gun that looks like a real gun and that makes a noise when it shoots, real cowboy boots and a real steering wheel. Only the props change, however. The underlying nature of the play and what play does for the child stay exactly the same.

Six-year-olds are as social as they ever were. They are still at the sheer beginning of their lifelong task of living with people and living with themselves. They are just starting to find some answers to the difficult questions of getting into a group, holding their own, being a follower, being a leader, sharing, waiting, giving and getting, using words instead of feet and fists. Some people assume that "social adjustment" is a simple task that kindergarten can take care of. This assumption is clearly wrong. Over-six children need ample time for social experimentation. They need time to practice their ways of getting along. Unfortunately, in many first grades, each child lives in the lonely island of his separate seat and desk. Even whispering is a crime! We turn children into isolationists when all of their urges are to work with others.

Six-, seven- and eight-year-olds love and need to talk together. They need to plan together seriously but they also need to giggle and rough-house a bit. They need to find a

299

friend or two. They need to work with those friends. Over-six children have fewer conflicts and are much more verbal than when they were younger. They need practice times to test out how words can solve problems and give direction to events.

As their bodies lengthen out and as they lose their baby teeth, these children take on a somewhat older look. They are as tender as ever inside, however. They somehow seem to sense that they are moving toward the end of the world of childhood, coming close to the edge. These youngsters want —as much as Threes did and Fours, sometimes even more— the reassurance that the big people around them are still friendly, still gentle and warm, ready to be helpful when they are needed.

Second graders write much more easily than first graders. Sevens are the love letter specialists. Their teachers receive real *billet-douxs*: "Dear Miss Smith: I love you." This is the giveaway to how *all* the children in this age range feel. They are ready to fall in love with their teachers and they hope their teachers will love them. The teacher of Sixes, Sevens, Eights —and parents too—must have a gentle touch, a soft way.

A class size that is not much larger than twenty is still important. These children are not yet the lecture-hall type. Small class size makes it possible for the teacher to prove her warmth, and to give these children a lot of individual attention. Compared to when they were one-year-olds, "school-age" children are amazingly skilled. Yet deep inside of themselves they know the truth; they are still relatively helpless! They are still dependent children. The time is coming—at year eight or nine or ten—when they will feel quite cocky, certain they can go it alone. They then will act as if they want none of us. Now they need to know we are around, and friendly and willing to help. They still want, at times, to slip their hand in ours.

On to Years Six, Seven and Eight

More Intellectual Drive—Yet the Same

Just as they did when they were younger, these children love to hear stories from books. Hardly any activity is more pleasurable. They have a slowly developing interest in reading for themselves, and in writing, and in mastering the symbols of quantity. But the interest in verbalism and symbolism is only a beginning bud in the child—a far cry from all of him! An absorption with words and word pictures seldom begins to blossom with any rich fullness until children are more nearly seven in their growing—not when they are barely six.

These youngsters are still egocentric. What *they* do is the most important thing in the world—what *they* see, what *they* hear, what goes on before *their* two eyes. No less than under-six children, Sixes and Sevens and Eights do their best learning from firsthand observation and personal participation and experimentation. Things make most sense when these children can see them close up—not at long range or vicariously —and when they can touch them, smell them, climb up and in and on them.

They are curious, just as they have been curious from birth. Facts fascinate them. These children are not content when their minds are idle, any more than they feel right when their bodies are still. They are thirsting to learn about the world. And an inviting world is at their doorstep. Their minds are beginning to range more and more but they are still here-and-now creatures, stirred most vividly by the life right around them. Airports, the railroad station, the river with its boats, the markets and produce terminals, farms and factories, printing shops, the firehouse and police station and post office—the whole life of our communities—could educate these children in science, in the social studies, *and* in reading, too.

301

To truly learn, these children must see the inner workings for themselves. They must get out on that doorstep, not stay locked inside the school. They really use their brains when they are "Johnny-on-the-spot." Without firsthand experiences, they become verbal but never *knowing* children. The greatest vice of our feverish efforts to teach reading early is that these beginning years in school become intellectually sterile years. No moving new ideas flow in: no vivid images, no concrete pictures, no deeply personal experiences.

Every Five carries within him much of what he was like when he was four and three and two. Every Five takes a plunge ahead now and again; an experimental venture into what he will become. So, too, every Six and Seven and Eight carries within him his five-ness and four-ness and his three-ish qualities. Our children will grow with more solid contentment —they will grow with strength and into greater effectiveness —if we can shake off the notion that birthdays make a big difference.

One day merges into the next, and brings with it the day just past. At no point in development are there sudden cliffs, sudden drop-offs, sudden changes. Certainly not at age six! Our ways of living with children must jibe with the gradual-ism of growth. We must let our children grow into their maturity, somehow curbing our impatience to shove them along. There are no shortcuts. A child can only skip being five or skip being six by carrying within him an emptiness that does no good.

FOR INDEPENDENT STUDY

1. Many excellent books carry their descriptions of children on into the over-six years. The two very well-known books by Dr. Arnold Gesell and Dr. Frances Ilg, *Infant and Child in the Culture of Today* and *The Child from Five to Ten*

are available between one set of covers: *Child Development* (New York: Harper, 1949). An excellent book, written by authors who know young children very well and who carry their sensitivity on into the later years, is *Childhood and Adolescence*, by L. Joseph Stone and Joseph Church (New York: Random House, 1957). Another very good book is *Behavior and Development From 5 to 12*, by Glenn R. Hawkes and Damaris Pease (New York: Harper and Row, 1962).

2. A book, primarily for teachers, which stresses the continuity in schooling from kindergarten through the primary years is *Those First School Years*, a publication of the Department of Elementary School Principals (Washington: National Education Association, 1960). Parents and teachers will be interested in comparing this book with a similar book originally published in England: *Learning and Teaching in the Infants' School*, by E. G. Hume (New York: Longmans' Green, 1952. rev. ed.).

3. Be sure to observe some six-, seven- or eight-year-olds at play—not on a school playground under an adult's supervision, but playing on their own: out of school, on Saturdays or holidays. Look for the similarities between what these older children do and how three-, four- and five-year-olds play. You will, of course, see differences, too. As you watch children going their natural gait, think about their usual school experiences and compare the two settings.

What would you do?

Question 30 A young three-year-old in the bathroom in nursery school suddenly discovers how to flush the toilet all by himself. He flushes it three and four times, even though there is nothing in the bowl to flush. What is your inclination: *a*) Let him. What's the harm? *b*) Stop him. What is a school for if not to teach him? Be very specific: Once is enough! *c*) Tell him that once is enough but if he wants to go on flushing the toilet, don't make an issue of it. Let him do it, if he wants to. *d*) Lead him gently but firmly away from the bowl and the next time be on your toes. *You* flush the toilet so this kind of incident doesn't arise.

the larger family of the child

Chapter 33

During the whole span of the early childhood years one dominant and enduring characteristic of children is their dependence. At two, at eight, youngsters must look to their parents for protection. They must look to them for practical help in doing all the things they cannot yet do for themselves.

The parents of young children are themselves dependent, however. No mother and father, alone and unaided, can provide all that a child needs. Just as the youngster turns time after time plaintively to mother or father to say: "Fix it, please," so the immediate family must turn to the larger family —the community, the state, the nation—for services and support.

If the young child is ignored by his mother and father, or neglected, or turned loose with too little help and protection, he is sure to be harmed. Just as certainly, if the mother and father are given inadequate aid by all the rest of us, the child is sure to be harmed. A child needs *two* good families. He

305

needs loving parents, willing and generous parents, thoughtful parents, responsive parents—a mother and father glad to make the adjustments that the young child's immaturity demands. But the young child also needs a larger family—equally pleased and proud of its children, equally concerned, equally willing to invest itself in their well-being.

The great benefits that come to children when the community and the state and the nation are "good parents" are dramatically demonstrated in the field of health. In one brief twenty-year span, 1930-1950, we reduced infant mortality from 64.6 to 29.2 per 1,000 live births. The number of reported cases of smallpox dropped from 102,000 in 1920 to only four in 1953. The reported incidence of whooping cough decreased from over 160 cases per 100,000 in the population in the 1930's to 18.6 in 1958. Diphtheria hit more than 140 per 100,000 in the 1920's; in 1958 the incidence was 0.5 per 100,000!

In very recent years, when retrolental fibroplasia was blinding youngsters, the larger family of the child mobilized its resources and stuck at the problem until it uncovered the cause: the excess of oxygen being supplied to premature children. When large numbers of babies were being born with defective limbs the protective services of the larger family went into action to dig out and expose the source of the trouble: the drug thalidomide taken by mothers during the early months of pregnancy.

No individual family, no mother or father alone could bring these advances to childhood. Only the larger family—spending money, spending time, pooling skills, doing research, enacting legislation—could act effectively on children's behalf.

In the field of physical health the efforts of the larger family go on. One cause of mental retardation—phenylketonuria—has recently been identified, and the means for early diagnosis and for preventing damage have been developed. So, too, with another genetic cause of retardation, galactosemia. There are well publicized successes—the development of protection against poliomyelitis, as one example. There are more obscure but significant successes—the enactment of legislation about the doors of refrigerators to lessen the danger that young children, playing, will be locked inside.

Jobs remain to be done. The death rates for babies less than three days old have hardly dropped at all in the past two decades. The hazards of premature birth remain high; in 1957 premature birth was an underlying cause in 43.9% of all deaths of infants under one year of age. Little progress has been made in coping with cancer, the second most important cause of death among children after the age of four. But the larger family of the child is at work, *in health*. The average life expectancy of a child born in 1958 was almost 70 years, contrasted with the less-than-50-year average for the child born in 1900. This great gift of twenty years of life symbolizes the good that can come when the larger family extends its helping hand to the immediate family.

Unfortunately, in many other areas of life the larger family does not back up the immediate family of the child with this same strength and concern and support. There are glaring gaps where we leave parents too much on their own, expecting them to cope by themselves with their problems. Children pay a price for this neglect by their larger family.

No Preparation for Parenthood

The absence of preparation for parenthood is an example of neglect. Raising children can be the most satisfying and rewarding aspect of adult life. Yet almost everyone takes on the challenge of parenthood as a rank amateur. And almost everyone fumbles and stumbles with the job, learning what he can as he goes along. We give parents almost no helping

307

hand in advance. We turn young people loose to work out, hit or miss, whatever approaches they can.

Unprepared, with little know-how, too many parents worry needlessly about healthy, normal and even very promising responses on their child's part. Anxiety takes the place of pride and pleasure.

Unprepared, too many parents are blind to beginning signs of trouble. They settle, usually with a bothered unhappiness, for less satisfactory performance than their child could achieve. Because they are unprepared, some parents give too little guidance and direction. Too many others slap their children needlessly. They spank their children needlessly. They yell at their children and nag their children needlessly, fruitlessly—and harmfully.

The larger family of the child could make preparation for parenthood a fundamental part of all secondary education. We could insist that every high school in America have a major program—not a minor or an elective, not an occasional unit, not for girls alone—concentrating on building the skills and understanding needed for living happily with that complex creature, the human child.

We now offer a little help. The federal government distributed 1,629,313 copies of the Children's Bureau book, *Infant Care*, during 1960. Some state and local departments of health distribute other valuable booklets and pamphlets. But we—through our federal government and through our state governments and through our public school systems—are not doing enough to prepare young men and women for the most significant job they will undertake in their lives.

Nor is advance preparation the only help mothers and fathers need. Even with the best possible start, problems in living with young children are bound to arise. But parents have much too little "in-service education" and much too little friendly and supporting supervision.

The road through early childhood covers a tricky and troublesome terrain. The child must move from complete dependence toward growing independence. He must move from complete egocentricity toward a growing social concern, and from instant gratification toward a growing capacity for postponement and control. He must move from his world of imagination to everyone's world of reality. Under the best of conditions these are mountainous assignments, and few families today work "under the best of conditions."

The great mobility of our population is one handicap. Many young mothers and fathers are raising their children in new communities, separated from the "old hands," grandparents, who in other years would have been available for counsel. In the new suburbs, the blind often are leading the blind. Decisions about child rearing stem not from inner conviction but from peeking over one's shoulder to see what the neighbors are doing.

Upward social mobility can be an added complication. Life in the suburbs can be subtly yet intensely competitive. The child unwittingly may be the family's Buick or Oldsmobile, its Thunderbird or Cadillac or even its 1957 Chevrolet. It can be exceedingly hard for families alone to keep a level head and to make wise decisions in a highly competitive climate.

The recent trend toward early marriages presents still another complexity. Many young parents are trying to help their children through the developmental tasks of early childhood while they themselves are still confronting some of the unfinished tasks of their own growing up. The young child's natural "no" can be taken as a direct personal confrontation by the young father who is not solidly sure of his own independence. The young child's natural clinging can be distasteful and frightening to the young mother still seeking her own satisfactions.

Parents are tremendously interested in their children,

309

deeply motivated to do a good job. Young married America talks constantly about its children but it talks to itself—over the fence, over the bridge table, over the dinner table, at the shopping center. The larger family of the child lets these young parents down by providing only an echo chamber for the talk. There is almost no helpful feedback.

The larger family of the child could and should provide a network of consultation services. We need many more family service centers where parents could comfortably check on their experiences and check their reactions, and find a listening ear more skilled than that of the "lady next door." We need countless more child guidance clinics, especially centers concerned with the "little" problems of early childhood. Where clinics do exist today their waiting lists are interminable. And their focus has to be on the almost unsolvable problems that have grown so severe that they now trouble the community, after years of having troubled the family alone and the child alone.

Parents whose children differ especially need supporting consultation: the parents of the retarded child, of the cerebral palsied child and the crippled child, the parents of the young child with a vision or hearing loss or with a speech defect. But all parents at times need some perspective, some encouragement, a point of view to challenge and enlarge their own, occasionally a sound practical down-to-earth suggestion. The larger family is stingy with this kind of help.

MORE THAN CONSULTATION

Many parents need concrete services that go beyond consultation. The three million and more mothers-of-children-under-six who work need a dramatic increase in Aid to Dependent Children. They need publicly aided child care centers. They need the protection of laws to insure the quality of foster day homes and of private child care centers. They need efficient enforcement of these laws.

Most of these three million mothers work because their life is already complicated. They have faced some nasty problem: death or illness in their family, divorce or separation or desertion, and poverty. They work as a partial solution to one difficulty but, without a stronger helping hand from the larger family, their work often only opens the door to more troubles.

We now do so little for working mothers: a small deduction on income tax for child care expenses, a few state and local laws but usually with feeble enforcement, only a very few public child-care centers and only a few good programs sponsored by churches and by charitable organizations. We act as if working and raising children was a simple problem, on a par with other routine minor complications of life. We forget the extent of the problem, the severity of the problem.

The larger family of the child forgets that mass poverty still exists in America, too. One recent report estimates that between forty and fifty million Americans, about one-fourth of us, are living in poverty. Another study estimates that 77,000,-000—almost one half of us—live in poverty or "deprivation," a level of existence slightly better than being abysmally poor.

Many of our aged are included in these figures; many who are not responsible for children. But these figures also stand for young boys and girls: children in city slums, in rural slums, children of migratory workers, children of unskilled and unorganized urban workers, the children of the unemployed. Some parents puzzle over which creative toy to buy for their child. Millions of other parents are desperately worried about rats and cockroaches, about a roof over their heads, food on the table, running water, a little heat, some warm clothing.

To do its job, a child's family must be surrounded by a live and vigorous economy. When the productive life of a society is sluggish or stagnant, families are let down. The home—it is so easy to sing sweet songs about the home!—can become an intolerable place for children. Youngsters breathe despair and inherit their parents' poverty. This is the fate of millions of children today.

The High Cost of Children

The solution is not easy to see. But one inescapable fact is clear: The solution, the many approaches to solutions, will cost money. Our unique mixture of private enterprise and government spending has produced an amazing standard of living for some of us, unparalleled in its comfort and ease. But it has not been able to provide a decent life for all of us. Some form of massive governmental aid is surely needed if massive poverty is to be ended. The rest of us—the one-half who do not live in poverty and deprivation—must sacrifice some of our luxuries if the millions of children in "the other America" are to have a fair chance at life.

We now feel burdened by taxes. We must recognize that this is not because we are splurging on services for children. We are actually starving most such services. Some children early become the direct responsibility of the community. These children are orphaned; they are abandoned; their own parents are unable to care for them. The publicly supported institutions which become the "parents" of these children are always short of money. We will not tax ourselves enough or give enough through charity to provide adequate staffs or to pay the staffs decently. Children are trapped in these institutions, staying far too long, because we will not provide the money for enough good foster homes.

We have almost no publicly supported nursery schools because we are not willing to tax ourselves for them.

Less than 50% of our five-year-olds have public kindergartens to go to for the same reason. Far too many of our kindergartens operate only on half-shifts and are over-crowded for the same simple reason: We do not want to spend more public money.

The blunt fact is: Children cost money. This is the truest single generalization about all ages—children under six, children over six: *They are expensive!* Individual mothers and fathers know this well, but the larger family of the child has yet to face up to this fact. We have to learn to like spending tax money on the common good and the common welfare. We have to learn to feel pleased and rewarded by public expenditures, just as many well-to-do parents feel pleased with spending money on their own child. But each child is to a real extent the child of all of us.

CHANGES IN ATTITUTE

This sense of all-encompassing concern must be especially extended to America's non-white families and children. Non-white families face the greater poverty. In 1957, the median family income for the United States as a whole was $4,971; for the non-white family the median income was $2,764. Non-white families face the greater health hazards. In 1957 the infant mortality rate for white infants was 23.3 per 1,000 live births; it was 43.7 for non-white infants. In 1954 the maternal mortality rate for non-white mothers was about 15 per 10,000 live births; it was slightly under 4 per 10,000 live births for white mothers.

Non-white mothers are often working mothers, hurt by the absence of good child-care facilities. Their children's schooling is less adequate and, as the children mature, job opportunities for them will be more limited. Every white family ought to look with awe and respect at every non-white family that succeeds, in the face of obstacles such as these, in raising good and healthy children.

313

Within the individual family the non-white mother and father may be every bit as skilled and as understanding as anyone else, but the white family with its white child gets the fuller support from the rest of us. The white child is more apt to have the two families he needs. Until we accept that white is not necessarily God's favorite color, we will continue to make it harder for many of our children to grow up sturdily and to achieve their potential.

One other change in attitude is urgent. The essential need for change stems from the fact that we have finally created the perfectly unprejudiced instrument: total war. The threat of war today touches all children: white and non-white, the children of the poor and of the well-to-do, urban children and rural children, America's children and the world's children. We must make sure that this blindly universal destroyer is never put to use.

This may be the hardest task that the larger family has to undertake. It certainly calls for patience. It calls for daring innovation in new political organization. It calls for the highest creativity in devising effective machinery for the settlement of disputes. It may well call for vast investments of money to create peace. But the initial and fundamental change must be a change of attitude—a commitment that there can no longer be a resort to force. There has to be a new and consuming determination to insure that there will be a tomorrow for children.

The years under six should be years of satisfaction and contentment. Important as these years are, however, they should be just the beginning. A child has a right to a future. That right is uniquely in jeopardy today. Individual mothers and fathers alone cannot guarantee it. Together all of us—parents and non-parents, the larger family of the child—may succeed if we face up to the urgency of the task. And if we don't, all our other efforts for children can only fail.

314

FOR INDEPENDENT STUDY

1. A good film which symbolizes the needed protective efforts of the larger family of the child is *PKU: Preventable Mental Retardation*. This fifteen minute color film, usually available from state departments of health, shows the exciting results of early diagnosis and dietary treatment of phenylketonuria. It is useful too for its excellent contrast of normal and retarded development.

2. Two recent books may trouble you but serve as very useful prods to your conscience and awaken you to the plight of the disadvantaged in our American society: *The Other America: Poverty In the United States*, by Michael Harrington (New York: Macmillan, 1962), a very readable and moving report packed with disturbing statistics, and *The Fire Next Time*, by James Baldwin (New York: Dial Press, 1963), two personal essays.

3. The National Committee for the Day Care of Children, 44 E. 23 Street, New York 10, New York and the Child Welfare League of America, 345 E. 46 Street, New York 17, New York, are especially concerned with the working mother and the services needed by her children. If you don't know what a good child-care center looks like—you probably won't be able to find out by looking around in your own community!—borrow the film, *Little World*. This picture of a child-care center in a New York City housing development shows one of the most needed supports which we are not now giving our young children in any appreciable quantity.

4. Novels, movies, books by scientists, many organizations are all trying to help us realize our new dilemma: We still

315

have international conflicts but we can no longer afford to settle them in the old ways of force. If you are not yet caught up in this awareness, take two minutes to listen to the song, "What Have They Done To The Rain," sung by Joan Baez on Vanguard VRS-9112.

WHAT I WOULD DO

Some of the persisting themes of this book ought to make it clear that the thirty questions asked at the conclusion of the preceding chapters are by no means a test in the usual sense of the word, with one infallibly "right" answer, the perfect and pat solution for each problem. If you have been tremendously eager to find out what the "book" says is the "right" thing to do, the following quotations may be more important for you to memorize than the "answers" which are given: "In every part of child rearing, at every age, there never is some one procedure which *must* be followed or a child is doomed. There is no technique which must *never* be used . . ." (p. 47); "If you try to 'follow the book' when the book doesn't jibe with your own common sense, you are headed for trouble. And your child is headed for trouble, too. . . ." (p. 261); "Babies do not need . . . angels to raise them, nor paragons . . . People will do. Ordinary people are all a baby asks for. We can be ourselves. We each have our own sense of humor, our own special tolerances where we are easygoing, and our own sore spots where we are touchy. There is no one golden pattern we each must follow . . ." (p. 41); Perhaps most important of all: *"At any one moment the best thing to do is whatever seems the best thing to do. Your feelings, your instincts, what makes sense to you are the very best guides to follow"* (p. 261).

The reason why "answers" are given below is not because they are the perfect solutions which everyone must follow. The reason is that "doing what comes naturally" does not mean that you must go on, forever and ever, always doing the same thing. At the time, you have to do what looks best. But adults can change. There is no need to get stuck in a rut (p. 262) and ". . . the real 'children's hour' comes after the youngsters are in bed. This is the time when adults talk to-

317

gether, and go over what happened during the day to build some guidelines for the future. Mothers (and fathers and teachers and all of us!) . . . need to 'see the movies of the game.' They need the chance to . . . test their solutions on a fresh person who wasn't involved in each incident" (p. 247).

This is now the "children's hour"—the time to take stock and think. "When everyone is so completely sure that what he is doing is right, and never feels puzzled or any need to talk over what has gone on, the chances are that thinking has stopped." (p. 248). "No child gains if he meets only pigheadedness and stubbornness . . . A sense of justice and a sense of right are much more important than simply holding the line forever . . . Pooled thinking sometimes reinforces the old approaches. Sometimes it develops a new consistency, a new line of strength that can be solidly held to because it represents the best judgments . . ." of mother and father and teacher and a lot of people who care about children's well being (p. 248). So: What would I do? The following are my inclinations and the people with whom I would tend to agree:

1. *b*. See pp. 64, 88 and 164 for my reasons why. *d*, my other possible choice, seems to me to over-do things a bit. It sounds like more comfort than the child is asking for!

2. *b*, *c* and *d* don't fit in with my understandings; *a* comes closest but it has a stingy, irritable sound. I would "give in" but gladly—this girl shows that she needs a lot of love. See pp. 77-81.

3. *a*, *b*, *c* and *d* all seem to me to miss the boat. Pages 77-81 and 268 tell why I think so. This looks to me like clear "self-demand" behavior and I think I know what this boy is demanding: not things, but love!

4. *c* is my clear choice. Pages 88 and 240 tell why.

5. I go along with father, *c*, for the reasons expressed on pages 70 and 77.

6. *d* looks right to me partly because I know there is no such man as "J. Ellington Whitehurst"! And partly because he sounds so much like someone imbued with an awe of habits. The job isn't to "bend twigs" but to nourish trees!

7. The nice relaxed neighbor, *c*, is on the right track, I think. I am all for the mother's goals but she should read the part of Chapter 31 beginning near the bottom of page 290 as well as page 137.

8. "Hogwash and baloney and sweet talk and soft soap" is my thought, too. *d* sounds right. This may be the mother's natural, honest style but I suspect that the points involved on pages 25 and 38 come closer to the truth.

9. I am all for relaxed mothers! But that terrible-sounding mother-in-law—*c*—says what I would do and for the reasons expressed on page 279.

10. *b* is my preference—that looks like good teaching to me, and wonderful child-experimentation. This is a small example of the kind of thing I try to suggest on the pages beginning with 189.

11. *a:* "Let them do what they want to do" and silently sing the Star Spangled Banner! If you chose another path, re-read pages 258 and 259.

12. *a*, and I try to tell why on page 197.

13. *a.* again. These sound like very healthy children to me. They are "growing more and more talky (but) they are holding on to their fists and their feet a lot better. You have to think of their words as typical age-level language; as such, they are just a bit 'nice'." (p. 264).

14. In all honesty, my answer here would depend a lot on my own mood at the moment! And I am seldom in a good frame of mind when I try to cook supper! But even if I am not feeling healthy, the child certainly is (See page 172). On my "good" days I would stay as cheerful as I could. *c* comes closest, if I could say it with a smile!

15. Everyone is off-base here, I think. The approach on page 278 seems like the best one to me.

16. *b* would be my way, but not because I feel cornered and am wailing, "What can you do with them!" I go along with what has been said on pages 42, 89, 182.

17. *b.* "Keep peace in the family," and *peace in the child!* This youngster certainly has the beginnings of an idea! See pages 172-173.

18. In a way this is a very silly question. All through the book we have said that things don't mean a thing! But I like this question anyhow! It is a kind of a test of how easily you react to what makes a child feel good. I strongly go along with *a.*

19. *a, b, c,* and *d* all seem to me to miss the mark. Pages 213, 268 and 323 all seem relevant here but I think this boy needs some expert help, and needs it now! He sounds as if he has been hurt already, and it would be so easy to hurt him some more.

20. *d,* and without any hesitancy! Page 42 tells why.

21. After all that has been said about identification, this is a really tricky question! If you want to produce a law-abiding child, shouldn't you be law-abiding yourself? But I would still go along with *a.* Flexibility—giving to children the best of our heads and the best of our hearts—seems tops to me. Page 248 tries to state this point of view.

22. *d* would be my approach. And page 266 tells why.

23. *d* again. And with no trouble at all in reaching a decision, for the reasons stated on pages 64, 88, and 238.

24. *a* seems right. If you disagree, read pages 99 and 121 again.

25. I side with *a,* for the reasons expressed on page 266.

26. *c* seems to me like the best way. Pages 196 and 197 express my point of view.

27. "That's a fine way to bring up stupid children."

c is exactly how I feel. Page 185 expresses the reason why very well: "Under-six children are realists. They are concerned with the truth. This age is made up of hard-boiled detectives: They just want the facts!"

28. From my standpoint, this is one of the "rigged" questions; neither *a, b, c* or *d* seems right. I would find my answer by putting pages 148-149 and 279 together.

29. *b,* and with an exclamation mark! But I think mother underplays what she is doing. Her efforts seem to me to add up to something really "special." The section beginning on page 208 makes clear why I am so enthusiastic, plus the section beginning on the bottom of page 325.

30. *a.* Pages 190 and 195 support this approach. This isn't "just" water down the drain or "water" under the bridge —but the kind of water that really nourishes a child. No one incident makes much difference one way or the other, but if we can only find ways of letting children live lives that are right for them—with all their energy and curiosity and eagerness—the children won't simply be breathing (there is no trick to that!) but they will be and grow vigorously *alive,* truly operating with all they have to give.

the big ideas: a summary

Chapter 34

Just as there is no dramatic developmental change between year five and year six, there is no change at all in the fundamental principles that underlie growth and development at *any* age—infancy, early childhood, middle childhood, preadolescence, adolescence, and in our adulthood. One set of laws does not govern the growth of young children and a different set apply to older youngsters. *The same big ideas that hold true under six hold true after six.*

These ideas stand out more clearly when the child is young. Behavior is open. Changes in behavior come in a compact span of years, unrolling so that it becomes more easy to see them. Now is a good time to highlight these big ideas so they can guide us, under six and after six.

The child wants to grow. From the instant of conception, this is the child's fate: to grow. He is bound and determined to move along the human path toward maturity. He carries

322

inside of him the vital energy of life that pushes him, drives him, propels him ever onward toward his ultimate end.

Once you are impressed with the tremendous strength of maturation, your whole attitude toward children changes. You relax a bit. You feel more faith, more confidence. You are in a thousand times better position to enjoy each stage of growth as it comes along. You know that you have a great ally on your side: growth. Children do not stay the same forever. Sometimes before our very eyes they mature physically. Always, whether we see it at the moment or not, they are in the process of maturing socially, intellectually, emotionally.

When you work with humans, you are not dealing with dead, inert matter but with live, changing organisms. Our role is *not* to provide the engine power. We need not push or prod or punish children into maturing. We guide children, yes. We remove roadblocks from their path. We make sure they have the emotional nourishment so their growth continues. Now and again we have to help all children get back on the main track of growth. These are tremendously important, yet relatively easy jobs. The child himself takes care of the biggest job of all: To grow! The human must grow. He wants to, with the fiercest kind of fervor.

Growth has direction. As long as a youngster is surrounded by humans in a reasonably decent setting, he goes in the direction that makes living with humans possible. Growth does not mean that the child gets bigger and grabs more, that he gets bigger and hits more, that he gets bigger and hurts more. He does not move toward more selfishness, toward more isolation, away from reality. The child's normal growth propels him toward all those skills and attitudes upon which human society is based. A child is conceived a human; he grows into his humanity.

As long as he stays emotionally and physically well, as long as he lives with good people, the child moves toward rationality. He wants to think more and to talk things over. He moves toward wider social relationships, away and out of himself, ever expanding so that more and more people are his brothers. He moves toward finer emotional expression. He becomes capable of a wider range of feeling, of a more effective expression of feeling. The child does not stay belly-centered, feeling only when an event hits him directly, personally, in his own private little world. As he grows he can bleed when another bleeds.

Once we realize that there is a social direction to growth, once again our posture toward children is affected. We have more faith in them and we get more enjoyment from living with them. *They* want what we want for them: to become useful, contributing and decent members of human society.

Growth has order. The child's move toward maturity does not take place in a helter-skelter way. Each child moves along the human track of development. There is a fixed order to maturing, just as there is a set path of tracks each train must follow as it moves from Washington to New York. The stops are determined in advance, by our human nature, just as the railroad stations are clearly marked: Washington, Baltimore, Wilmington, Philadelphia, North Philadelphia, Trenton, Newark and New York, etc.

A child cannot skip being five and doing what five-year-olds do, any more than the train can skirt Baltimore and go to Annapolis instead. He cannot skip being four. He cannot skip being three. The final stop is New York—the final stop is adult maturity. But each station along the way plays its essential part in bringing the child closer and closer to the ultimate end.

At each stage in development there are unique opportunities special to that particular time. There are appropriate tasks to be done and appropriate ways to act. Only in Baltimore can you see Fort McHenry. Only in Philadelphia can

324

you see Independence Hall. The search for a sense of trust, autonomy, initiative can best be pursued in the early years. Other jobs come along later in their own good time. The challenge is not to rush the "train" through each station stop. Life is not a race. We must keep our eye on where we are headed *and at the same time* be glad we are where we are. Death is not the goal of life; living is.

The years of early childhood have a very special significance in the human order of growth. They are the beginning years. The child who gets off to a good start has made a good start —no one can take that away from him. He moves on into his future with all the confidence and ease that a good start can give. A winning "first quarter" of the game increases the likelihood that the "second quarter" will be a winning period, too.

The satisfactions of early childhood are so basic that the child who rushes through these years, unfulfilled, must always and persistently come back until his early needs have been met. He goes on "acting like a two-year-old," until he lives a satisfying two-year-oldness, if it takes to the end of his days.

The years of early childhood have another special significance. These beginning years—"just" the baby years, the simple-sounding "pre-school" years—have their unique challenges and opportunities. Under-six has *its* days to be lived. This is a sharp reminder at the very start of life that *all* stages of growth are important: early childhood *and* the middle years, pre-adolescence and adolescence, and adulthood.

Each child is an individual. The human track is the same for all. But each train—each child—has its very special qualities. Each child gets off to a completely unique start. He begins life with a highly selective pooling of chromosomes, his inheritance from two never-ending, never-the-same lines of humans. From the start, the experiences of life are never the same for any two people—not even for the most identical

325

twins! We all follow the same human path, but we differ from the instant of conception and our differences continue to multiply.

We inherit differences in intelligence and in our rate of growing, in the depth of our feelings and the strength of our drives. We inherit our susceptibilities; some of us hurt more than others and bruise more easily. We bring into the world unique strengths, talent potentials and interest potentials that are private to us alone. We inherit "blind spots," just as we inherit our height, hair color and texture, and the color of our eyes.

Then life's experiences play on these initial inborn differences. We are the only child, the middle one; the first boy; the "war baby"; rich, poor; minority, majority; slum child, favored child. With inborn differences and imposed differences, each child leads a different life. No event is ever the same for any two children. Each feels his life differently and takes different meanings from it.

We must "nurse" each child along. We must operate with a fine feeling for each child's special qualities, giving to each what he needs, drawing from each what he can give. Every single youngster needs to feel understood and accepted for what he is—in his age, his sex, his interests, his style—to make the best use of his powers. If we treat each one the same, no child gets his due. If we are dissatisfied with a child's *self*, he is dissatisfied with himself. If we ask more than he can do, he does less than he can do. Only the youngster who is accepted for what he is, as he is, in his unique personality, can use all the engine power at his command.

Growth is indivisible. Inevitably, inescapably, whether we know it or not, or like it or not, intellectual and social and emotional and physical development inextricably merge. There is no way to slice a child into separate parts.

326

The baby's first physical gains—sitting, crawling, standing, walking—stimulate his intellectual growth. His early language —an intellectual development—triggers his social interests. His beginning social play is completely intermeshed with emotional, intellectual and physical components. Always—and we all know this!—how a child feels affects how he thinks and how he acts. Fear freezes us; confidence frees us. Anger blinds our thinking. The child who is at peace with himself and the world moves better, plans better, acts better.

Physical feelings seep into the brain just as easily as the emotions do. The hard-of-hearing child has trouble with his speech. The malnourished children, the tired and the sick, cannot learn as well as they otherwise could. And social responses affect learning, too. The lonely outcast on the fringes of a group cannot use his brain power. The youngster with physical ease builds social ease and emotional ease and greases his own path to learning. The pressured child—ill at ease emotionally—is ill at ease socially and physically, and he "cannot keep his mind on his work."

Each child is a whole. We can separate him into his parts only so that we can talk about those parts. In his actual living, the child is always *one*, an integrated human. We fool ourselves when we think we can concentrate on *teaching* the brain, and not the feelings or the body or social attitudes. This is sheer wishful thinking. In every experience a child ever has—in school, at home or anywhere—all of him is involved. The only question is whether we will realize that children are wholes and make wise plans for children with their wholeness in mind. Or, whether we will close our eyes to the integration of the human and let our efforts fall where they may, doing good or evil simply by chance.

Growth is uneven. The main stops along the human track are clearly marked: Washington, Baltimore, Wilmington,

327

Philadelphia . . . but the rate of speed is not a steady, even thirty miles an hour. Nor are there consistent and regular ten-minute station stops.

Normal growth includes *plateaus*. Children seem to stand still for a while, consolidating gains and gathering strength for the long haul ahead. At other times in growth some things steal the show. Youngsters go on *jags*. They become more absorbed (maybe more than we would like them to be) with interests and activities that for them have special meaning. All children spurt at times. Momentarily they leap ahead, for quick tastes of new behavior and, at times, they simply grow faster almost as if they were making up for lost time or saving time for later use. Some regression—a backing up for safety—is also completely normal. The human way of growing is *not*: "Day by day in every way we get better and better."

Plateaus, jags, spurts, regressions all serve, in the long run, to move the child ahead. The overall pattern is forward but at any one moment each child has his own movement, and for his own good purposes. Standing still to feel safe—drinking deeply to get his fill—spurting to test out the land ahead—going back to build up reserves. This is the human way of moving forward.

You must stand back from a child to get perspective. And you must keep your faith in the child's urge to grow and in the social direction of his growth. With these supports you can keep your tolerance and your patience, and ward off the temptation to nag a child into strength. A youngster grows strong only when he is true to himself.

Growth does not always glitter like gold. The stages of growth so important to a child are not necessarily easy for us. There is a difference between behavior that is developmentally healthy and significant—*good for the child*—and behavior that is good for us—pleasant to live with. Young children wet. They have to, but wetting is a nuisance. Young children spit up. They have to, but what a nuisance! Young children wake up in the middle of the night; they cry because they cannot talk; they must be carried because they cannot walk. At every age children do what they must do, because they are who they are. Their normal behavior does not always check with our convenience.

Sometimes we know why children do what they do. We accept their crying, for example, when we *know* they are teething. But the times when we *know* the reason are few compared to those times when we do not. You get no medals for siding with children when the reason for their behavior is obvious. Then the gold glitters—anyone at all can see it. The real trick to living well with youngsters lies in our willingness to give them a little free rein. Can you go along with them, even when you *don't* know why they do what they do, and when their behavior certainly isn't what we would do at our advanced age?

Living well with children calls for faith as well as facts. You need a conviction that there is a plan to growth and some point to all behavior—the faith that "God works in wondrous ways his miracles to perform." It is this faith that breeds humility. Our task is not to play God. Our task is not to end those acts that don't happen to please us, although they please the child very deeply.

We each have our tolerances, peculiar to us, and our special tender spots. Some of us can live with the young child's noise and activity with never a qualm. Some of us can tolerate the four-year-old's verbal "outrages" without breaking stride. Some of us are not bothered in the least by the young child's love of water, mud, and gush. The job we face is to extend our tolerances. We have to learn to take children as they come. Many of their most persisting acts do not come clearly

329

marked: "Good." "Important." "Developmentally significant." The behavior is sheer gold for the child's well-being but it does not always glitter like gold.

Behavior talks. The clue to what counts in development is what a child does. As we live with children—infants or adolescents, it makes no difference—we must be alert to those things they persistently seek, over and over, time after time. And we must respect their seeking. We must be alert to those things they shrink from, not once but time and time again. And we must respect their shrinking. The significant evidence on what is developmentally significant is not what a child says or the reasons he can verbalize. His behavior talks, more than his words ever can.

Children tell us when all is right with their world. They tell us through their contentment. They tell us through a comfortable quality that permeates their whole bodies. You sense an at-ease feeling, a deep down note of joy in themselves and in their world.

Just as clearly, children tell us when life is awry. Their bodies speak with tightness and tension. Their bodies speak with awkwardness and lack of smoothness. A thousand and one signs all say: "The parts are not meshing smoothly." A mechanic listens for the purr of an engine. We have to listen for the purr of childhood. We must be glad to do those things that clearly make a child feel good. But the good sound of childhood is not a momentary giggle nor does it mean that life is always soft and easy. Children—bound to grow—purr only when they find their lives full of challenge, as much as they can take. They purr only when they give all they have to give—but not more than is within them.

No one can know in advance all there is to know about children. No book can tell it all. To live well with youngsters you need your memory and your brain but you also need heart and sensitivity. Your willingness to give whatever a child's behavior shows that he needs is your best tool for producing a healthy child—a child who feels pleased with himself and pleased with others, a child who can live with himself and live with others.

Appendix

Chapter 2 discusses the many different ways in which children have been studied. The following is a list of books which illustrate each of these methods which have thrown some light on childhood. The list is a long one, but still highly selective. Many, many other books could have been included. The books that follow are good illustrations of the methods by which our knowledge of children has been built up *and* likely to be available in most libraries. I am very grateful to Laura Dittmann for her invaluable help in preparing this Appendix.

Adults have looked back on their childhoods

Bagnold, Enid, *National Velvet*. New York. Grosset, 1938.

Benson, Sally, *Meet Me in St. Louis*. New York: Random House, 1942.

Burnett, Whit (ed.) *Time to Be Young*. Philadelphia: Lippincott, 1945.

Cary, Joyce. *House of Children*. New York: Harper, 1956.

Coffin, Robert P. T. *Lost Paradise*. New York: Macmillan, 1934

Dermout, Maria. *Yesterday.* New York: Simon and Schuster, 1959.

Gilbreth, F. A. and E. G. Cory. *Cheaper by the Dozen.* New York: Crowell, 1949.

Godden, Rumer. *The River.* New York: Little, Brown, 1948.

Green, Anne. *With Much Love.* New York: Harper, 1948.

Lewis, C. S. *Surprised by Joy.* New York: Harcourt, Brace, 1956.

Milne, A. A. *Year in, Year out.* New York: Dutton, 1952.

Roosevelt, Eleanor: *This I Remember.* New York: Harper, 1949.

Smith, Betty. *A Tree Grows in Brooklyn.* New York: Harper, 1943.

Smith, R. P. *Where Did You Go? Out. What Did You Do? Nothing.* New York: Norton, 1958.

Psychiatrists and other therapists hear the stories of childhood

Axline, V. *Play Therapy.* Boston: Houghton Mifflin, 1947.

Bettelheim, B. *Love Is not Enough.* Glencoe, Ill.: Free Press, 1950.

Horney, K. *Our Inner Conflicts.* New York: Norton, 1945.

——————. *The Neurotic Personality of Our Time.* New York: Norton, 1937.

Kanner, L. *Child Psychiatry.* Springfield, Ill.: Thomas, 1950.

Menninger, K. *The Human Mind.* New York: Knopf, 1945.

——————. *Man Against Himself.* New York: Harcourt Brace, 1956.

Pearson, G. H. J. *Emotional Disorders of Childhood.* New York: Norton, 1949.

Redl, F. and D. Wineman. *The Aggressive Child.* Glencoe, Ill.: Free Press, 1957.

Slavson, S. R. *Child Psychotherapy.* New York: Columbia University Press, 1952.

Sullivan, H. S. *An Interpersonal Theory of Psychiatry.* New York: Norton, 1953.

Case studies of children

Baruch, D. *One Little Boy.* New York: Julian Press, 1952.

Bettelheim, B. *Truants from Life.* Glencoe, Ill.: Free Press, 1955.

Moustakas, C. E. *Children in Play Therapy*. New York: McGraw-Hill, 1953.

Murphy, L. B. *Personality in Young Children*. Vol. II, *Colin, A Normal Child*. New York: Basic Books, 1956.

Murray, H. A. *Explorations in Personality*. Cambridge: Harvard University Press, 1936.

Shirley, M. M. *The First Two Years: A Study of Twenty-five Babies*. Vols. I, II, III. Minneapolis: University of Minnesota Press.

Normal children have been followed over the years

Barker, R. G. and F. H. Wright. *Midwest and Its Children: The Psychological Ecology of an American Town*, Evanston, Ill.: Row, Peterson, 1955.

Bayley, N. "Factors Influencing the Growth of Intelligence in Young Children," in Thirty-ninth Yearbook, National Society for the Study of Education, Bloomington, Ill.: Public School Publishing Co., 1940.

Gray, G. W. "Human Growth. The complete physical, physiological and psychological histories of 160 boys and girls recorded by the Denver Child Research Council." *Scientific American*, October, 1953.

Macfarlane, J. W. *et al. A Developmental Study of the Behavior Problems of Normal Children Between 21 Months and 14 Years*. Berkeley: University of California Press, 1954.

Sontag, L. W., C. T. Baker and V. L. Nelson. *Mental Growth and Personality Development: A Longitudinal Study*. Lafayette, Ind.: Child Development Publications, 1958.

Spence, J. C., et al. *A Thousand Families in Newcastle on Tyne*. London: Oxford University Press, 1954.

——————. *Growing Up in Newcastle on Tyne*. London: Oxford University Press, 1960.

Stott, L. H. *The Longitudinal Study of Individual Development*. Detroit: Merrill Palmer School, 1955.

Stuart, H. C. and D. G. Prugh, eds. *The Healthy Child*. Cambridge: Harvard University Press, 1960.

337

Parents have informally recorded their own children's growth

Bates, M. and P. S. Humphrey, eds. *The Darwin Reader.* Contains Charles Darwin's "Biographical Sketch of an Infant." New York: Scribners, 1956.

Kellogg, W. N. and L. A. Kellogg. *The Ape and the Child.* New York: Whittlesey, 1933.

Miller, Wayne. *The World Is Young.* New York: Ridge Press, 1958.

Shinn, M. W. *The Biography of a Baby.* Boston: Houghton Mifflin, 1900.

Time samples of children's behavior

Barker, R. G. and Wright, H. F. *One Boy's Day.* New York: Harper, 1951.

Brody, S. *Patterns of Mothering.* New York: International Universities Press, 1956.

Gesell, A. *An Atlas of Infant Behavior.* (3,200 photographs.) New Haven: Yale University Press, 1934.

Grief. 16 mm. silent film.

Starting Nursery School: Patterns of Beginnings. 16 mm. sound film.

This Is Robert, 16 mm. sound film.

The Two Year Old Goes to the Hospital. 16 mm. silent film.

The experiences of many professions have enlarged our understanding

Aldrich, A. A. and M. M. Aldrich. *Babies Are Human Beings.* New York: Macmillan, 1954.

Balint, A. *The Early Years of Life.* New York: Basic Books, 1955.

Bossard, James H. S. *The Sociology of Child Development.* New York: Harper, 1948.

Freud, Anna and Dorothy Burlingham. *Infants Without Families.* New York: International Universities Press, 1944.

Jersild, Arthur. *Child Psychology.* Englewood Cliffs, N.J.: Prentice-Hall, 1960.

Josselyn, Irene. *Psychosocial Development of Children.* New York: Family Service Association of America, 1948.

Mitchell, Lucy Sprague. *Here and Now Story Book*. New York: Dutton, 1921, 1948.

Plant, James. *The Envelope*. New York: Commonwealth Fund, 1950.

Rasey, M. I. and J. W. Menge. *What We Learn from Children*. New York: Harper, 1956.

Sheehy, Emma. *There's Music in Children*. New York: Holt, 1952.

Woodcock, L. *Life and Ways of the Two Year Old*. New York: Basic Books, 1941.

Understanding children through tests

Anastasi, A. *Psychological Testing*. New York: Macmillan, 1954.

Cattell, P. *The Measurement of Intelligence of Infants and Young Children*. New York: Psychological Corporation, 1940.

Doll, E. *The Measurement of Social Competence*. Minneapolis: Educational Test Bureau Publications, 1953.

Gesell, A. and C. Amatruda. *Developmental Diagnosis*. New York: Hoeber, 1947.

Goodenough, F. L. and K. M. Maurer. *The Mental Growth of Children from 2 to 14 Years*. Minneapolis: University of Minnesota Press, 1942.

Stutsman, R. *Mental Measurement of Preschool Children*. Yonkers, N.Y.: World Book, 1931.

Terman, L. M. and M. A. Merrill. *Measuring Intelligence*. Boston: Houghton Mifflin, 1916.

Wechsler, D. *The Wechsler Intelligence Scale for Children*. New York: Psychological Corporation, 1949.

Controlled research on children

Blatz, W. E. et al. *Collected Studies of the Dionne Quintuplets*. Toronto: University of Toronto Press, 1937.

Burlingham, D. *Twins: A Study of Three Pairs of Identical Twins*. New York: International Universities Press, 1952.

Lippitt, R. and R. K. White. "An Experimental Study of Leadership and Group Life," in *Readings in Social Psychology*, by

G. Swanson, T. Newcomb, and E. Hartley, eds. New York: Holt, 1952.

McGraw, M. B. *Growth: A Study of Johnny and Jimmy.* New York: Appleton-Century-Crofts, 1935.

Stolz, L. M. *Father Relations of War-Born Children.* Stanford, Cal.: Stanford University Press, 1954.

Experiments with animals

Harlow, H. K. "Love in Infant Monkeys," in *Scientific American,* June, 1959.

Hayes, C. *The Ape in Our House.* New York: Harper, 1951.

Lorenz, K. Z. *King Solomon's Ring.* New York: Crowell, 1952.

Anthropologists study children around the world

Erikson, E. *Childhood and Society.* New York: Norton, 1950.

Leighton, D. and C. Kluckhohn. *Children of the People.* Cambridge: Harvard University Press, 1947.

Mead, M. and M. Wolfenstein, eds. *Childhood in Contemporary Cultures.* Chicago: University of Chicago Press, 1955.

Mead, M. *Coming of Age in Samoa.* New York: Morrow, 1928.

——————. *Growing Up in New Guinea.* New York: Morrow, 1930.

Whiting, J. W. M. and I. L. Child. *Child Training and Personality.* New Haven: Yale University Press, 1953.

Sociologists study children

Glueck, S. and E. Glueck. *Delinquents in the Making.* New York: Harper, 1952.

Goodman, M. E. *Race Awareness in Young Children.* Cambridge: Addison-Wesley, 1952.

Lewis, C. *Children of the Cumberland.* New York: Columbia University Press, 1946.

Miller, D. R. and G. E. Swanson. *The Changing American Parent.* New York: Wiley, 1958.

Padilla, E. *Up from Puerto Rico.* New York: Columbia University Press, 1958.

Stendler, C. B. *Children of Brasstown.* Urbana, Ill.: University of Illinois Press, 1949.

Whyte, W. F. *Street Corner Society*. Chicago: University of Chicago Press, 1955.

Studies of physical growth

Bayley, N. "Growth Curves of Height and Weight by Age for Boys and Girls Scaled According to Physical Maturity," in *Journal of Pediatrics* 48: 187-194, 1956.

Greulich, W. A. and S. I. Pyle. *Radiographic Atlas of Skeletal Development of the Hand and Wrist*. Stanford, Cal.: Stanford University Press, 1950.

Krogman, W. M. *Handbook of Measurement and Interpretation of Height and Weight in the Growing Child*. Monograph XIII (3). Lafayette, Ind.: Society for Research in Child Development, 1950.

Stuart, H. C. and S. S. Stevenson. "Physical Growth and Development," in *Textbook in Pediatrics*, by Nelson, W. E., ed. Philadelphia: Saunders, 1959.

Talbot, N. B., E. H. Sobel, J. W. McArthur, and J. D. Crawford. *Functional Endocrinology from Birth through Adolescence*. Cambridge: Harvard University Press, 1952.

Wetzel, N. C. "The Baby Grid," in *Journal of Pediatrics* 29: 439-454, 1946.

The products of children have been analyzed

Alschuler, R. H. and L. W. Hattwick. *Painting and Personality*. Vol. I, II. Chicago: University of Chicago Press, 1947.

Hartley, R., L. K. Frank, and R. M. Goldenson. *Understanding Children's Play*. New York: Columbia University Press, 1952.

Johnson, H. M. *The Art of Block Building*. New York: Day, 1933.

Wolfenstein, M. *Children's Humor*. Glencoe, Ill.: Free Press, 1954.

Projective tests probe beneath the surface

Abt, L. E. and L. Bellac. *Projective Psychology*. New York: Knopf, 1950.

Ames, L. B., J. Learned, R. Metraux, and W. Walker. *Children's Rorschach Responses*. New York: Harper, 1952.

Anderson, H. H. and G. L. Anderson. *An Introduction to Pro-*

341

jective Techniques. Englewood Cliffs, N.J.: Prentice-Hall, 1951.

Frank, L. K. *Projective Methods.* Springfield, Ill.: Thomas, 1948.

Murphy, L. B. *Personality in Young Children.* Vol. I. New York: Basic Books, 1956.